Emperor and Galilean

╼ 1873 ╾

Smith and Kraus *Books for Actors*

GREAT TRANSLATIONS FOR ACTORS SERIES

Anthologies

Chekhov's Early Plays, tr. by Carol Rocamora

Chekhov: Four Plays, tr. by Carol Rocamora

Chekhov's Vaudevilles, tr. by Carol Rocamora

Ibsen: Four Major Plays, tr. by R. Davis & B. Johnston

Ibsen Volume II: Four Plays, tr. by Brian Johnston

Ibsen Volume III: Four Plays, tr. by Brian Johnston

Marivaux: Three Plays, tr. by Stephen Wadsworth

Arthur Schnitzler: Four Major Plays, tr. by Carl Mueller

Villeggiatura: The Trilogy by Carlo Goldoni, tr. by Robert Cornthwaite

Classics

The Coffee Shop by Carlo Goldoni, tr. by Robert Cornthwaite

Cyrano de Bergerac by Edmond Rostand, tr. by Charles Marowitz

A Glass of Water by Eugene Scribe, tr. by Robert Cornthwaite

Mercadet by Honoré de Balzac, tr. by Robert Cornthwaite

The Sea Gull by Anton Chekhov, tr. by N. Saunders & F. Dwyer

Spite for Spite by Agustin Moreto, tr. by Dakin Matthews

The Summer People by Maxim Gorky, tr. by N. Saunders & F. Dwyer

Three Sisters by Anton Chekhov, tr. by Lanford Wilson

The Wood Demon by Anton Chekhov, tr. by N. Saunders & F. Dwyer

Zoyka's Apartment by Mikhail Bulgakov, tr. by N. Saunders & F. Dwyer

If you require pre-publication information about upcoming Smith and Kraus books, you may receive our semiannual catalogue, free of charge, by sending your name and address to *Smith and Kraus Catalogue, P.O. Box 127, Lyme, NH 03768. Or call us at (603) 643-6431, fax (603) 922-3348. WWW.SmithKraus.Com*

Emperor and Galilean

A WORLD HISTORICAL DRAMA

—— 1873 ——

translated by Brian Johnston

Great Translations for Actors

SK
A Smith and Kraus Book

A Smith and Kraus Book
One Main Street, PO Box 127, Lyme, NH 03768
603.643.6431

Cover and Book Design By Julia Hill Gignoux, Freedom Hill Design

First Edition: September 1999
9 8 7 6 5 4 3 2 1

Library of Congress Cataloging-in-Publication Data
Ibsen, Henrik, 1828–1906.
[Kejser og Galilaeer. English]
Emperor and Galilean: a world historical drama, 1873 / translated by Brian Johnston. —1st d.
p.   cm.   — (Great translations for actors)
ISBN 1-57525-194-9
1. Julian, Emperor of Rome, 331–363 Drama. I. Johnston, Brian, 1932– .   II. Title.
III. Series: Great translations for actors series.
PT8870.J64   1999
839.8'226—dc21   99-16975

CONTENTS

INTRODUCTION

Ibsen's career, with almost uncanny symmetry, can be divided into two equal parts. The first extends from his first play, *Catiline*, (1850) to *Emperor and Galilean* (1873). The second half comprises the great twelve-play Realist Cycle, from *Pillars of Society* (1877) to *When We Dead Awaken*, (1899). The first half opens and closes with plays on classical, Roman themes and features two rebel heroes, Catiline, who shook republican Rome in the first century B.C.E.; and Julian the Apostate who attempted to destroy the Christian hegemony of the Byzantine and Roman empires in the fourth century A.D. and thus to change the entire course of Western history. While we think of Ibsen as the creator of modern prose drama, this first half of his career—23 years—is almost entirely given over to poetic and historical plays.

It also is possible to see that career as dividing into three parts. Here, the first section would be those plays written in Norway, from *Catiline* to *The Pretenders* (1863). Then would come the great "middle period" plays written in exile, from *Brand* (1866) through *Peer Gynt* (1867) and *The League of Youth* (1869) to *Emperor and Galilean*, to be followed by the Realist Cycle. In either scheme of division it will be seen that *Emperor and Galilean* occupies a pivotal position. It is both the culmination of the first phase of his creativity and the synthesis of the great middle plays—with their "galilean" (*Brand*) and "emperor" (*Peer Gynt*) themes—into the vision of "the third empire." It is Ibsen's last overtly historical drama and signals his decisive adoption of prose as the medium for his future drama.

Ibsen insisted *Emperor and Galilean* was his masterwork, upon which his fame would rest. So overwhelming has been the impact upon the world of his modern realist plays, that this claim often has been met with bemusement and even some condescension. Yet Ibsen's claim for the play is, I believe, sustainable. It is a magnificent work, huge in conception, intensely and urgently dramatic, and containing as wide-ranging an overview of human history and destiny as can be found only in the most supreme artworks.

Though planned as early as 1864, *Emperor and Galilean* remained fermenting in Ibsen's imagination for nine years until it was published in 1873. It is the work on which he spent by far the most time. When he completed it, he was at the height of his creative powers. He saw it as the cornerstone of his entire dramatic output. "This book will be my masterpiece," he declared. He already had completed the two great poetic dramas, *Brand* and *Peer Gynt* and was about to embark on the Cycle of twelve modern plays, which were to establish his international fame. Dramatizing the tragic career of Julian the Apostate in the fourth century A.D., *Emperor and Galilean* presents Western Civilization itself at one of its most crucial turning points.

The play also stands as the watershed of Ibsen's career: It is his last historical drama and it represents his decisive final break with verse drama. At the same time it lays the foundation for all the plays to follow. While the plays of the Realist Cycle are well known, *Emperor and Galilean* still awaits discovery by modern readers, actors, and directors. To the end of his life Ibsen insisted it was his greatest work. The Shakespearean scholar, G. Wilson Knight has written of the play, "it is certainly the greatest dramatic document of its century....it is stageworthy...[it is] conceived dramatically, even theatrically...under a spectacular production the result could be triumphant....all depends on our interest in the one grand opposition. That granted, Julian and his plight are humanly drawn, and so are the rest. Excitement is maintained; new events, new life, seethe and crash, all history is before us, turning on the one axial problem."

Ibsen's biographer, Michael Meyer declared, "Of all Ibsen's plays...*Emperor and Galilean* is the one most underrated by posterity." Ibsen himself believed— and nothing in subsequent history has proved him wrong—that the play dramatizes "the struggle between two irreconcilable powers in the life of the world, something which will in all ages repeat itself; and because of this universality, I call the book a 'world-historic' play." Much of our world still suffers under ideologies that seek to simplify, distort, reduce, and mutilate our full human identity and potentiality. The forces seeking to replace this awkward and diverse human identity with a less complex, more pliant one are not just totalitarian but are active in our own culture; they can be heard baying at diversity as degeneracy, deploring nonconformity, continually narrowing the permissible range of human action and expression. The historical situation the play dramatizes is one of multiple heroisms, crimes, follies, fanaticisms, massacres, and confusions throughout an entire empire—and as topical as the latest news today.

While working on the play Ibsen moved from Rome, the ancient "southern" scene of the Roman (and later Christian) empire, the greatest organizer and shaper of European cultural identity in the past, to Bismarck's Germany in the north, already reshaping the modern world as an intellectual and as a major political and military force. Ibsen maintained this residential oscillation between Rome and Germany for a number of years. And an interplay of metaphoric "north" and "south" informs many of the plays in the later Cycle— in Rosmer and Rebekka, for example in *Rosmersholm,* where the north (Rebekka) stands for radical and ruthless energies and forces that disturb and agitate a settled, ancient, traditional, and civilized order. Such a contrast—the ancient Roman world and Bismarck's Germany—would suggest that Ibsen conceived his play on a huge time scale: and that the "'world-will's" unfinished business in the play—the goal of "the third empire of spirit and flesh, Galilean and Emperor"—was now to be handed over to the modern world to accomplish. He told a correspondent, Julius Hoffory, that *Emperor and Galilean* was "the first work I wrote under German intellectual influences" and he goes on to describe "Germany's great time" which has expanded his "theory of history and of human life" from a national one (which had informed his earlier historical plays, such as *The Pretenders*) to one of a whole race. It was then, he continues, that he could write the play. Ibsen, therefore, expects us to read the drama of the modern world in the drama of the ancient one it has inherited.

THE VISIONARY SCALE OF *EMPEROR AND GALILEAN*

In Part Two Act Four of *Emperor and Galilean*, Emperor Julian—attempting radically to steer the entire course of Western history—and his spiritual advisor, Maximus—seeking into the mystery of the world-spirit's direction—gaze far down into a ravine where Julian's army, filing in a snakelike column, prepares to do battle with the Persian army of King Sapor. Looking at the multitude reduced to ant-like figures in the distance Julian observes how, when the soldiers reached a gap in the pass, every man rushed into it because "it cut the marching time by an hour, a fragment of effort saved—on the journey to death." To Julian, it is an image of human history itself. The soldiers, in their immediate preoccupation, "can't see how they've shrunk the heavens over them and don't know there are heights where it's vaster....isn't it as if men live only so that they die? The Galilean's ghost's in this."

The primary quests of modern thought and modern history are in that image: the search for "direction" beyond the visionless present of the god that failed. The quest is pursued in the world of thought (Hegel, Nietzsche, Marx); in the world of action (Lenin, Hitler, or Mao)—all variously and fatefully lured to understand, predict, or to steer the world-spirit, the "weltgeist," each to his own interpretation of history and destiny. When Julian descends from the heights into the arena of actual life, that vision becomes entangled in ferocious conflict, fanatic oppositions, tyranny, pedantry, superstitions, sycophancy, partisan blindnesses, everyday absurdity—all that bedevils the "vision" in the world we have to live in. That confusion is our condition and why Ibsen felt *Emperor and Galilean* to be his most modern play. Ibsen's pronouncements on his age ("the whole history of the world seems to me like a sinking ship") show how he looked on the triumphant materialism and emasculated "Christendom" of his own day as a level of subhumanity for which the trolls of *Peer Gynt* were the appropriate emblem. He wrote much of the play in Rome: once the center of the renaissance, which also, like Maximus in this play, tried to forge a synthesis between classical paganism and Christianity. Most of the artworks—by Michelangelo, Leonardo, Raphael, the great church of St. Peter itself—surrounding Ibsen in Italy were all witnesses to that effort.

THE HUMAN CONTEXT OF THE VISIONARY DRAMA

The distinguished thing about the play is that while it struggles to formulate its vision it does not deliver it in high-minded didacticism or poetic rhapsody, in the manner of the Romantic historical drama of which it is the culmination: It dramatizes its visionary quest only in its baffled, infinitely painful, human context. It is the baffled human context that makes for great drama, and, in Part Two in particular, this involves a dazzling variety of performance styles: Brechtian "demonstration" satire, broad comedy, elegiac poignancy, visionary utterance, and desolate tragedy. Both Part One and Part Two contain Ibsen's most powerful writing and have a rare almost confessional quality. "In the character of Julian," he confessed to Ludvig Daae, "there is much more of what I have lived through in spirit than I care to acknowledge to the public." He wrote to Edmund Gosse, "What I depict I have, under different conditions, lived through myself; and the historical subject I have chosen has a much closer connection with the movements of our own time than one might at first imagine."

Julian sought to counter the narrow vision and life-renunciation of the "Galilean" (Christian) revolution with a liberating and life-affirming alternative: drawing upon Greek Hellenism and looking for guidance in the spiritual mysteries explored by Maximus. Near the end of his life he is forced to witness the failure of his entire endeavor. "It was this lost treasure I wanted to give back to mankind. Like Dionysos before, I came to them full of joy and youth, with vine leaves on my brow and with grapes full and ripe in my arms. But they rejected my gifts, and I am mocked and hated and reviled by friends and enemies." Ibsen, in his lifelong struggle with and against his culture, must have identified with Julian's project and with his tragedy. Early in life, scarcely fifteen years old, he left forever his repressive, pietistic little birthplace of Skien in Norway for one of the most remarkable acts of self-determination on record. The Skien Ibsen left behind him was convulsed by the strictly pietistic evangelism of the pastor G. A. Lammers under whose spell Ibsen's own family soon succumbed. As Michael Meyer observes, "to the free thinking disciple of Voltaire [whom the youthful Ibsen especially admired] such an atmosphere must have seemed peculiarly intolerable." By choosing poetry and theatre as his vocation, Ibsen, like Julian, battled throughout his life to establish his alternative, liberating vision: to carve out for himself and for his nation, a larger, more liberating imaginative terrain for the spirit to inhabit.

The scene of Julian gazing down upon his army is one of many repeated moments of "vertical scenography" in the play—of abysses and heights—when its whole "argument" repeatedly is regathered together in a single, profound and visionary cluster, like the continual contrapuntal regathering of themes or leitmotivs in a musical composition. The scene goes back to the most ambitious imagery of Romantic poetry and drama: to the contrast between the heroic heights and the visionless depths of the valley-dwellers in *Brand* and *Peer Gynt*—scenes which themselves look back to the global cultural consciousness of Goethe's *Faust*; to the outlaws and outcasts of Byron's plays, such as *Cain* and *Manfred*, and to the huge natural perspectives brought to bear on ordinary human life in the poetry of William Wordsworth. The play is structured upon a series of such polarities, beginning with the title itself. From the antinomies of "Emperor" and "Galilean" we find a succession of vast divisions: the continual interplay of heights and depths, inner and outer worlds, flesh and spirit, life-renunciation and joy of life. What makes the psychology of the play so fascinating—and so "actable"—is that these antinomies are present not just externally between opposing individuals and groups: The individuals and groups themselves are riven intolerably between these competing and warring antinomies within their own identities.

This can be seen at once in the portrait of the Emperor Constantius in the first scene in the play. He appears onstage in a condition of near-schizophrenia, heading a Christian procession itself riven by division and disorder in its members as the stage directions make manifest. The all-powerful Emperor, as he walks fearfully toward the Christian chapel, is under the control of his slave, Memnon; at one point he screams in terror at the remembrance of the massacres that got him in power and now torment his Christian conscience. Later, in telling contrast, we see him exit the chapel, having atoned in prayer for his terrible crimes, emerging ruthless, decisive, deadly: The lethal "Emperor" identity re-established over the guilty Galilean one. The division continues in such ironic and almost Dostoevskyean portraits as the conflicted Julian—a would-be pagan more puritanical than the Christians—and wedded to the ardent Christian, Helena, more passionately sensuous than the pagans. Julian, the intellectual and emotional epicenter of the huge play, arguably is the most complex hero in all drama. His tormented consciousness combines the visionary and the petty, the lyrical and the pedantic, the idealistic and the Machiavellian, the heroic and the vacillating. These very complexities, together with his qualities of cunning, allow him to survive where simpler-minded, confident creatures such as Gallus and Helena go under. His ardent espousal of a sensuous world he yet shrinks from entering; his poignant desire for approval and love making him an easy prey to sycophants; his genuinely visionary contact with a spiritual world coupled with a gullibility before omens and frauds, reveals Julian to be the most self-conscious and adequate representative of his extraordinarily schizophrenic culture.

This pervasive cultural schizophrenia continues even as satirical comedy in such portraits as the deliciously hypocritical Christian tutor, Hecebolious—prefiguring Rørlund of *Pillars of Society* and Pastor Manders of *Ghosts;* the duplicitous philosopher, Libanius, and the sycophantic flatterers, rhetoricians, and philosophers who surround Julian when he is emperor. The satire broadens in the depiction of such figures as the hilariously lascivious Christian barber, Eunapius, frequenter of whorehouses and later an opportunistic but enthusiastic convert to the cult of Venus, who describes directing his "reverent thoughts in devotion" to the statue of "that entrancing goddess, whom I especially honor and worship..." This last instance is an example of how we have to be on the alert for the pervasive play of Ibsen's satiric humor throughout the drama, (what George Bernard Shaw, writing of this play, called his "grim hoaxing humor") and which often goes undetected by those with a far too solemn idea of Ibsen's art. Eunapius "reverent thoughts" obviously are tumescent raptures.

THE VIVIDLY DRAMATIC PORTRAITURE OF THE PLAY

There is a crowded and complex portraiture in the play, an immensely rich array of types (and actable "parts"), a fine specificity in its immensely varied actions, which prevent the grand antinomies of the play's argument from thinning into abstraction. Such firmly grounded specificity prepares us for Ibsen's next great work—the huge twelve-play Realist Cycle that follows. Julian's more universal quest continually will haunt the modern realist plays: Nora Helmer's sense of a reality whose glimpsed dimensions shatter her doll house; Osvald Alving's baffled "joy-of-life" whose exoneration emerges only after the tragic demolition of all that had suppressed it; Rosmer and Rebecca's bid for spiritual authenticity and liberation in *Rosmersholm;* the mysterious realm from which the Stranger emerges in *The Lady from the Sea,* (which "quotes" directly from this play); the "vine-leaves in the hair" by which Hedda Gabler, too, sought to resurrect Dionysos in her despiritualized world. And, in the last four plays, the collision between baffled and tormented everyday reality on one side and, on the other, the transcendent forces that invade and set out to transfigure that reality. Quite apart from its own commanding achievement, *Emperor and Galilean* is indispensable for understanding the plays of the Realist Cycle.

THE HISTORICAL VERACITY OF *EMPEROR AND GALILEAN*

It might surprise readers that this "world-historic" play stays very close to the historical facts while "shaping" them dialectically, tragically, and theatrically. A sympathetic commentator on Julian such as Edward Gibbon in *The Decline and Fall of the Roman Empire* records the same positive and negative aspects of Julian's career that we find Ibsen re-imagining. Miracle-workers like Maximus, did instruct Julian into Neo-Platonic theurgic mysteries and séances, and Julian, with most of his extraordinary culture—the opposite of our relentlessly materialist one—wholeheartedly went along with this entire spiritualist procedure of magic, séances, and miracle mongering. Julian, who attempted to combine the offices of Supreme Pontiff and of Emperor—commander of the spiritual and the political empires, continually consulted magicians and soothsayers as well as philosophers and made his most important decisions only after such consultations. He did try to rebuild the temple of Jerusalem to prove Jesus a liar, and the effort was disastrously defeated in the dubiously "miraculous" manner described in the play. Pagan temples and statues were destroyed, some by earthquake others by fanatic Christians, like Agathon who ecstatically tells Julian of his divinely inspired massacre of pagans and destruction of their temples. The Christians did react to Julian's endeavor with the fanatic fortitude the play records. Ibsen has dramatically heightened some incidents and has shaped others to emphasize the overall conflict of the play; but the extraordinary events he dramatizes are part of the historical record. It was an age in which miracles were ardently looked for and triumphantly discovered by both Christians and Pagans: in which omens and visions on both sides were clamorously proclaimed and remembered when extraordinary events seemed to confirm them.

To a truly wonderful extent, Ibsen has imagined himself into this culture and its habits of thought and feeling. What Ibsen said of his procedure in such earlier historical dramas as *Lady Inger of Ostraat* is even more true of *Emperor and Galilean:* "I tried as far as possible to live myself into the ways and customs of that period, into the emotional life of the people, into their patterns of thought and modes of expression." To his publisher, Frederick Hegel, he wrote, "This drama (*Emperor and Galilean*) has been a Herculean labor—not the writing of it; that has been easy—but because of the trouble it has cost me to revivify in my own mind an age so remote and alien." To imaginatively inhabit a world so different from Ibsen's own culture as that of fourth century A.D. Byzantium must have seemed to the poet the greatest possible liberation from the suffocating pietism of his own background in Skien and from the parochialism of his contemporaries at large.

The success with which Ibsen enters into the world of *Emperor and Galilean* gives the play a "closeness" and immediacy, a sense of being directly caught up, confused, baffled and moved by events along with the hero that is, I think, unusual in Ibsen's writing. From the massacre by Constantius of Julian's entire family in his childhood to his death on the battlefield, Julian lived and died much as Ibsen portrays him. This raw engagement with its subject makes this play intended for readers at least as histrionic and as *passionately* actable, I think, as the plays of the Realist Cycle. In the modern realist plays Ibsen brings to bear upon events ironic perspectives, including archetypal forces, of which the protagonists are unaware, and the audience gradually has a view, denied to the protagonists, of the evolving dialectic. In *Emperor and Galilean* such a "Sophoclean" advantage is denied us. Julian's engagement with the archetypal realm is alarmingly, disconcertingly direct, (more Aeschylean than Sophoclean) and his quest, all the time wrapped in agonizing uncertainty, is highly conscious and dramatic. We are in the thick of events with the hero, whether in an unnervingly ambiguous séance or on the battlefield—much as in Shakespeare's *Macbeth*, a drama that often haunts this play. Indeed, the reader will pick up many Shakespearean echoes throughout both parts of the play: Macbeth's compact with ambiguous powers and ascendancy to the throne; his defeat and death in battle; the introspective vacillations of both Julian and Hamlet; and Macbeth's recognition that the powers he trusted have toyed with him as Julian at the end, discovers himself to have been ambushed by the world-will.

HISTORY RECREATED AS TRAGEDY

Emperor and Galilean is drama conceived on the hugest possible human scale, involving all of Western civilization at its most crucial turning point: The moment when Julian the Apostate attempted to remake our humanity by undoing the Christian revolution. With astonishing hubris Julian sets out to remake humanity itself. Working more directly upon the world than Goethe's Faust, he sets himself up as the deliberate and principled Anti-Christ. The play is the quintessential historical drama because it makes the possibility of understanding the historical process itself the very heart of the play's quest. It is History re-created as Tragedy. Aeschylus already had shown the way in the first Greek tragedy we possess: *The Persians,* where, dramatizing a war in which he took part, he nevertheless re-imagines the "facts" to bring out the universal drama (of Persian hubris punished by Zeus) "behind" the facts as he knew them. Ever since Aristotle's dictum that Poetry is more true than History (because, while history must show what happened, Poetry can show what *ought to* have happened), history and drama have maintained an ambivalent symbiosis. Shakespeare rewrote English History in terms of Tudor ideology. In the modern period, Friedrich Schiller was the first to recreate History as tragic myth, like Aeschylus "correcting" historical fact by showing the universal forces behind the historical details in such plays as *Don Carlos, Wallenstein,* and *Mary Stuart..* Though *Emperor and Galilean* sticks closer than Schiller to the historical accounts, Ibsen clearly is recreating history as tragic myth, discovering the tragic pattern, the tragic "argument" behind the "facts."

This clearly is evident in the *shaping* of the play. First is the division into the contrasting Parts One and Two. Part One dramatizes Julian's gradual rebellion against and ultimate onslaught upon the Christian world. In this section, Julian 'trajectory' is dynamic and expanding: He leaves corrupt Constantinople first for the learning of Athens, then for the mystery of Ephesus. Unexpectedly, he is proclaimed Caesar, and at this moment he has been deflected from his *spiritual* quest and caught in the treacherous snares of the political world that ultimately will destroy him. As Caesar he gathers military strength and Part One ends with his preparations for war as he *advances* against Constantius and the Christian order.

Part Two records an opposite trajectory: the Christian world's huge counterattack descending upon the now increasingly *retreating* Julian. Julian, in power, finds his quest baffled, confused, and undermined, both by the feebleness and sycophancy of his supporters (with the exception of a few such as Nevita and Maximus) and by the ferocity of his Christian opponents whose once-flagging cause ironically is rejuvenated by Julian's offensive. As G. Wilson Knight observes: "There is more of the ecstatic Dionysos in the Christians than in the intellectual Julian." Julian's own character struggles against disintegration and utter disillusion until he finally dies, defeated but still clinging to the forlorn dream of a revived Hellenism. Part Two gives rise to more dramatic styles than the more unitary Part One: satiric, comedic, elegiac, mock-polemical and tragic. The two Parts of the play, then, stand in ironic contrast to each other, like a huge diptych.

As a historical *tragedy* the drama must record its hero's defeat: Otherwise the action would not be tragic. As a Hegelian *historical* tragedy it must discover an illuminating (universal) pattern beneath all the confusion of details that go into that defeat. Hegel distinguished between individuals who, from the highest and noblest motives, "have resisted that which the advance of the spiritual idea makes necessary" and who thereby tragically fail, and those "whose crimes have been turned into the means—under the direction of a superior principle—of realizing the purpose of that principle" and so succeed despite manifest inferiorities. The former, nobler characters, possess only "a formal rectitude—deserted by the living spirit and by God." Julian, I would claim, is this tragically nobler character: One whose highest motives only serve the inscrutable designs of the *Weltgeist* (world-spirit) and who finds himself "deserted by the living spirit and by God" while inferior figures, like Jovian, succeed. In the séance of Part One, Act III, Julian finds himself linked with such great "negative but necessary" figures as Cain and Judas. In the course of the play, he will have served the purposes of the world-will by bringing about the opposite of what he intended.

THE SYMMETRICAL STRUCTURING OF THE PLAY

The symmetrical contrast of the two Parts of the play is repeated in a careful structuring of each act in both Parts One and Two. Part One, Act One is built around two imperial processions: the first, in the opening scene, in drastic disarray, entering the Chapel and the world of spiritual communion; the second, toward the close, in deadly decisiveness, exiting the Chapel and into the world of political action. Act Two opens with Julian's celebration in Athens of Hellenic culture, including the mock trial of the Christian Gregory; it ends with his disillusioned rejection of Athens and its moribund, book-dominated classicism and with his departure for the mysteries of Ephesus. Act Three begins with a séance in which Julian and Maximus ponder the *spiritual* secrets of the world-will and its mysterious destiny and ends with Julian's investiture as Caesar in the dangerous *material* world of imperial power: the most fatally decisive event in the play. In Act Four, we see Julian at first fleeing the disastrous consequences of his military victory over the Gauls that will bring down upon him the dreadful wrath of Constantius; but the act ends with him brilliantly controlling his army and embarking upon his campaign against the Emperor: as in *Macbeth* a sinister luring of the hero to treacherous reality. Act Five shows him first searching *below* in the depths and darkness "for light" and direction, then concludes with his emerging and *ascending* into the light and ready to advance upon Constantius and Constantinople and claim the imperial throne.

Part Two reveals the same pattern of contrasting opening and closing scenes to each act. Each decisive action of Julian is countered with a devastating reaction; each attempt at restoring the old ceremonies degenerates into farce and brings about a Christian revival; each reluctant persecution only inspires his Christian opponents to martyrdom; and on the battlefield there is the same pattern of reversals. In Act Five Julian, at first lost in a fog of paranoid delusions, at the end dies clearly reaffirming the vision that has animated him from the beginning. It is by such thematic shaping of each act and of the whole play that Ibsen is able to achieve firm aesthetic control over such a mass of historical detail.

THE CHARACTER OF JULIAN

Julian's "finely-tuned inadequacies," as Wilson Knight termed them, are in a sense virtues—even, at first, survival skills. Unlike his brother Gallus and his wife Helena, two uncomplicatedly ruthless (and adulterous) pagans-at-heart who are ardently faithful Christians, the rigidly virtuous, abstemious (and pagan) Julian is a complex but canny survivor. More honest and self-aware than Constantius, he is driven to injustice by the fanaticism and ferocity of his opponents. Ibsen does not minimize the historical record of Julian's defects that accompanied his undeniable virtues and gifts: his superstitious reliance, born from his painful human isolation, on omens and oracles; his learning that degenerates into pedantry; the injustices and cruelties he is exasperated into committing; his susceptibility to flattery. He is the most complex dramatic character ever created: As a thinker, Hamlet is a mere freshman beside him, Macbeth a barbarian, and Marlowe's and Goethe's Fausts—his closest competitors—are never serious world-agents able to act decisively upon historical reality.

The portrait of the tortured intellectual, Julian, vainly fighting the world-spirit with pen and sword, stands out strikingly from the portrait gallery of earlier heroes in history and drama: and this is his modern aspect. An adequate modern world leader—a Lenin or Mao—must try to understand his or her world "theoretically" as well as practically. Such a leader must not only act, but, like Julian, act with a theoretical underpinning to ensure that the actions undertaken are those the nature of reality requires. The volumes of writings left by Lenin, and the fierce ideological and pedantic disputes entered into by rival modern revolutionary leaders, would have astonished such successful but nonintellectual world-shapers as Alexander, Julius Caesar, Tamburlaine and Napoleon. Julian the Apostate Ideologue might be the first such modern portrait in drama.

But Julian, who wishes to emulate the Stoic Marcus Aurelius, also resembles Nero, the Emperor as Artist. He continually is regarding himself in the mirror held up by his revered ancients. His painfully self-conscious ceremonies and sacrifices are desperate histrionic "stagings," craving to achieve authenticity; yet, as director of each show, he always is being let down by the shabby materials he has to work with: sycophants and flatterers instead of courageous comrades, half-hearted and venal fellow-celebrants instead of true believers. Nor do his enemies allow him even the consolation of ennobling combat, being hostile and fanatic zealots with no sense of beauty, reason, nor any of the values Julian seeks to re-establish. The situation is repeated in *Rosmersholm* where another apostate, Rosmer, is horrified by the savagery his apostasy has aroused in his opponents. The Galileans do not have the "truth" against his "illusion": They prove to have only the more secure illusion. Julian finds himself fighting, not "God" but the more potent idea of God in the minds of his opponents.

Puritanical, abstemious, and chaste, he pedantically plays the part of the priest of Venus, goddess of sexual love and of Dionysos, god of wine, intoxication, and the passions. His bacchanals degenerate into travesties because, under him, they become academic charades pursued by charlatans and pedants. No one was less equipped to inspire a revival of Hellenic joy-of-life. With more reason than Hamlet he could lament:

> The time is out of joint. O cursèd spite
> That ever I was born to set it right.

This is his tragi-comedy. His hatred of Christianity seems a stronger force in him than his love of paganism. The "artist" aspect of Julian accounts for much of his rhetoric, especially in his empty contests with Libanius; by attempting to recreate the *spirit* of the old Athenians, he can only parody their style. It is in the duels of eloquence with Libanius, applauded by his sycophantic courtiers, that Julian most pathetically is depicted *savoring* the once-living but now moribund spirit of the pagan past. The desperate artificiality of it all shows how futile Julian's revivalism (like Hedda Gabler's attempt to resurrect Dionysos in Eilert Løvborg) actually is.

Julian himself becomes at times a somewhat comic-pathetic figure. At the opening of Act III, (Part Two) a band of recalcitrant and hungry scholars in ragged cloaks and with matted hair and beards, grumbling, sarcastic and mutinous are gathered around a similarly ragged and unkempt Julian with ink on his fingers, still futilely urging by persuasive pamphlets the fatally wounded Pegasus of paganism to fly. Yet something of the beauty and courage of Julian's quest again and again is conveyed: We sense the beauty, in lyric moments when his yearning for a numinous world manages repeatedly to rise above the most disheartening reversals he suffers; we sense the courage when he doggedly pursues his lonely, often desolating and terrifying path into the heart of darkness. Ibsen maintains our sympathy, admiration, and interest in this figure even at his most ludicrous moments. These qualities make for a quite unique form of tragedy: a tragedy of the intellect. It is a very subtle portrait of a baffled mind.

ON CUTTING THE TEXT

With its great length and its huge cast, *Emperor and Galilean* is not performable without extensive cutting, (though it was successfully performed at length as a radio play by the British Broadcasting Company many years ago). Julian's long speeches in Part Two, many of them directly lifted from his writings, are suitable candidates for reduction. One might dream of some enlightened film producer, armed with an intellect and abetted by a similarly imaginative director (a Scorcese or Bertolucci, perhaps), creating a movie epic out of the play; it splendidly has the "scenes" and confrontations; but until that miracle, a theatrical production with huge excisions is all that can be hoped for. All such cuts, however, must be left to directors. The translator needs to provide the fullest and most accurate text possible, leaving it to the theatre professionals to decide what to leave out. Any reading of the play will confirm its superbly histrionic qualities: There are scenes that cry out for performance and dramatic confrontations as compelling as any in Ibsen—or in drama.

Emperor and Galilean

PART ONE

CAESAR'S APOSTASY

"CAESARS FRAFALL"

A Drama in Five Acts

CHARACTERS

THE EMPEROR CONSTANTIUS
THE EMPRESS EUSEBIA
PRINCESS HELENA, the Emperor's sister
PRINCE GALLUS, the Emperor's cousin
PRINCE JULIAN, Gallus's younger half-brother
MEMNON, an Ethiopian, the Emperor's slave
POTAMON, a goldsmith
PHOCION, a dyer
EUNAPIUS, a barber
A fruit seller
A Captain of the Guard
A soldier
A painted woman
A paralyzed man
A blind beggar
AGATHON, son of a vine-grower from Cappadocia
LIBANIUS, a philosopher
GREGORY, of Nazianzus
BASIL, from Caesarea
SALLUST, from Perusia
HECEBOLIUS, theology teacher
MAXIMUS, a mystic
EUTHERIUS, a chamberlain
LEONTES, a quaestor
MYRRHA, a slave woman
DECENTIUS, a tribune
SINTULA, master of the horse
FLORENTIUS, a general
SEVERUS, a general
ORIBASES, a doctor
LAIPSO, a centurion
VARRO, a centurion
MAURUS, a standard-bearer

Soldiers, churchgoers, pagan onlookers, courtiers, priests, philosophy students, dancing-girls, servants, the quaestor's attendants, Gaulish warriors.
Visions and voices.

SETTING

The events occur between A.D. 351 and A.D. 361.

ACT ONE

Easter night in Constantinople. The setting represents an open garden with trees, bushes, and overturned statues, close to the Imperial Palace. In the background, brilliantly lit, stands the imperial chapel. To the right, a marble balustrade whose steps lead down to the water. Between the pines and the cypresses are glimpses of the Bosphorus and the Asiatic coast.

Divine service. Imperial troops of the household on the church steps. Huge crowds of worshippers are streaming in. Beggars, cripples, and blind people are at the entrance. Pagan onlookers and sellers of fruit and of water crowd the place.

ANTHEM: *(From within the Chapel.)*
  In glory shall endure
  The Cross for evermore!
  The serpent, vanquished, lies
  In torment without cease.
  Oh blessed Lamb arise!
  The earth now dwells in peace!

POTOMAN: *(The goldsmith, with a paper lantern, enters from the left and taps a soldier on the shoulder.)* Hsst! my good friend—is the emperor on his way here?

SOLDIER: I don't know.

PHOKION: *(The dyer, in the crowd, turns his head.)* Emperor? Do I hear someone asking after the Emperor? The Emperor's arriving just before midnight—maybe even a bit earlier. I got it from Memnon himself.

EUNAPIOS: *(A barber, rushes in furiously, shoving a fruit seller aside.)* Out of the way, pagan!

FRUIT SELLER: Gently, sir.

POTOMAN: What's the pig whining about?

EUNAPIOS: Dog!

PHOKION: Whining against a well-dressed Christian, a man of the Emperor's own faith!

EUNAPIOS: *(Knocking the fruit seller down.)* Go on—into the muck!

POTOMAN: That's it! Wallow in it—just like your gods.

PHOKION: *(Striking him with his stick.)* There! Take that—and that!

EUNAPIOS: *(Kicking him.)* And that; and that! You'll feel this on your god-forsaken hide! *(The fruit seller hurries away.)*

PHOKION: *(With the obvious intention of being heard by the Captain of the Guard.)* I earnestly wish someone would bring this incident to the blessed ears of our Emperor. Only recently the Emperor expressed his displeasure at how we Christians associate with the pagans as if there were no distinction between us—

POTOMAN: You mean the notice posted in the marketplace? I've read it too. What I think is—just as you find true and worthless gold in the world—

EUNAPIOS:—so we shouldn't all be tarred with the same brush. My thoughts entirely. Thank God a few zealous souls are still to be found among us.

PHOKION: We're far from being zealous enough, dear brethren! Just look at the airs these blasphemers give themselves! How many in this mob, do you imagine, carry the sign of the cross and the fish on their arms?

POTOMAN: No. Yet they dare to swarm in front of the holy Chapel itself—!

PHOKION: On such a sacred night as this—

EUNAPIOS:—blocking the path of the Church's true followers.

A PAINTED WOMAN: *(In the crowd.)* The Donatists are true?

PHOKION: What? Donatist! You're a Donatist?

EUNAPIOS: What's this? You're not the same?

PHOKION: I? I! May hellfire blast your tongue!

POTAMON: *(Crossing himself.)* Let plague and pestilence—

PHOKION: Donatist! You carrion! You rotten tree!

POTOMAN: Well said! Well said!

PHOKION: Fuel for Satan's furnace.

POTOMAN: That's right! Give it him, give it him, dear brother!

PHOKION: *(Pushing the goldsmith away.)* Hold your tongue! Get away from me. I know you, now—you're Potoman, the Manichaean!

EUNAPIOS: A Manichaean? A stinking heretic. Ecch! Ecch!

POTOMAN: *(Holding up his paper lantern.)* Ah! That's Phokion, the dyer from Antioch! The Cainite!

EUNAPIOS: Horrible! I've fallen among a band of liars.

PHOKION: Horrible! I've aided the seed of the devil!

EUNAPIOS: *(Boxes his ear.)* That's for helping me!

PHOKION: *(Strikes him back.)* Oh, you rotten cur!

POTOMAN: Damn you—damn you both!

(Free-for-all; laughter and jeers from the crowd.)

CAPTAIN OF THE GUARD: *(Calling to the soldiers.)* The Emperor!

ANTHEM: *(From the high altar.)*

The serpent, vanquished, lies
In torment without cease.
Oh blessed Lamb arise!
The earth now dwells in peace!

(The Court enters in splendid procession from the left, led by Priests with censers. They are followed by soldiers, torchbearers, courtiers, and bodyguards. At

the center of the procession, the EMPEROR CONSTANTIUS. Thirty-four
years old, of distinguished bearing, beardless and with brown, curly hair. His eyes
have a gloomy and mistrustful expression and his walk and demeanor betray
uneasiness and infirmity. The EMPRESS EUSEBIA walks on his left, a pale and
delicate woman, the same age as the Emperor. Behind the royal couple walks
PRINCE JULIAN, a youth of nineteen, not yet fully developed. He is dark-
haired, with the beginnings of a beard, and sparkling, brown eyes, that glance
restlessly about. The Court dress seems to encumber him; his manner is strikingly
awkward and intense. The Emperor's sister, HELENA, a voluptuous, twenty-
five-year-old beauty, follows next, attended by girls and older women. Courtiers
and soldiers bring the procession to a close. The Emperor's personal slave,
MEMNON, a huge and magnificently clad Ethiopian, is among the followers.)

CONSTANTIUS: *(Suddenly halts, turning round to PRINCE JULIAN, and asks*
  sharply.) Where is Gallus?

JULIAN: *(Turning pale.)* Gallus? Why do you want Gallus?

CONSTANTIUS: There! I caught you out!

JULIAN: My lord—!

EUSEBIA: *(Taking the emperor's hand.)* Come now, come now.

CONSTANTIUS: Your conscience cried out! What are you two plotting?

JULIAN: We?

CONSTANTIUS: You and he!

EUSEBIA: Hush! Come now, come now, Constantius

CONSTANTIUS: Such a wicked act! What was the oracle's answer?

JULIAN: Oracle? By the Blessed Savior—.

CONSTANTIUS: If anyone's lying about you, he'll pay at the stake. *(Pulls*
  JULIAN aside.) Let's hold fast together, Julian! Dear cousin, let's do that!

JULIAN: It all lies in your hands, my dearest lord!

CONSTANTIUS: My hands—!

JULIAN: Oh, stretch them in mercy over us!

CONSTANTIUS: My hands? What were you thinking about my hands?

JULIAN: *(Grasps his hands and kisses them.)* The emperor's hands are white
  and cool.

CONSTANTIUS: What else should they be? What were you thinking? Now I've
  caught you again.

JULIAN: *(Kissing them once more.)* They're like rose petals here in the moonlight.

CONSTANTIUS: Yes, yes, yes, Julian!

EUSEBIA: Let's go. It's now time.

CONSTANTIUS: Into the presence of the Lord! I! I! Oh, pray for me, Julian!
  They will offer me the holy wine. I can see it! It gleams like a serpent's eyes,
  in the golden chalice—*(Screams.)* Ah! Jesus Christ, pray for me!

EUSEBIA: The Emperor is sick—

HELENA: Where is Caesarius? The doctor, the doctor—fetch him—!

EUSEBIA: *(Softly.)* Memnon, good Memnon!

(She talks quietly to the slave.)

JULIAN: *(In a low voice.)* My lord, be merciful—send me far from here.

CONSTANTIUS: Where do you want to go?

JULIAN: To Egypt. If you'll agree. So many are going there now—into the great solitude.

CONSTANTIUS: Into the solitude? Hah! In the solitude, one broods. I forbid you to brood.

JULIAN: I won't brood—if you'd just allow me—. Here, my soul's hunger grows every day. Evil thoughts crowd in on me. For nine days I've worn a hairshirt—but it hasn't protected me. For nine nights I've whipped myself with scourges, but they won't drive those evil thoughts away.

CONSTANTIUS: We need to be steadfast, Julian! The devil's diligently at work in all of us. Talk to Hecebolius—

MEMNON: *(To the EMPEROR.)* Now it's time to—

CONSTANTIUS: No, no, I don't want to—

MEMNON: *(Taking him by the wrist.)* Come, gracious lord—come, I say.

CONSTANTIUS: *(Composes himself, and says with dignity.)* Into the House of the Lord!

MEMNON: *(Softly.)* And afterwards—that other matter—

CONSTANTIUS: *(To Julian.)* Gallus shall attend on me.

(Behind the EMPEROR'S back, JULIAN clasps his hands imploringly to the EMPRESS.)

EUSEBIA: *(Quickly, whispering.)* Don't be afraid!

CONSTANTIUS: Stay outside. You can't enter church in the state of mind you're in now. Were you to kneel at the altar, it would be only to call down evil on me. Oh, don't nurse such guilt inside you, my beloved cousin.

(The procession heads for the Chapel. On the steps, beggars, cripples, and blind men throng round the EMPEROR.)

A DEFORMED CRIPPLE: Great Lord of the world, let me touch the hem of your robe, that I may be healed.

A BLIND MAN: Pray for me, O Lord's anointed, that I may see again.

CONSTANTIUS: Have faith, my son! Memnon, scatter silver among them. In, now! In!

(The Court proceeds into the Chapel while the doors are closing. The swarm of people disperses soon after. Only JULIAN remains behind, in one of the streets.)

JULIAN: *(Gazing at the Chapel.)* Why would he want Gallus? On this holy night, surely he's not thinking of—! Oh, only to *know*—! *(He turns and bumps into the retreating blind man.)* Watch where you're going, friend!

BLIND MAN: I am blind, sir!

JULIAN: Blind still? Can you really not see even that shining star? Shame on you—of so little faith. After God's anointed promised to pray for your sight!

BLIND MAN: Who are you, mocking a blind brother?

JULIAN: Your brother in unbelief and blindness.

(He moves to go out to the left.)

A VOICE: *(Softly, behind him, in the bushes.)* Julian, Julian!

JULIAN: *(With a cry.)* Ah!

THE VOICE: *(Closer.)* Julian!

JULIAN: Stay where you are—I'm armed! Take care!

A YOUNG MAN: *(Meanly dressed, with a traveler's staff, comes into sight among the trees.)* Be easy; it's me—

JULIAN: Stay right there! Don't come near me, man!

THE YOUNG MAN: You don't remember Agathon, then—?

JULIAN: Agathon! What are you saying? Agathon was just a boy—

AGATHON: Six years ago. I recognized you straight away. *(Comes closer.)*

JULIAN: Agathon! Yes, by the Holy Cross, if I don't believe it's really you!

AGATHON: Look at me—take a good look—

JULIAN: *(Embracing and kissing him.)* My childhood friend, my—brother! Dearest of them all! And you're here? Of all the miracles! You've come the whole way over the mountains, and then across the sea—all the way from Cappadocia!

AGATHON: I got here two days ago, by boat from Ephesus. Oh, how I've been trying to find you these two days. At the palace gates, the guards wouldn't let me in and so—

JULIAN: Did you give my name to anyone? Or say you were looking for me?

AGATHON: No, I didn't dare give your name because—

JULIAN: You did the right thing. Never give out more than is absolutely necessary. Over here, Agathon—in the full moonlight where I can see you. Agathon, Agathon! How you've grown, Agathon. How strong you look.

AGATHON: And you're paler.

JULIAN: I don't thrive in this palace air. It's unhealthy here, I think. Not like Macellum. Macellum lies high up. Not another town in Cappadocia lies as high as Macellum. How fresh those snow winds blow, down from the Taurus mountains—! Are you tired, Agathon?

AGATHON: Not a bit.

JULIAN: Let's sit down, just the same. It's so quiet and peaceful, here. Close together, like this! *(He pulls him down to a seat by the balustrade.)* "Can anything good come from Cappadocia" they say. Yes, friends can come. Can anything be better? *(Gazes at him awhile.)* Incredible, that I didn't recognize you straight away. You, my own dearest friend—isn't this just as if we were boys again—?

AGATHON: *(Kneeling before him.)* With me at your feet, just as before.

JULIAN: No, no, no—

AGATHON: Oh, let me—like this!

JULIAN: Ah, Agathon, it's both sinful and blasphemous—you kneeling to me. If you only knew the load of guilt I carry! Hecebolius, my worthy teacher, suffers agonies over me. Why, he could tell you—! How thick and glossy your hair's grown. How curly it is. But Mardonius—how is it with him? *His* hair must be almost white by now.

AGATHON: Completely white.

JULIAN: How Mardonius knew how to interpret Homer! I don't believe anyone can come near to him at that! "Hero against hero in battle. And the bright gods above, urging them on." I could see it before my very eyes!

AGATHON: At that time your were set on becoming a great and successful warrior.

JULIAN: Those were happy years—those six in Cappadocia. Were the years longer, then, than now? It seems so, when I call to mind all we crowded into them. Yes, they were happy years. We with our books, and Gallus on his Persian horse. Like the shadow of a cloud—that's how he sped across the plain. Ah, but there's *one* thing you must tell me. The church—?

AGATHON: The church? Over the grave of St. Mamas?

JULIAN: *(With a faint smile.)* That Gallus and I built. Gallus finished his wing; but I—it would never come right. How did it work out later?

AGATHON: It didn't. The builders said it was impractical doing it that way.

JULIAN: *(Thoughtfully.)* Just so; just so. It was wrong of me to think they were incompetent. I know now why it couldn't work out. I must tell you, Agathon. Mamas was a false saint.

AGATHON: St. Mamas?

JULIAN: That Mamas was never a martyr. The whole legend about him's an absurd heresy. Hecebolius, with that tremendous learning of his, found out the truth of the matter; and I myself recently have written a slight piece on this subject, Agathon, which some philosophers, oddly enough, have spoken highly of in the classrooms. The Lord keep my heart free from all vanity! The evil tempter is everywhere, sneaking his way into—one can never be sure. To think Gallus succeeded, not I. Oh, Agathon, when I think about that church, I see Cain's altar—

AGATHON: Julian!

JULIAN: God won't acknowledge me, Agathon!

AGATHON: Don't talk that way! Wasn't God mighty in you when you led me out of the darkness of paganism and into the light for all eternity? And you, then, no more than a child!

JULIAN: Yes, all that now seems just a dream.

AGATHON: And yet, it was the redeeming truth!

JULIAN: *(Gloomily.)* If it were that *now!* Where did I find those words of fire? The air filled with hymns—a ladder between heaven and earth—*(Stares.)* Did you see that?

AGATHON: See what?

JULIAN: A star, falling—*there,* behind the two cypresses. *(Silent awhile, then says, abruptly.)* Did I ever tell you what my mother dreamt, the night before I was born?

AGATHON: I don't remember.

JULIAN: No, no, that's right. I learned about it later.

AGATHON: What did she dream?

JULIAN: My mother dreamt she was giving birth to Achilles.

AGATHON: *(Eagerly.)* You believe in dreams as much as ever?

JULIAN: Why do you ask?

AGATHON: You'll get to hear. It all fits in with what drove me across the sea—

JULIAN: You've a special reason for coming? I didn't think of asking why—

AGATHON: A strange reason, but one which keeps me hovering in a state of uncertainty and fear. There's so much I ought to know first—about life in this city—about yourself—about the Emperor—

JULIAN: *(Looks searchingly at him.)* Tell the truth, Agathon; who've you spoken to here before you met me?

AGATHON: Not with anyone.

JULIAN: When did you get here?

AGATHON: I told you before—two days ago.

JULIAN: And right away you want to know—? What kind of things do you want to know about the Emperor? Is there somebody who asked you—? *(Flings his arms about him.)* Oh, Agathon, my friend, forgive me!

AGATHON: Forgive what? Why?

JULIAN: *(Rising, alert and listening.)* Hush! No, it's nothing—just a bird somewhere in the bushes. I'm truly happy here. Why would you think I'm not? Why shouldn't I be happy? Don't I have all my family here? Well, that is, all those our blessed Savior's arm was able to protect.

AGATHON: And the Emperor has taken your father's place?

JULIAN: In all things the Emperor is wise and good.

AGATHON: *(Who also has risen.)* Is it true—the rumor that one day you'll become the Emperor's successor?

JULIAN: *(Quickly.)* Don't speak such dangerous things. I've no idea what foolish rumors are going around. Why are you asking me all these questions? You'll not get another word out of me until you tell me what you want here in Constantinople.

AGATHON: I come in the service of the Lord God.

JULIAN: If you hold dear your Savior and your salvation, get back home again. *(Leaning over the balustrade.)* Speak softly, there's a boat down there. *(He draws him over to the other side.)* What do you want, here? To kiss a splinter of the holy cross? Get back home again, I tell you! Do you know what Constantinople's become these last fifteen months? A blasphemous Babylon. You haven't heard? You know that Libanius is here?

AGATHON: But, Julian, I don't know Libanius.

JULIAN: You sheltered Cappadocian! Lucky the land where his voice and teaching haven't yet struck deep!

AGATHON: Ah, he's one of those heretical pagan teachers!

JULIAN: The most dangerous of the lot.

AGATHON: Surely not more dangerous than Aedesius of Pergamon?

JULIAN: Him? Who thinks any more about Aedesius of Pergamon? Aedesius is in his dotage.

AGATHON: More dangerous yet than that mysterious Maximus?

JULIAN: Maximus! Don't speak of that charlatan. Who really knows anything for certain about Maximus?

AGATHON: He claims he slept three years in a cave the other side of Jordan.

JULIAN: Hecebolious holds him to be an impostor, and he's probably not far wrong. No, no, Agathon, Libanius is the most dangerous. Our sinful earth seems to be convulsed in agony under this scourge. There were signs foretelling his coming. Men and women suddenly were struck down by a dreadful pestilence. And then, when that was over, in November, every night, there rained down fire from heaven. You mustn't doubt it, Agathon! I myself have seen the stars break from their spheres and plunge down to the earth, flaming as they fell. Since then, he's been teaching here—he, the philosopher, the orator. Here, everyone calls him the king of eloquence. And well they might. I tell you, he is terrible. Youths and men flock to him; he binds their souls so they *must* follow him . Heresy flows seductively from his lips, like the poems and songs of the Trojans and Greeks.

AGATHON: *(In alarm.)* Oh, you've sought him out too, Julian!

JULIAN: *(Recoiling.)* I! God protect me from all such acts. If you hear any rumors to that effect, pay no attention to them. It isn't true I've sought out

Libanius, in the night—or in disguise. Just to approach him would appall me. In any case, the Emperor's forbidden it, and Hecebolius is even more adamant. Any of the faithful need only come near him to become apostates and blasphemers. And they're not the only ones. His words are carried from mouth to mouth right into the palace itself. His playful scorn, his irrefutable logic, his satiric verses—these break into my prayers. They crowd in on me like those hideous, birdlike creatures who sought to befoul the food of the adventuring hero. There are times, to my horror, I feel repelled by the very Faith and Word that should nourish me. *(With an uncontrollable outburst.)* If I had the Emperor's power, I'd send you the head of Libanius on a silver platter.

AGATHON: But how can the Emperor possibly allow this? How can our devoted, God-fearing Emperor—?

JULIAN: The Emperor? All praise to our Emperor's faith and piety. But the Emperor has no mind for anything except this wretched Persian war. It fills everyone's thoughts. No one cares about the war waged here against the Prince of Golgotha. Ah, my dear Agathon, it's no longer like it was two years ago. Then, that mystic Maximus's own two brothers paid with their lives for their false doctrines. You've no idea what powerful supporters Libanius now has. One or two small-fry philosophers might get chased out of the city—but no one dares touch *him*. I've pleaded and I've prayed to both Hecebolius and the Empress to get him banished. But no, no! What good does it do to get rid of the others? This one man poisons the air for us all. Oh, You my Savior, if I could only fly from all this heathen hideousness! Living here is living in the lions' den.

AGATHON: *(Eagerly.)* Julian—what was that you said?

JULIAN: Yes, yes. Only a miracle can save us.

AGATHON: Oh, then listen! The miracle's happened.

JULIAN: What do you mean?

AGATHON: I'll tell you, Julian, because I can't doubt any longer you're the one who is meant. What brought me to Constantinople was a vision—

JULIAN: You say a vision?

AGATHON: A divine revelation—

JULIAN: Then, by the grace of God, speak! No, hush, don't speak. Wait. Someone's coming. Stay here—look unconcerned—as if there's nothing— *(They both remain standing by the balustrade. A tall, handsome middle-aged man, dressed in the customary short cloak of the philosophy teacher, enters through the avenue on the left. A flock of young men accompany him, all with their clothes tucked up short, with ivy wreaths in their hair and carrying books, papers, and parchments. They are laughing and talking animatedly as they enter.)*

PHILOSOPHER: Don't drop anything into the water, Gregory, my happy friend! Remember, what you're carrying's worth more than gold.

JULIAN: *(Who is standing close by him.)* With all respect—is there any good worth gaining more than gold.

PHILOSOPHER: The fruits of your lifetime's labor—can you buy those back with gold?

JULIAN: True, true. But just for that reason you shouldn't risk them on the treacherous waters.

PHILOSOPHER: Man's favor is more treacherous.

JULIAN: That was wisely said. And where are you sailing with your riches?

PHILOSOPHER: To Athens. *(He makes to walk on.)*

JULIAN: *(Suppressing a laugh.)* To Athens? Then, O man of wealth, you don't value your own riches.

PHILOSOPHER: *(Halting.)* How so?

JULIAN: Is it a wise man's labor to bear owls to Athens?

PHILOSOPHER: My owls can't adjust to the ecclesiastical light of this imperial city. *(To one of the young men.)* Take my hand, Sallust. *(About to descend the steps.)*

SALLUST, A STUDENT: *(Halfway down the steps.)* By the gods, it's *him!*

PHILOSOPHER: Him—?

SALLUST: As truly as I live. I know him—I've seen him going around with Hecebolius.

PHILOSOPHER: Ah! *(He scrutinizes JULIAN with concealed interest; then comes a step nearer, saying.)* You smiled just then. What were you smiling at?

JULIAN: You were lamenting the ecclesiastical light. I rather imagine it was the regal light from the king of the classrooms that proved too strong for your eyes.

PHILOSOPHER: Envy can find no place under the short cloak.

JULIAN: What finds no place, reveals itself.

PHILOSOPHER: You've a sharp tongue, noble Galilean!

JULIAN: Why Galilean? What are my Galilean features?

PHILOSOPHER: Your smart court dress.

JULIAN: I'm a friend of wisdom, under all this. I even wear a coarse shirt. But, tell me: What are you looking for in Athens?

PHILOSOPHER: What did Pontius Pilate look for?

JULIAN: Wait now! Isn't truth here where Libanius is?

PHILOSOPHER: *(Looks coldly at him.)* Hm! Ah yes, Libanius! Libanius will soon be silent. Libanius is tired of the struggle, sir.

JULIAN: Tired? He, the invulnerable, the all-conquering—

PHILOSOPHER: He is tired of waiting for his equal.

JULIAN: You're joking, stranger! Where does Libanius imagine he'll find his equal?

PHILOSOPHER: His equal has been found.

JULIAN: Who? Where? Name him!

PHILOSOPHER: That could prove dangerous.

JULIAN: Why so?

PHILOSOPHER: Aren't you a courtier?

JULIAN: What of it?

PHILOSOPHER: *(Softly.)* Are you yourself bold enough to name the Emperor's successor?

JULIAN: *(Thoroughly shaken.)* Ah!

PHILOSOPHER: *(Hastily.)* If you betray me, I'll deny everything!

JULIAN: I'll betray no one. Definitely not, definitely not! The Emperor's successor, you say? I don't know who you mean. The Emperor's not elected anyone. But why did you joke just now? Why did you speak of Libanius's equal?

PHILOSOPHER: Tell me yes or no—is there a young man living at court, kept by strict orders, prayers, and prohibition, from approaching the light of the classrooms?

JULIAN: *(Quickly.)* That's done to keep his faith pure.

PHILOSOPHER: *(Smiling.)* So the young man has such weak faith in his faith? What can he know of his faith? What does a warrior know of his shield until he's tested it?

JULIAN: True, true. But these are loving kinsmen and teachers, you must know—

PHILOSOPHER: Mere phrases, sir. I'll tell you what it is. It's for the Emperor's sake his young cousin's kept away from the lovers of wisdom. The Emperor doesn't possess the divine gift of words. Of course, the Emperor's great—but he can't bear that his successor might shine out over the empire—

JULIAN: *(Confused.)* And you dare to—!

PHILOSOPHER: Yes, you're indignant on your ruler's behalf, but—

JULIAN: Far from it; on the contrary; Yes, it could be—. Listen, I stand quite close to this young prince. It would interest me dearly to know—*(Turns round.)* Stand to one side, Agathon; I must talk in private with this man. *(Goes several steps with the stranger.)* You said "shine out"? Shine out over the empire? What do you know—what do any of you know—about Prince Julian?

PHILOSOPHER: Can Sirius be concealed by a cloud? Won't the wind driving here and there rip open the cloud, so that—

JULIAN: Straight to the point, I beg you.

PHILOSOPHER: The Palace and Church are like a twofold cage in which the prince is held prisoner. That cage is not tight enough. At times he lets mysterious words fall; the court toadies—forgive me, sir, the court-followers—take up these and deride them to outsiders. Their deeper meaning escapes these gentlemen—pardon me sir—for few of them does it exist.

JULIAN: For none of them. You can safely say for none—

PHILOSOPHER: It seems to for you. And in any case, for us. Yes, he could shine out over the empire! Aren't there stories told of his childhood years in Cappadocia, when in a debate with his brother Gallus he took the part of the gods and defended them against the Galilean?

JULIAN: That was just a game: a rhetorical exercise—

PHILOSOPHER: And what didn't Mardonius report of him. And Hecebolius after! What artistry already lay in the boy's speech—what beauty, what grace in the play of his thought!

JULIAN: Is that what you think?

PHILOSOPHER: Yes, he could well become an opponent we'd both fear and desire. What does it need for him to reach such an honorable height? He need only go through the same school Paul went through, so unharmed that he later could join with the Galileans, outshining all the other apostles combined, because he had knowledge and eloquence! Hecebolius is fearful for his pupil's faith. Oh, I know so well how that comes from him. But does this overscrupulous man forget he once drank from the springs he now denies his pupil? Wasn't it from us he learned those weapons of speech he now so skillfully launches against us?

JULIAN: Oh, true, undeniably true!

PHILOSOPHER: And what are the gifts of Hecebolius compared with the gifts so wonderfully revealed in this princely child who, from reports in Cappadocia, proclaimed a doctrine over the graves of the martyred Galileans which, though I hold to be wrong—and just for that reason all the harder to carry to victory—yet proclaimed with such spiritual fervor that—if I dare trust a widespread rumor—great numbers of children of his own age accepted his leadership and followed him like disciples. Ah, Hecebolius, just like the others, is more jealous than zealous; and therefore Libanius has waited in vain.

JULIAN: *(Grasping his arm.)* What has Libanius said? For God's—I implore you, tell me!

PHILOSOPHER: He's said everything you've just heard. And said more. He's said, "Watch that princely Galilean; he is a spiritual Achilles."

JULIAN: Achilles! *(Quietly.)* My mother's dream!

PHILOSOPHER: There, in the open classrooms, the battle is fought. Day breaks in joy over the combat and the combatants. Word-weapons whirl; keen shafts of knowledge engage in battle; the blessed gods sit smiling from the clouds—

JULIAN: Away from me with your paganism—!

PHILOSOPHER: And the heroes return to camp, arms entwined, without rancor, their cheeks flushed, their blood pulsing through every vein, with the trophies of knowledge and with laurels on their brows. Ah, where is Achilles? I do not see him. Achilles is angry—

JULIAN: Achilles is unhappy! But can I believe this? Tell me—my head is swimming—did Libanius say all this?

PHILOSOPHER: Why did Libanius come to Constantinople? Did he come with any purpose other than to seek out a certain noble youth's friendship?

JULIAN: *(Tense.)* Speak the truth! No, no, it can't be true. How should this square with all the contempt and mockery—one doesn't mock a man whose friendship one seeks.

PHILOSOPHER: Galilean calumnies, to build a wall of hatred and anger between the two champions.

JULIAN: You're surely not denying it was Libanius—?

PHILOSOPHER: I deny it all absolutely.

JULIAN: You mean those lampoons didn't come from him?

PHILOSOPHER: Not a single one. They all originated in the Emperor's palace and were sent out in his name.

JULIAN: Ah, what are you saying—?

PHILOSOPHER: What I'd dare defend against anyone. You have a sharp tongue—who knows if it wasn't you—

JULIAN: I! But can I believe this? That Libanius didn't write them? None of them?

PHILOSOPHER: No, no.

JULIAN: Not even that shameful poem about Atlas with his twisted shoulders.

PHILOSOPHER: No, no I tell you.

JULIAN: Nor even that stupid and insolent piece about the monkey in court dress.

PHILOSOPHER: Ha! ha! Written in the church, not in the classroom. You don't believe it? I tell you, it was Hecebolius—

JULIAN: Hecebolius!

PHILOSOPHER: Yes, Hecebolius; Hecebolius himself, to create ill will between his enemy and his pupil.

JULIAN: *(With clenched fists.)* Ah, if that's true—!

PHILOSOPHER: If this blinded and betrayed young man knew us philosophers better he'd not have acted so harshly against us.

JULIAN: What are you saying?

PHILOSOPHER: Now it's too late. Farewell, sir.*(He is about to leave.)*

JULIAN: *(Grasping his hand.)* Friend or brother—who are you?

PHILOSOPHER: A man who grieves to see one born of the godhead perish.

JULIAN: What do you mean by "born of the godhead"?

PHILOSOPHER: The uncreated in the changing.

JULIAN: I'm still in the dark.

PHILOSOPHER: A great and glorious world exists to which you Galileans are blind. Life, in that world, is a celebration among statues and sounds of temple songs, with goblets filled to the brim and hair decked with roses. Bridges dizzily span from soul across to soul even to the furthest light in space. I know One who could be ruler of this great and sunlit kingdom.

JULIAN: *(Fearfully.)* Yes, at the cost of his salvation.

PHILOSOPHER: What is salvation? Reunion with the source of life.

JULIAN: Yes, but in full consciousness. Reunion for *me*, just as I am!

PHILOSOPHER: Reunion, like the raindrop with the ocean, or the rotting leaf with the earth that nourished it.

JULIAN: Oh, if only I had knowledge. Had the weapons to raise against you!

PHILOSOPHER: Win those weapons young man! The classroom is the fencing school of the intellect—

JULIAN: *(Shrinks back.)* Ah!

PHILOSOPHER: See those joyful young men there! There are Galileans among them. We can talk of divine matters without quarreling. Farewell! You Galileans have driven truth into exile. Look how we deal with our destiny; how we keep our heads erect and wear the laurel on our brows. That's how we depart, shortening the night with song and awaiting the arrival of Helios.

(He descends the steps, to where his pupils have been waiting for him; then the boat is heard rowing them away.)

JULIAN: *(Gazing long across the water.)* Who was he, that enigmatic man?

AGATHON: *(Approaching.)* Listen to me, Julian—!

JULIAN: *(Excitedly aroused.)* *He* understood me! And Libanius himself; the great, the incomparable Libanius! Imagine it, Agathon, Libanius has said— oh, how keen those pagan eyes must be.

AGATHON: The tempter's method, believe me!

JULIAN: *(Ignoring him.)* I can't bear any longer to be here among these people. They're the originators of all those vile satires. Here I'm ridiculed, treated with contempt while they laugh behind my back. No one here respects what I bear within me. They mock me, my speech, my gestures. Hecebolius himself—! Yes, I can feel it, Christ is leaving me; I am becoming evil here.

AGATHON: Oh, you don't understand. You are marked out for God's grace.

JULIAN: *(Pacing up and down the balustrade.)* I am the one Libanius wishes to combat. What a strange wish. Libanius holds me to be his equal. It's *me* he's waiting for—

AGATHON: Listen and obey. Christ is waiting for you!

JULIAN: What do you mean, friend?

AGATHON: The vision that drove me to Constantinople—

JULIAN: Yes, yes, the vision; I'd nearly forgot. A revelation, you said? Oh, tell me, tell me.

AGATHON: It was back home in Cappadocia, just over a month ago. A rumor got around that the pagans had started holding secret meetings at night in the temple of Cybele—

JULIAN: The fools! That has been most strictly forbidden—

AGATHON: All the faithful rose up in rage. The authorities ordered the temple torn down and we smashed the abominable idols. The more zealous of us were driven by the spirit of the Lord to go further. Singing hymns and carrying our holy banners before us, we marched through the city and fell like agents of wrath on the ungodly; we took their costly possessions from them; many houses were set on fire; many pagans perished in the flames; we pursued still more through the city and killed them as they fled. Oh, that was a great day for the Lord!

JULIAN: And then? The vision, Agathon!

AGATHON: For three whole days and nights the Lord of Vengeance was strong in us. But then, the frailty of the flesh couldn't keep up with the ardor of the spirit, and we gave up the pursuit. I lay on my bed, unable to wake or sleep. It felt I was hollowed out inside, as if the spirit had left me. I lay burning with fever; I tore my hair, wept, prayed, sang—I no longer know what I went through—then, all at once, I saw in front of me by the wall, a white, shining light and in its blaze stood a man in a robe that reached down to his feet. Rays of light streamed from his head; he held a scroll and fastened his eyes gently on me.

JULIAN: You saw that!

AGATHON: I saw it. And then he spoke saying: "Rise up, Agathon; seek him who shall inherit the empire. Bid him enter the den and wrestle with the lions."

JULIAN: Wrestle with the lions? Strange, how strange! Ah, if it were—! The encounter with that wise man. A revelation, a message to me—*I* should be the chosen one?

AGATHON: It is certain.

JULIAN: Wrestle with the lions! Yes, I see it. So it shall be, Agathon. It's God's will I should seek out Libanius—

AGATHON: No, no, hear me to the end.

JULIAN:—steal his skill and his learning from him—smite the unbelievers with their own weapons—strike, strike like Paul—conquer like Paul in the cause of the Lord.

AGATHON: No, no, that's not how it's meant!

JULIAN: How can you doubt it? Libanius—isn't he as strong as the mountain lion and isn't the classroom—

AGATHON: No, I tell you, that's not it; for the apparition continued: "Say to the chosen one he shall shake the dust of the imperial city from his feet, and never more enter its gates."

JULIAN: And you're certain of this, Agathon?

AGATHON: Yes, absolutely.

JULIAN: Not here, then. Wrestle with the lions? Where, where? Where is the light to be found in all this!

(PRINCE GALLUS, a handsome, powerfully built man of twenty-five, with fair, curly hair, and fully armed, comes along the avenue on the left.)

JULIAN: *(Going to him.)* Gallus!

GALLUS: What is it? *(Pointing to AGATHON.)* Who is this person?

JULIAN: Agathon.

GALLUS: Which Agathon? You seek out so many kinds of—ah, for God's sake, it's the Cappadocian! You've actually grown into a man—

JULIAN: Did you know, Gallus, the Emperor's been asking after you.

GALLUS: *(Tense.)* Now? This night?

JULIAN: Yes, yes. He wants to speak with you. He seemed in a fearful rage.

GALLUS: How do you know that? What did he say?

JULIAN: I didn't understand. He wants to know what a certain oracle has answered.

GALLUS: Ah!

JULIAN: Hide nothing from me. What does it mean?

GALLUS: It means either death or banishment.

AGATHON: Merciful Savior!

JULIAN: I suspected as much. But no, the Empress was confident. You must tell me, tell me.

GALLUS: What can I tell? I know no more than you. If the Emperor spoke of an

oracle, then a certain messenger must be in prison, or someone's betrayed
me—

JULIAN: Messenger! Gallus, what is it you've risked?

GALLUS: Oh, how can I go on any longer living this life of uncertainty and fear?
Let him do what he wants with me; any alternative is better than this—.

JULIAN: *(Quietly, drawing him a little to one side.)* Careful, Gallus. What's all this
about a messenger?

GALLUS: I directed a question to the priests of Osiris in Abydos.

JULIAN: Ah! the oracle. And this paganism—

GALLUS: The pagan part of it could be overlooked, but—yes, now you might as
well know—I asked about the outcome of the Persian War.

JULIAN: What madness! Gallus, I can tell looking at you—you asked about
more than that!

GALLUS: Steady! I didn't ask—

JULIAN: Oh, yes! You asked about a certain powerful man's life or death.

GALLUS: And if it were true? What lies closer to both our hearts than that?

JULIAN: *(Clasps his arm.)* Be quiet, you madman!

GALLUS: Get away from me! Crawl to him like a dog if you want to—I'm in no
mind to put up with it any longer. I'll cry it out in every marketplace—
(Shouting to AGATHON.) Have you seen him, my Cappadocian? Have you
seen the murderer?

JULIAN: Gallus! Brother!

AGATHON: Murderer!

GALLUS: The murderer in the red robe; my father's murderer, my stepmother's,
my elder brother's—

JULIAN: Oh, you'll bring destruction down on us!

GALLUS: Eleven heads in a single night, eleven bodies, our whole family. Ah,
but you can be sure his conscience is convulsing him, writhing through his
veins like a nest of serpents.

JULIAN: Don't listen to him! Come away! Come away!

GALLUS: *(Grasping JULIAN by the shoulder.)* Stay—you look pale and uncomfortable;
is it you, perhaps, who's betrayed me?

JULIAN: I! Your own brother—!

GALLUS: Brother, what brother! Kinship's no shield in our family. If you've
been secretly spying on my actions, say it! Who else could it be? Do you
think I don't know what's being whispered here? The Emperor's thinking of
making you his successor.

JULIAN: Never. Dear Gallus, I swear it will never happen. A still greater one has
called me. Oh, believe me, Gallus, my path's set out for me. I'll not go that

way, I tell you. Oh, you Lord of the Hosts—I on the Emperor's throne—no, no, no!

GALLUS: Ha-ha! A good performance, hypocrite!

JULIAN: Yes, it's easy for you to laugh, when you don't know what's happened. I hardly know myself. Oh, Agathon—if this head of mine were anointed! Wouldn't that be an apostasy—a deadly sin? Wouldn't the Lord's holy oil burn me like molten lead?

GALLUS: Making our noble cousin balder than Julius Caesar!

JULIAN: Don't talk like that! Render unto Caesar that which is Caesar's.

GALLUS: My father's blood—your father's and your mother's—!

JULIAN: Oh, what do we know of those horrors? We were only little, at the time. Most was the work of the soldiers; it was the rioters, the evil advisers—

GALLUS: *(Laughing.)* The successor's already rehearsing!

JULIAN: *(In tears.)* Oh, Gallus, if only I could die or be banished in your place. I'm endangering my soul, here. I ought to forgive—and I can't. Evil's growing in me, hatred and revenge are whispering—

GALLUS: *(Quickly, looking toward the Chapel.)* Here he comes!

JULIAN: Be careful, dear brother! Ah, Hecebolius!

(The Chapel door meanwhile has been opened. The congregation streams out; some go away, others remain standing outside to see the court procession pass by. Among them is HECEBOLIUS, the tutor, dressed as a priest.)

HECEBOLIUS: *(About to pass by on the left.)* Is that you, Julian. I fear I've spent another painful hour on your behalf.

JULIAN: Unfortunately, you spend far too many.

HECEBOLIUS: Christ is displeased with you, my son. It is your obstinate spirit that angers him—your disrespectful thoughts, all your worldly vanity—

JULIAN: I know, Hecebolius, you tell me that so often.

HECEBOLIUS: Only just now I sent up my prayers for your improvement. Oh, it was as if our otherwise so merciful redeemer sent them back down again—as if he would not listen to me. He let vain and distracting trifles creep into my thoughts—

JULIAN: You prayed for me? Oh, most loving Hecebolius, praying even for us inarticulate animals—at least, when we go in court dress!

HECEBOLIUS: What are you saying, my son?

JULIAN: Hecebolius, how could you write that slanderous poem?

HECEBOLIUS: I! I swear to you by all that's high and holy—

JULIAN: It's clear from your eyes you're lying! I know for certain you wrote it. How could you, I ask you—and in Libanius name as well?

HECEBOLIUS: Well then, my dearly beloved, since you know about it—

JULIAN: Ah, Hecebolius! Deception, lies, falsehood—!

HECEBOLIUS: See, precious soul, how dearly I love you! I'd dare anything for the soul of the man the Lord one day will anoint. If I lied and deceived out of care for you, I know a merciful God looked down with indulgence on my deeds and stretched his approving arm over them.

JULIAN: How blind I've been! Let me clasp these perjured fingers—

HECEBOLIUS: The Emperor!

(EMPEROR CONSTANTIUS, with all his retinue, enters from the Chapel. AGATHON, during the foregoing, had already withdrawn among the bushes on the right.)

CONSTANTIUS: Oh, this blessed, heavenly peace that's now upon me!

EUSEBIA: You feel strong now, my Constantius?

CONSTANTIUS: Yes, yes! I saw the living dove descend upon me! It took away all my burden of guilt. Now, there's much I dare do, Memnon!

MEMNON: *(Softly.)* Dare at once, my lord.

CONSTANTIUS: There they stand, the pair of them. *(He goes forward toward them.)*

GALLUS: *(Involuntarily reaching for his sword and crying out in alarm.)* Don't try to harm me!

CONSTANTIUS: *(With outstretched arms.)* Gallus! Cousin! *(Embraces and kisses him.)* See, by this starlit Easter night I choose him who lies near my heart. Bow down to the ground all of you. Hail Gallus Caesar!

(General amazement among the followers; involuntary cries can be heard.)

EUSEBIA: *(Crying out.)* Constantius!

GALLUS: *(Bewildered.)* Caesar!

JULIAN: Ah! *(As though in joy, he seizes the Emperor's hands.)*

CONSTANTIUS: *(Pushes him away dismissively.)* Don't come near me! What is it you want? Isn't Gallus the elder? What hope have you allowed yourself? What rumors has your blind arrogance encouraged—? Away, get away!

GALLUS: I—I Caesar!

CONSTANTIUS: My heir and my successor. Within three days you'll join the army in Asia. The Persian war is very close to your heart—

GALLUS: Oh, my most gracious lord—!

CONSTANTIUS: Thank me with actions, beloved Gallus! King Sapor's army lies west of the Euphrates. I know how concerned you are for my life; so make it your mission to destroy him. *(He turns round, takes JULIAN'S head in both hands, and kisses him.)* And you, Julian, my devout friend and brother—that's how it must be.

JULIAN: Blessings on the Emperor's will!

CONSTANTIUS: No requests! Listen, though, I've been thinking of you also. Know, Julian, you now can breathe more freely in Constantinople—

JULIAN: Yes, praise to Christ and the Emperor!

CONSTANTIUS: You know already? Who has told you?

JULIAN: What, my lord?

CONSTANTIUS: That Libanius is banished?

JULIAN: Libanius—banished!

CONSTANTIUS: I've banished him to Athens.

JULIAN: Ah!

CONSTANTIUS: Out there lies his ship; he sails tonight.

JULIAN: He himself! He himself!

CONSTANTIUS: You've wished that for so long. I couldn't arrange it for you before, but now—let this be a small compensation, my dear Julian.

JULIAN: (Seizing his hand.) My lord, grant me one more favor!

CONSTANTIUS: Ask whatever you wish.

JULIAN: Let me journey to Pergamon. You know old Aedesius teaches there.

CONSTANTIUS: A most extraordinary wish; you, among the pagans—?

JULIAN: Aedesius is not dangerous. He's a noble-minded old fellow, and now quite feeble.

CONSTANTIUS: Then what do you want with him, brother?

JULIAN: To learn to wrestle with the lions.

CONSTANTIUS: I understand your pious wish. And you're not afraid; you're sure you're strong enough?

JULIAN: The Lord God has called to me with a clear voice. Like Daniel, I'll go calm and joyful into the lions' den.

CONSTANTIUS: Julian!

JULIAN: This very night you have been His instrument, without knowing it. Let me go forth and cleanse the world!

GALLUS: (Softly, to the EMPEROR.) Humor him, my lord. It will distract him from thinking about greater things.

EUSEBIA: I beg you, Constantius, don't stand in the way of this fervent desire.

HECEBOLIUS: (Quietly.) Noble Emperor, let him go to Pergamon. I give up trying to influence him, here, and now it hardly seems that important—

CONSTANTIUS: How can I deny you anything at a time like this? Go with God, Julian.

JULIAN: (Kisses his hands.) Thank you, thank you.

CONSTANTIUS: And now, on to the banquet to celebrate. My Capuan cook has discovered some new dishes for Lent: carp necks in Chian wine and… Let's proceed, and with you following next to me, Gallus Caesar!
    (The procession moves off.)

GALLUS: (Softly.) Helena, what a miraculous turnaround!

HELENA: Oh, Gallus, it's the dawn of our hopes.

GALLUS: I can hardly believe it! Who brought it about?

HELENA: Ssh!

GALLUS: *You*, my love? Or who—who?

HELENA: Memnon's Spartan dog.

GALLUS: What do you mean?

HELENA: Memnon's dog. Julian gave it a kick; *this* is the revenge.

CONSTANTIUS: Why so silent, Eusebia?

EUSEBIA: *(Quietly, in tears.)* Oh, Constantius—that you could make such a choice!

CONSTANTIUS: Eleven ghosts demanded it.

EUSEBIA: Sadly for us, this won't appease the ghosts.

CONSTANTIUS: *(Calling.)* Flute players! Why are the wretches silent? Play, play!

(All, with the exception of JULIAN, go out to the left. AGATHON emerges from between the trees.)

JULIAN: Gallus the successor; and I—free, free, free!

AGATHON: Wonderful how the Lord's purposes are revealed!

JULIAN: You heard what's come about?

AGATHON: Yes, everything.

JULIAN: And now tomorrow, Agathon—tomorrow, to Athens!

AGATHON: To Athens? But you're going to Pergamon.

JULIAN: Ssh! You don't know what I'm up to—we must be cunning as serpents. First to Pergamon—and then on to Athens!

AGATHON: Farewell, my friend and lord.

JULIAN: You won't come with me to Athens?

AGATHON: I cannot. I must go home; I've my little brother to look after.

JULIAN: *(By the balustrade.)* They're weighing anchor. Fair winds, my winged lion; Achilles follows in your wake. *(Cries out, softly.)* Ah!

AGATHON: What is it?

JULIAN: A falling star.

END OF ACT ONE

ACT TWO

Athens. An open square, surrounded by colonnades. In the square, statues and a fountain. In the corner to the left an opening onto a narrow street. Sunset. BASIL from Caesarea, a slenderly built young man, is sitting reading at the base of a column. GREGORY from Nazianzus is at the center of a group of students who are strolling up and down among the columns. A larger group runs, shouting, across the square and out to the right. Much shouting in the distance.

BASIL: *(Looking up from his book.)* Why all the shouting?

GREGORY: A ship's put in from Ephesus.

BASIL: With new students?

GREGORY: Yes.

BASIL: *(Getting up.)* So, we're in for a raucous night. Let's go, Gregory, we don't need to witness their obscenities.

GREGORY: *(Pointing to the left.)* Look over there. Is that a pleasanter sight?

BASIL: Prince Julian—with roses in his hair and his face flushed—

GREGORY: Yes, and right behind him that rowdy, wild-eyed crowd. Just listen to their drunken babbling! They've been drinking all day in Lycon's wine shop.

BASIL: And many of our own—young Christians—among them, Gregory.

GREGORY: So they call themselves. Didn't Lampon claim to be a Christian—he who violated the daughter of Zeno, the oil-seller? And Hilarion of Agrigentum and the two others, who did things too nauseous to name—

JULIAN: *(Heard calling from offstage, left.)* Hey, now! Just look, it's Castor and Pollux from Cappadocia!

BASIL: He's caught sight of us. I'm going. I can't stand seeing him like this.

GREGORY: I'll stay. He'll be needing a friend, I think.

(BASIL goes out to the right. At the same moment JULIAN, with a group of young men, come out of the narrow street. He has untidy hair and wears a short cloak like the others. Among the students is SALLUST from Perusia.)

MANY IN THE CROWD: Long live the light of Athens! Long live the lover of wisdom and eloquence!

JULIAN: All your flattery's futile. You don't get another verse today.

SALLUST: When our leader falls silent, we feel empty, like the morning after a night of feasting.

JULIAN: Well, if it's what you want, let it be something new. Let's stage a mock trial.

THE WHOLE CROWD: Yes, yes, yes; Prince Julian in the judge's seat!

JULIAN: Cut out the prince, good friends—

SALLUST: Climb up, incomparable man!

JULIAN: Should I presume—? There stands the man. Who knows the law better than Gregory from Nazianzus?

SALLUST: That's true!

JULIAN: To the Judge's seat, my wise Gregory; I'm the defendant.

GREGORY: I beg you, friend, let me stay out of this.

JULIAN: To the Judge's seat, I tell you. *(To the others.)* What shall be my offense?

A FEW VOICES: Yes, what shall it be? You make the choice!

SALLUST: Let it be something Galilean, as we the ungodly call it.

JULIAN: Right, something Galilean. I have it! I've refused to pay taxes to the Emperor—

MANY VOICES: Ha! ha! Not bad! Splendid!

JULIAN: So here I am—dragged in, shoved by the neck, hands bound together—

SALLUST: *(To GREGORY.)* Blind Judge—well, I mean—insofar as Justice is blind, behold this audacious man; he's refused to pay the imperial tax.

JULIAN: Allow me to cast a word onto the scales of your deliberations. I am a Greek citizen. How much does a Greek citizen owe the Emperor?

GREGORY: Whatever the Emperor demands.

JULIAN: Good; but how much—and now answer as though the Emperor himself were present—how much is the Emperor entitled to demand?

GREGORY: All.

JULIAN: Truly, that was answered as though the Emperor himself were present. But now comes the snag; for it stands written: "Render unto Caesar that which is Caesar's; and unto God, that which is God's."

GREGORY: And so?

JULIAN: Then tell me, O wise judge, how much of mine belongs to God?

GREGORY: All.

JULIAN: And how much of this "all" of God's have I leave to give the Emperor?

GREGORY: Dear friends, no more of this game!

THE STUDENTS: *(Shouting and laughing.)* Come on, answer him!

JULIAN: How much of God's can the Emperor demand?

GREGORY: I'll not answer. It's unseemly, both toward God and the Emperor. Let me go from here.

MANY VOICES: Form a ring around him!

JULIAN: Keep hold of him! What's this, O unfortunate judge! You've botched the Emperor's brief, and hope to scuttle off scot-free? So you want to escape? To where? To where? To the Scythians? Gather before me! Answer me, you future servants of the Emperor and of wisdom—didn't he seek to escape from the Emperor's authority?

THE STUDENTS: Yes, yes!

JULIAN: And what penalty would you impose for such a crime?

VOICES: Death! Death in a wine vat!

JULIAN: Let us reflect. Let us answer as though the Emperor himself were present. What is the limit of the Emperor's authority?

A FEW VOICES: The Emperor's authority is without limit.

JULIAN: So I'd assume. But to seek to escape from the limitless, O friends, is that not madness?

THE STUDENTS: Yes, yes! The Cappadocian is mad!

JULIAN: And what, therefore, is madness? How did our forefathers reckon this condition? What did the Egyptian priests teach? And what say Maximus the mystic and the other philosophers of the east? They say that in the madman heavenly secrets are revealed. Our Gregory—since he's set himself against the Emperor—is consequently in special accord with heavenly powers. Pour out wine for the Cappadocian; sing songs in Gregory's praise. A statue in honor of Gregory from Nazianzus!

THE STUDENTS: (*Amid laughter and shouting.*) All praise to the Cappadocian! All praise for the Cappadocian's judgment!

(*LIBANIUS, surrounded by students, crosses the square.*)

LIBANIUS: Well now, I do believe my brother Julian's proclaiming wisdom in the marketplace!

JULIAN: Call it foolishness, rather; wisdom's wandered off.

LIBANIUS: Wisdom has wandered off?

JULIAN: Or about to wander off; that's so, isn't it—because surely you're also off to the Piraeus?

LIBANIUS: I, brother? What would I want in the Piraeus?

JULIAN: Then is our Libanius the only teacher who doesn't know a ship from Ephesus has just put in?

LIBANIUS: Huh! Why should I bother about such a ship!

JULIAN: It's crammed to the brim with would-be students.

LIBANIUS: (*Scornfully.*) Because it comes from Ephesus!

JULIAN: Doesn't gold weigh just as heavy, wherever it comes from?

LIBANIUS: Gold? Ha! ha! Whatever gold there is, Maximus keeps for himself. He'll let none of it go. And the students that come here from Ephesus, what are they like? Shopkeepers' sons, first sons of tradesmen. Gold, did you say, my dear Julian? I say lack of gold. But I'll put this lack of gold to use, to stamp a truly minted coin for you, young men! For isn't a precious lesson for your lives—when presented in a thoughtful and attractive form—as worthy as well-weighted gold? Listen, then, if you've ears to hear. Here it's been said that certain men have sped down to the Piraeus. Who are they, these hasty ones? Far be it for me to name names: They term themselves lovers and teachers of wisdom. Fly now in your thoughts down to the Piraeus. What's going on down there at this moment, while I'm standing here in this friendly gathering? I'll tell you what's going on. Those men who claim to love and impart wisdom are bustling onto gangplanks, shoving, squabbling, snapping at each other, forgetting all decency and dignity alike. And why, I ask you? Just to be the first on the boat—to grab hold of the most smartly dressed youngsters for themselves, drag them back to their houses, take them in, hoping to tempt them in every kind of way. What embarrassment, what an awakening, like the morning after the party, when in good time it's revealed—ha! ha!—that those youngsters brought with them hardly enough to pay for the welcoming banquet. Learn from this, young men, how ill it becomes a philosopher, and how meagerly it profits you, to pursue any good other than the truth.

JULIAN: Oh, my Libanius, when I listen to you with closed eyes, I find myself drifting into a sweet dream imagining Diogenes born again among us.

LIBANIUS: Your speech has the prodigality of a prince, my dearest friend.

JULIAN: Not in the least. And yet I was about to break into your discourse; *this* time at least, one of your colleagues will hardly feel himself short-changed.

LIBANIUS: My friend is joking.

JULIAN: Your friend assures you that two sons of Governor Milo are on board.

LIBANIUS: *(Gripping his arm.)* What are you saying?

JULIAN: The successor of Diogenes, who gets his hands on *them* to educate will never need eat the bread and drink the water of poverty.

LIBANIUS: Governor Milo's sons! That noble Milo who sent the Emperor seven Persian horses with saddles embroidered with pearls.

JULIAN: Many considered it too mean a gift for Milo.

LIBANIUS: Very true. Milo should have sent a poem, or a finely composed address or a letter. Milo's a richly accomplished man; the entire family of Governor Milo is richly accomplished.

JULIAN: Especially the two young sons.

LIBANIUS: That I can believe. May the gods guarantee, for the sake of their benevolent and generous father, they fall into good hands You were certainly right then, Julian; the ship has brought true gold from Ephesus. Aren't intellectual gifts the purest gold? But I can't rest easy; the young men's welfare is truly a serious matter. So much depends on who gets hold of them first. My young friends, if you believe as I do, then let's extend to these two strangers a friendly and guiding hand, and help them choose the best teacher and lodgings—

SALLUST: I'm with you!

THE STUDENTS: To the Piraeus! To the Piraeus!

SALLUST: We'll battle like wild beasts for Milo's sons!

(They all leave, to the right, with LIBANIUS; only JULIAN and GREGORY stay behind in the colonnade.)

JULIAN: *(Following them with his eyes.)* Look at them, capering about like a flock of fauns. Licking their lips in anticipation of the banquet to be served tonight. *(Turns to GREGORY.)* Were they to send up a sigh to God at this moment, it would be to empty their bellies of breakfast.

GREGORY: Julian—

JULIAN: Yet just look at me. I am sober.

GREGORY: I know that. You are moderate in all things. And yet you live this life with them.

JULIAN: And why not? Do you or I know when the lightning next will strike? Then why not live one shining, sunlit day. Do you forget how I dragged out both my childhood and my early youth in gilded slavery? For me it had become a habit, I can even say a necessity, to feel this palpable terror over me. And now? A sepulchral silence from the Emperor—this sinister stillness! I left Pergamon without the Emperor's permission: The Emperor ignores it. On my own decision I go to Nicomedia: I lived there and was taught by Nicocles and others: The Emperor let's it pass. I came to Athens and sought out Libanius whom the Emperor's forbidden me to see: The Emperor's remained silent to this day. How should I interpret this?

GREGORY: You should interpret it in a loving spirit, Julian!

JULIAN: Oh, you don't know—! I dread this power hanging over me—terrifying when it acts, all the more terrifying when it's at rest.

GREGORY: Be honest, my friend, and tell me if this alone has led you onto these strange paths.

JULIAN: What do you mean by strange paths?

GREGORY: Is what rumor says true—that you occupy your evenings exploring the pagan mysteries in Eleusis?

JULIAN: Hah! Be assured there's little to be learnt from those mystery-mongering dreamers. No need to speak of them.

GREGORY: Then it's true! Oh, Julian, how could you seek out such infamous contacts?

JULIAN: I have to live, Gregory—and all this school of philosophy stuff is not life. Take Libanius! I can never forgive him that I've loved him so dearly! With what humility and trembling joy I approached that man when I arrived here, bowed down before him, kissed him and called him my elder brother.

GREGOR: Yes, all the Christians felt you went much too far.

JULIAN: And yet I came here so elated in spirit. I saw in my mind a tremendous battle between us two—the world's wisdom wrestling with God's truth. What became of it? Libanius never seriously intended this battle. He never wanted to fight at all; he only seeks self-interest. I tell you, Gregory— Libanius is not a great man.

GREGORY: Yet he is praised as such by all enlightened Greece.

JULIAN: Yet still he's not a great man, I tell you. Just once I saw Libanius great. That night in Constantinople. Then he was great, because he'd suffered a great wrong and so a mighty anger filled him. But here! Oh, what have I been witness to! Libanius has great learning, but he's not a great man. Libanius is greedy; he's conceited; he's filled with envy. Do you imagine he's been able to accept the reputation—I admit, greatly due to the partiality of my friends—I've been able to make for myself? If you come to Libanius, he'll describe to you the essentials of all the virtues and how to recognize them. He's got it all at his fingertips, just like the books in his library. But does he live these virtues? Is his life like his learning? He, the successor to Socrates and Plato—? Ha! Ha! Didn't he flatter the Emperor until he was banished? Didn't he flatter me at our meeting in Constantinople—a meeting he's since tried in vain to depict in a ludicrous light. And what am I to him now? Now he's writing to Gallus, to Gallus Caesar, to the Emperor's heir, to wish him success with his campaign against the Persians—despite the fact the campaign's been indifferent enough, and Gallus is not exactly conspicuous for his learning or any particular eloquence. And this Libanius continues to be hailed by the Greeks as the king of philosophers. Oh, I won't deny it irritates me. To speak frankly, I'd have thought the Greeks would choose better by fastening their eyes on those devotees of philosophy and eloquence who in recent years—

BASIL: *(Entering from the right.)* Letters! Letters from Cappadocia!

GREGORY: For me too?

BASIL: See here—from your mother.

GREGORY: My pious mother!

JULIAN: Is it your sister who writes?

BASIL: *(Who entered with his own letter opened.)* Yes, it's Macrina. She reports some serious and then some strange news.

JULIAN: What news?

BASIL: First about your exalted brother Gallus. He's enforcing harsh rule in Antioch.

JULIAN: Yes, Gallus is hard. Macrina writes "harsh rule"?

BASIL: *(Looking at him.)* Macrina writes "bloody"—

JULIAN: Ah, it's as I thought! Why ever did the Emperor marry him to that depraved widow, Constantina?

GREGORY: *(Reading.)* Oh, what unheard of abomination!

JULIAN: What is it, friend?

GREGORY: *(To Basil.)* Doesn't Macrina mention anything about what is going on in Antioch?

BASIL: Nothing explicitly. What is it? You've gone pale—

GREGORY: You know Clematius, that upright man from Alexandria?

BASIL: Yes, yes. What of him??

GREGORY: He's been murdered.

BASIL: What's that you say? Murdered?

GREGORY: I call it murder; they've executed him without charge or trial.

BASIL: Who executed him?

GREGORY: Yes, who? How can I tell you who? My mother describes the situation this way: Clematius's mother-in-law was filled with an unholy passion for her daughter's husband, but since she could not get her way with him, she sneaked a way through a backdoor entrance to the palace—

JULIAN: Which palace?

GREGORY: My mother only writes "the palace."

JULIAN: Well? What next?

GREGORY: All that's known is she gave a prominent and powerful lady a very precious jewel in order to procure a death warrant—

JULIAN: But they didn't get it?

GREGORY: They got it, Julian!

JULIAN: Oh, Jesus!

BASIL: Appalling! And Clematius—?

GREGORY: The death warrant was sent to the governor, Honoratus. This weak individual dared not oppose a command from so high an authority. Clematius was imprisoned and executed early next morning without, writes my mother, being able to speak in his own defense.

JULIAN: *(Quietly, going pale.)* Burn these dangerous letters. They could bring disaster down on all of us.

BASIL: Such naked violence—and all within a great city. What's become of us?

JULIAN: Yes, you may well ask what's become of us! A Christian murderer, a Christian adulteress, a Christian—

GREGORY: Lamenting won't put these things right. What do you intend doing?

JULIAN: I? I'll not go to Eleusis any more. I'll break off all association with the pagans, and thank the Lord my God who has removed the temptation of power from me.

GREGORY: Good. And then?

JULIAN: I don't understand you—

GREGORY: Then listen. You mustn't think that's the end of it, this murder of Clematius. Reaction to this despicable outrage has erupted like a plague all over Antioch. All manner of evil things have awakened to swarm out of their hiding places. My mother writes it's as if a stinking sewer had opened up. Wives betray their husbands, sons their fathers, priests the members of their own congregations—

JULIAN: This will spread further. The abomination will corrupt us all. Oh, Gregory, if only I could fly to the end of the earth—

GREGORY: Your place is at the earth's navel, Julian!

JULIAN: What is it you expect of me?

GREGORY: You're the brother of this bloody Caesar. Seek him out—he calls himself a Christian after all. Cast his crime in his face; strike him to the ground with fear and shame.

JULIAN: *(Shrinking.)* That's insane! What are you thinking of?

GREGORY: Do you love your brother? Do you wish to save him?

JULIAN: I loved Gallus more than anyone—

GREGORY: You *loved*—

JULIAN: As long as he was just my brother. But now—is he not Caesar? Gregory—Basil—O my dear friends—I tremble for my life, I draw my breath in fear of Gallus Caesar. That I should even think of stepping into his presence—I—whose very existence is a menace to him!

GREGORY: Why did you come to Athens? You announced to the world with a great fanfare: "Prince Julian is departing from Constantinople to do battle against the false philosophy—to exalt Christian truth over the heathen lie." What have you achieved to this effect?

JULIAN: Oh, it was not here that the battle was to be fought.

GREGORY: No, it wasn't here. Not with eloquence against eloquence; not with book against book, not with verbal fencing matches in the classroom! No, Julian, it's out there into the real world you should be venturing, your life in your hands—

JULIAN: I see that! I see that!

GREGORY: Yes, in the way Libanius sees it. You derided him. He knew how to list the essentials of all the virtues, and how to recognize them. But by rote, only by rote. How much of what you are belongs to God: How much can the Emperor demand?

JULIAN: You said yourself it was unseemly.

GREGORY: Against whom: God or the Emperor?

JULIAN: *(Quickly.)* Well then, shall we go forward?

GREGORY: *(Drawing back.)* I have my own little circle; I've my family to consider. To do more is beyond my power and my ability.

JULIAN: *(About to answer; suddenly listens to the right and shouts.)* To the bacchanal, friends!

(GREGORY stares at him for a moment; then departs through the colonnade to the left. A large crowd of students, with the newcomers among them, storm shouting wildly, into the marketplace.)

BASIL: *(Approaching.)* Julian, will you listen to me?

JULIAN: See there! They've taken their new friends to the baths, anointed their hair. Look how they swing their staves; how they yell and pound the paving stones. What do you say, Pericles? I seem to see your angry ghost—

BASIL: Come away! Come away!

JULIAN: Ah, do you see that naked lad they're hurrying along with them? Now come the dancing girls. Ah, see now what—!

BASIL: Ecch! Ecch! Turn your eyes away!

(Evening has fallen. The whole crowd settles down in the marketplace by the fountain. Wine and fruit are brought in. Girls, heavily made up, dance by torchlight.)

JULIAN: *(After a short silence.)* Tell me, Basil, why was pagan sin so beautiful?

BASIL: You're wrong, my friend. Poems and legends have been beautifully composed about pagan sin: But it *wasn't* beautiful.

JULIAN: Oh, what are you saying? Wasn't Alcibiades beautiful that time he stormed through the streets of Athens by night, flushed with wine and like a young god? Wasn't he beautiful in his defiance when he mocked at Hermes and hammered on the citizens' doors, when he called out to their wives and daughters, while the women inside trembled and sighed in almost-breathless silence wishing nothing so much as to—

BASIL: Please, I beg you, listen to me.

JULIAN: And wasn't Socrates beautiful in the symposium. And Plato and all the joyful, reveling comrades. And yet they took part in things the Christian brutes over there would deny under oath if anyone accused them. And then think of Oedipus, Medea, Leda—

BASIL: Fictions, fictions—you're confusing poetry and truth.

JULIAN: Aren't both the poetic imagination and the will created from reality? Just look at our holy scriptures, both the old and the new. Was sin beautiful in Sodom and Gomorra? Didn't Jehovah's fire punish what Socrates did not turn away from? When I live this life of wildness and passion, then I question, again and again, why truth should be the enemy of beauty.

BASIL: And at a time like this you can sigh after beauty? Can you so easily forget what you've only just now heard?

JULIAN: *(His hands at his ears.)* Not another word about those horrors. We'll cast off all that filth from Antioch—tell me what more Macrina writes. There was something else, I thought you mentioned—what was it you called the other news?

BASIL: Strange.

JULIAN: Yes, yes—what was it?

BASIL: She writes about Maximus in Ephesus—

JULIAN: The mystic?

BASIL: Yes, that inscrutable man. Now he's shown up again; this time in Ephesus. All the surrounding countryside is in a ferment. Maximus's name's on everyone's lips. Either he's a charlatan or he's made some sinister pact with certain spirits. Christians themselves are strangely drawn to his blasphemous signs and practices.

JULIAN: More, more! I beg you!

BASIL: There's no more about him. Macrina writes only that she sees in Maximus's reappearance a sign that we are under the wrath of the Lord. She believes great hardships await us for our sins.

JULIAN: Yes, yes, yes. Believe me, Basil, your sister's an exceptional woman.

BASIL: In truth, she is.

JULIAN: When you relate her letter to me, it's as though I'm able to grasp something clearly and completely that I've long been searching after. Tell me, is she still determined to turn away from the world and live in the desert?

BASIL: She's as firmly committed as ever.

JULIAN: Really? She who's held to be so gifted in every way. We know she's both young and beautiful, has wealth waiting for her to control and—for a woman—the highest degree of learning. I tell you, Basil, I'm burning to see her! Why does she long for solitude?

BASIL: I've already told you; the man she was to marry, died. She considers him her husband, waiting, to whom she must devote all her thoughts. She believes her duty is to be pure when she joins him.

JULIAN: Strange, how many these days find themselves drawn to the solitude. When you write to Macrina, would you mention that I, too—

BASIL: She knows that, Julian; but she doesn't believe it.

JULIAN: Why not? What does she write?

BASIL: Please, my friend, spare me—

JULIAN: If you love me, don't conceal a word of what she's written.

BASIL: *(Giving him the letter.)* As you wish, read it. Start *there*.

JULIAN: *(Reading.)* "Every time you write about the Emperor's young cousin who is your friend, my mind is filled with a great and radiant joy—" Oh, Basil, you be my eyes; read on for me.

BASIL: *(Reading.)* "Your account of the confident resolve with which he arrived in Athens was like a scene from the time of the old scriptures. Yes, I believe he is a David reborn to destroy the champions of the pagans. God's spirit be upon him in this battle and all the days to come!"

JULIAN: *(Grasping his arm.)* Let that be enough! She as well? What is it all of you are demanding of me, as if with one voice? Have I given any written testament to wrestle with such powerful lions—?

BASIL: How has it come about that all the faithful look to you in breathless anticipation?

JULIAN: *(Walking briefly up and down among the colonnades, halts, and reaches for the letter.)* Give it here—let me see. *(Reads.)* "God's spirit be upon him in this battle and all the days to come!" If only I could, Basil—! Instead, I feel like Daedelos, between sky and sea. A dizzying height and a yawning abyss. What meaning's to be found in these voices proclaiming from east and west that I shall save Christendom. Where is it—this Christendom? Is it with the Emperor or with Caesar? I believe their actions cry out, "no! no!" Is it with the mighty and the prosperous, with those effete voluptuaries who fold their hands over their well-filled bellies and pipe: "Was God's son created out of nothing?" Or with the enlightened, with those, like you and me, who've drunk beauty and wisdom from the pagan springs? Don't most of our brethren tilt toward the Arian heresy, which the Emperor himself favors so strongly? And what of that slovenly rabble of the empire, who destroy the temples and then murder the pagans and their families! Is that in the cause of Christ? Ha!-ha! Straight afterwards they fight among themselves for the spoils of those they've massacred. You might ask Macrina if Christendom is to be found in solitude—up on a column where the pious saint of the pillar stands on one leg. Or in the cities? Perhaps among those bakers' houses in Constantinople, or those who recently beat up each other over whether the trinity is made up of three persons or three hypostases! Which of all these would Christ acknowledge if he came back to earth again? Bring out your Diogenes' lantern, Basil. Light up this pitch darkness. Where is Christianity?

BASIL: Look for the answer where it always is found in times of trouble.

JULIAN: Don't hold back your well of knowledge. Quench my thirst if you can. Where shall I both see and find?

BASIL: In the writings of the holy men.

JULIAN: The same counsel of despair. Books—always books! I went to Libanius: The answer was: books, books! I go to you: books, books, books! I've no use for books—it's life I hunger after: communion, face-to-face, with the spirit!

Did Saul come to see through books? Wasn't it rather a flood of light that devastated him, a vision, a voice—

BASIL: Are you forgetting the vision and the voice that Agathon from Macellum—

JULIAN: An obscure commandment, an oracular message I can't make out. Was *I* the one chosen? The heir to the empire, it said. And which empire—? The thing's shrouded in a thousand uncertainties. I know only this: The lions' den is not in Athens. Then where, where? Like Saul I'm groping in the dark. If Christ wants anything of me, then he must speak clearly. My fingers in his wounds.

BASIL: And yet, it is written—

JULIAN: I know everything that's written. What is written, that isn't the truth made flesh. Don't you feel nauseous and sick, as if on board a ship becalmed, always veering between life and scripture, pagan wisdom and beauty? There must be a new revelation. Or a revelation of something new. There *must* be, I tell you; the time has come. Yes, a revelation! If you could pray *that* for me, Basil! Martyrdom—if that's needed—! Martyrdom, ah, my head swims at its sweetness—the crown of thorns on my brow—! *(He clasps his head with both hands, encounters the rose-garland which he tears off, reflects at length and says, softly.)* This. I'd forgotten it. *(Throws the garland away.)* One thing at least I've learned in Athens.

BASIL: What, Julian?

JULIAN: The old beauty is no longer beautiful, and the new truth is no longer true.

(LIBANIUS comes in quickly through the colonnades from the right.)

LIBANIUS: *(Still at a distance.)* Now we've got him; now we've got him!

JULIAN: Him? I thought you'd bag them both.

LIBANIUS: What both?

JULIAN: Milo's sons.

LIBANIUS: Ah, yes! I've got them too. But it's *him* we now have, Julian!

JULIAN: Who, my dear brother?

LIBANIUS: He's caught himself in his own net!

JULIAN: Aha! A philosopher, then?

LIBANIUS: The enemy of all philosophy.

JULIAN: Who do you mean? Who?

LIBANIUS: You really don't know? You've not heard the news about Maximus?

JULIAN: About Maximus? Oh, have the goodness to—

LIBANIUS: He was bound to come to this, eventually, that rash visionary—step-by-step, right into madness.

JULIAN: Or, in other words—the highest wisdom.

LIBANIUS: It's one way of putting it. But now it's essential to get control of the situation at once. You, in your privileged position, Julian, you're the man. You're the Emperor's closest cousin. All true philosophers hope and depend on you, both here and in Nocomedia—

JULIAN: Listen, most excellent Libanius—since I'm not omniscient—

LIBANIUS: Then know that Maximus has just come clearly into the open with the foundations of his teaching.

JULIAN: And you blame him for that?

LIBANIUS: He claims he can call on spirits and shades.·

JULIAN: *(Grasping his cloak.)* Libanius!

LIBANIUS: All on board ship were bubbling over with the most fantastic accounts, and here *(Showing a letter.)* here my colleague Eusabius writes more on the matter.

JULIAN: Spirits and shades—

LIBANIUS: In Ephesus recently, before a large gathering both of followers and opponents, Maximus performed forbidden arts on the statue of Hecate. It happened in the goddess's temple. Eusebius writes that he himself was present and witnessed everything, from beginning to end. A pitch black night enveloped them. Maximus uttered a mysterious incantation; then sang a hymn that no one understood. The marble torch flamed in the statue's hand—

BASIL: Blasphemous act!

JULIAN: And then—?

LIBANIUS: And then, in the bright bluish light, everyone saw how the statue's face came to life and smiled upon them.

JULIAN: What else—?

LIBANIUS: Most were gripped by terror. Everyone rushed to the exit ways. Many have been lying in sickness or delirium after. But he himself—can you believe it, Julian—? In spite of the fate his two brothers met in Constantinople— still pursues this perilous and scandalous path.

JULIAN: Scandalous? You call that path a scandalous one? Isn't this the path all wisdom sets out for? Communion between spirit and spirit?

BASIL: Oh, my dearest, most reckless friend.

LIBANIUS: More than scandalous, I call it! What *is* this Hecate? What are the gods at all for the enlightened understanding? Thankfully, we're not living in the days of the blind old singer. Maximus should know better than that. Hasn't Plato—and after him we others—given a clear interpretation of all such matters. Isn't it scandalous, therefore, in these days, to cloud once more in the fog of riddles and obscure dreaming, that admirable, substantial and, I venture to claim, arduously achieved edifice of concepts and commentary which we, as lovers of wisdom, as scholars, as—?

JULIAN: *(Fervently.)* Good bye, Basil! I glimpse a light on my path!

BASIL: *(Casting his arms about him.)* I won't let you go. I'll hold on to you

JULIAN: *(Twisting free of him.)* No one will hold me back; it's useless to oppose me.

LIBANIUS: What an outbreak of madness! Friend, brother, comrade, where are you going?

JULIAN: There, where torches flare and statues smile!

LIBANIUS: And you can do this! You, Julian, you, our pride, our light, our hope—you can yearn for this benighted Ephesus and place yourself in a charlatan's power. Consider, at the very hour you sink so low, at that same hour you'll have forfeited the splendid reputation for learning and eloquence which, in these years in Pergamon and in Nicomedia and above all here in the schools of Athens—

JULIAN: Oh, schools, schools! Stay here among your books—you've pointed out the man I'm searching for. *(He hurries off through the colonnades to the left.)*

LIBANIUS: *(Gazing after him.)* That royal youngster's a menace to true knowledge.

BASIL: *(Half to himself.)* Prince Julian's a menace to a great deal more.

END OF ACT TWO

ACT THREE

Ephesus. A brightly lit hall in JULIAN'S house. The entrance from the main hall to the right; further back, a small door covered by a curtain. On the left side a door, leading to the house's inner rooms. The background of the hall consists of a wall with an opening through which can be seen a little enclosed courtyard, decorated with statuettes.

Servants are preparing a lavish supper and placing cushions around the table. The chamberlain, EUTHERIUS, stands at the entrance, greeting with elaborate courtesy GREGORY and BASIL.

EUTHERIUS: Yes, yes, I assure you, it's all as it should be.

GREGORY: Impossible! You really shouldn't try fooling us.

BASIL: You're trying to hoodwink us, my friend! How could your master be waiting for us? No one at all knows about our departure from Athens; nothing held us up on the way. Our ship raced in time with the clouds and the wild cranes.

EUTHERIUS: Look about you. See that table there. His usual meal is herbs and bread.

GREGORY: There's no doubting it; all my senses tell me you're right: Wine jugs decorated with flowers and leaves, lamps and fruit, incense filling the hall with its scent, fluteplayers out there at the door—

EUTHERIUS: Early this morning he sent for me. He seemed especially happy; walking up and down and rubbing his hands. "Prepare a lavish supper," he told me, "because this evening two friends from Athens will be arriving." *(Meanwhile he has cast his eye on the open door, suddenly becomes silent and draws back respectfully.)*

BASIL: Is that him?

EUTHERIUS: *(Nodding in answer; then he signals to the servants to withdraw; they go out through the larger door, right. He follows soon after. A moment later, JULIAN enters from the left. He is dressed in a long Oriental robe. His whole bearing is animated and betrays strong inward excitement.)*

JULIAN: *(Going toward them and greeting them with much warmth.)* There! I see you! I'm holding you! Thank you, thank you, for flying ahead in spirit before arriving in the flesh.

GREGORY: Julian!

BASIL: My friend and brother!

JULIAN: I've been like an impatient lover anticipating this handshake. The court sycophants, fawning after certain people's favors, called me a monkey—ah, if only I had that monkey's four hands to clasp your four all at once!

GREGORY: But you must explain—your servants met us at the door with flutes, wanted to lead us to the bath and to anoint our hair and crown us with roses—

JULIAN: I saw you both last night. It was full moon, you see—and that's when the spirit always is strangely active in me. I was sitting at my desk in the library and had fallen asleep tired, oh, my friends, so tired with studying and writing. Then the house was convulsed as if with a tempest; the curtain lifted, flapping wildly, and I looked out into the night and far out over the sea. I heard a blissful singing, but the song came from two birds with women's faces. They swooped down at an angle toward the coast, then settled gently to the ground; the bird shapes melted away like white mist and there, in the soft, dim light I saw the two of you.

GREGORY: Are you certain about all this?

JULIAN: Were you thinking of me; did you talk about me last night?

BASIL: Yes, yes—in the bow of the ship—

JULIAN: What time in the night was that?

GREGORY: What time in the night did you have your vision?

JULIAN: An hour after midnight.

GREGORY: *(Glancing at BASIL.)* Uncanny!

JULIAN: *(Rubbing his hands; walking up and down.)* You see! Ha!-ha! Don't you see?

BASIL: Oh, then it's actually true—

JULIAN: What is? What's true?

BASIL: The rumors about the secret arts you practice here.

JULIAN: Ah, what won't rumor exaggerate? But still, what do the rumors have to say about me? I've been told there're lots of reports going the rounds. If I gave any attention to some of the accounts, I'd have to conclude there were few men in the empire as much talked about as I am.

GREGORY: You can believe that, certainly.

JULIAN: So how does Libanius respond to all this? He never relished the idea of anyone getting as much attention as himself. And what do my many estimable friends in Athens say about it all? It's well known, I suppose, I'm in disgrace with the Emperor and the whole court?

GREGORY: You? I regularly get news from the court camp: but my brother Caesarius writes nothing about that.

JULIAN: I can't interpret it any other way, my good Gregory. From all quarters they consider it essential to keep an eye on me. Only recently Gallus Caesar sent his private chaplain Aetius here to ferret out if I was holding fast to the true faith.

BASIL: And—?

JULIAN: I don't lightheartedly miss out on the morning services in church. And I consider the martyrs the most excellent of men; it truly is no easy matter to suffer such great torments, oh yes, and even death, for the sake of one's convictions. On the whole, I really think Aetius was satisfied with me when he left.

BASIL: *(Grasping his hand.)* Julian, for the sake of our close friendship, tell us frankly where you stand.

JULIAN: Dear friends, I'm the happiest man on earth. And Maximus—yes, he has the right to that name—Maximus is the greatest man who's ever lived.

GREGORY: *(Preparing to leave.)* All we wanted was to see you, my lord!

JULIAN: Can you let this make brother stranger to brother? You shrink back in fear when faced with the mystery. That doesn't surprise me. That was how I retreated before I came to see, and before I understood what was the essence of life.

BASIL: What do you call the essence of life?

JULIAN: Maximus knows that. In him is the new revelation.

BASIL: And that has been granted you?

JULIAN: I stand at the edge of it. Even this very night, Maximus has promised me—

GREGORY: Maximus is a dreamer—or else he's deceiving you—!

JULIAN: How can you presume to judge such mysteries? They're not for your learning, my Gregory! The pathway into the great glory is terrifying. Those dreamers in Eleusis were close to the right track; Maximus found that track and I, soon after—with his help. Then I wandered through dark chasms. A heavy swamp of water was on my left—a stream, I think, that had forgotten to flow. Shrill voices spoke confusedly, all at once, and without any meaning. Every now and then I saw a bluish light; horrible shapes brushed past me; I went on and on in deathly fear; but I came through the ordeal. Since then, since then, oh, dear friends, with this spiritually transformed body of mine, I've been long in the realm of paradise; angels have sung their anthems to me; I've seen the innermost light—

GREGORY: Woe to this godless Maximus! To this damnable pagan impostor!

JULIAN: Blindness! blindness! Maximus honors his forerunners in faith; he honors both his great brothers, both the lawgiver of Sinai and the seer of Nazareth. Do you know how the spirit of understanding came to fill me? It happened one night during prayer and fasting. All at once I felt myself being swept away far—far into space and outside of time; a bright, shimmering, sunlit day spread all around me, and I stood alone on a ship with slackened sails in the midst of the clear, sparkling Greek sea. Islands like anchored, airy clouds, towered up in the distance and the ship lay heavy, as if asleep, on that wine-dark surface. Then see! That surface became more and more transparent; clearer, thinner, until at last it no longer was there, and my ship hung over an empty, terrifying abyss. No green life, no sun down there, only a lifeless, slimy, black seabed in all its horrible nakedness—

But above, in the infinite vault of the sky that before had seemed mere emptiness, *there* was life; there the invisible took on form, and the silence became sound—. Then I grasped the great, redeeming revelation.

GREGORY: What revelation do you mean?

JULIAN: That which is, is not; and that which is not, is.

BASIL: Oh, you're becoming lost and destroyed in this web of light and mist.

JULIAN: I? Haven't miracles taken place? Don't both omens and certain mysterious portents among the stars prophesy the divine will has some unrevealed destiny in store for me?

GREGORY: Don't believe such signs. You can't be sure whose work they are.

JULIAN: You mean I'm not to believe in favorable signs which already have revealed their truth? *(He draws them closer to him and says, quietly.)* I can assure you, my friends, a great transfiguration is at hand. Gallus Caesar and I shall in good time come to share the rulership of this world—he as Emperor and I—yes, what shall I call it? The unborn can't be known by name—because it has none. No more of this until the moment's ready. But I feel free to speak about Caesar. Do you know about that vision which caused the imprisonment and torture of Apollinaris of Sidon?

BASIL: No, no—how should we know—?

JULIAN: Apollinaris claimed he heard someone knocking repeatedly on his door in the night. He got up and went outside; and saw—outside there, he caught sight of a figure—man or women, he couldn't be sure which. And the figure spoke to him and told him to prepare a purple robe, the kind worn by newly crowned emperors. And when Apollinaris, in terror, was about to decline such a dangerous assignment, the figure was no longer there and only a voice called, "Go, go, Apollonaris, and get the purple robe ready."

GREGORY: Was this the sign you said revealed its truth?

JULIAN: *(Nodding slowly.)* Seven days later Caesar's wife died in Bithynia. Constantina had always been his evil genius, and that was why she had to—because of a change that's taken place in the divine will. Three weeks after Constantina's death the imperial messenger, Scudilo, arrived in Antioch with a large escort, paid Caesar royal honors and invited him in the Emperor's name to be a guest at the imperial palace in Rome. Caesar's journey's now a triumphal progress through the provinces. In Constantinople he organized races in the hippodrome and the crowd cheered wildly when though only

Emperor in name, he stepped forward like the early emperors, to award the crown to Corax, the winner. So wonderfully does God again raise up our family so long sunk under sin and persecution.

GREGORY: Strange. In Athens there were quite other rumors.

JULIAN: I know for certain. The purple robe is imminent, Gregory! And should I doubt what Maximus has prophesied is about to happen to *me?* Tonight the last veil will fall. It's in here the great mystery will be revealed. Oh, stay with me, my brothers—stay with me in this night of anxiety and anticipation! When Maximus appears you'll be witness to—

BASIL: Never!

GREGORY: It isn't possible. I'm returning home to Cappadocia!

JULIAN: What's driven you so suddenly from Greece?

BASIL: My mother's a widow, Julian!

GREGORY: My father's weak in mind and body; he's in great need of my support.

JULIAN: Oh, but stay at the inn, then. Only until tomorrow—!

GREGORY: Impossible; our traveling party sets off at daybreak.

JULIAN: At daybreak? Before midnight the day might break for you.

BASIL: Julian, I can't go away in such great anxiety. Tell me—when Maximus has interpreted all the mysteries for you—what then?

JULIAN: Do you remember that river Strabo writes about, the river with its source in the Libyan mountains? It grows and grows in its course; but just as it's at its greatest, it oozes away into the desert sand and buries itself in the womb of the earth from whence it came.

BASIL: Is it death you long for, Julian?

JULIAN: All that your slavish imagination hopes for after death is precisely what the great mystery aims to provide all initiates here in their earthly lives. To restore us—this is what Maximus and his disciples seek—to that likeness to the divine we have lost. Why so doubtful, brothers? Why do you stand there, as if before some impassable barrier? I know what I know. In each of the passing generations there has been *one* soul in which the pure Adam was reborn; he was great in Moses, the lawgiver; he had the power to make the world submit to him in the Macedonian Alexander; he was most perfected in Jesus of Nazareth. But you see, Basil, *(Gripping his arm.)* they all lacked what is promised me—the pure woman!

BASIL: *(Breaking away.)* Julian, Julian!

GREGORY: You blasphemer! This is where your arrogant heart has led you.

JULIAN: Why all this contemptuous disbelief? Is it my slight stature that tells against me? Ha-ha; I say to you: This coarse, carnal race shall pass away. The future shall be conceived more in the spirit than the flesh. In the first

Adam they were harmoniously united, as in the images of the god Apollo. Since, they've lacked this union. Didn't Moses have a stammering tongue? Didn't his arms need support when he tried to hold them upraised on the shore of the Red Sea. Didn't the Macedonian continually need inspiring with strong drinks and other artificial means? And what of Jesus of Nazareth? Didn't he possess a fragile body? Didn't he fall asleep in the boat while the others stayed awake? And collapse beneath the cross that Simon the Jew carried easily? The two thieves didn't collapse. You call yourselves believers, and yet have so little faith in the power of miracles to reveal. Wait, wait— you shall see;—the bride shall be bestowed on me, and then—hand in hand we will go to the East, there where some say Helios is born—into the solitude, to hide ourselves, as the deity hides, go seek the grove by the banks of the Euphrates, discover that, and *then*—oh, greatest of glories, from there a new race in beauty and harmony shall go forward over the earth; and there, you prisoners of the text, you disbelievers, the empire of the spirit shall be founded!

BASIL: Oh, I can only wring my hands in misery over you. Are you the same Julian who set out from Constantinople only three years ago?

JULIAN: At that time I was blind, as you are now. All I knew was the path that ends at learning.

GREGORY: You now know where your path will end?

JULIAN: Where the path and the destination are the same. For the last time, Gregory, Basil, I implore you, stay with me. The vision I had last night— both that and so much more—indicates a mysterious bond between us. To you, Basil, I had so much to say. You're the head of your family; and who knows whether or not all the prospects promised me; if they might not, through you and your family—

BASIL: Never! No one shall be drawn into your madness and your wild imaginings as far as my will is concerned.

JULIAN: Why do you talk of your will. I see a hand that writes on the wall; soon I shall interpret the writing.

GREGORY: Come, Basil!

JULIAN: *(With outstretched arms.)* Oh friends, friends!

GREGORY: From this day, there's an abyss between us.

(He draws BASIL away with him; they leave, right.)

JULIAN: Yes, go, go! What do you two pedants know? Did you gain anything from the city of wisdom? You, my strong, arrogant Gregory—and you, Basil, more a girl than a man—you know only two roads in Athens, the road of the schools and the road of the church; the third road, through Eleusis and beyond, that you don't know, and still less—. Ah!

(The curtain on the right side is drawn back. Two servants in oriental dress bring in a tall covered object, which they place in the corner behind the table. Soon after, MAXIMUS a mystic, enters through the same door. He is a slim figure, of middle height, and has brown, hawklike features. His hair and beard are graying, with the exception of his thick eyebrows and mustache that are still jet-black. He is wearing a pointed cap and a long black robe; in his hand he carries a white staff.)

(MAXIMUS, without attending to JULIAN, goes over to the covered object, halts and gives a sign to the servants. They silently withdraw.)

JULIAN: *(Softly.)* At last!

(MAXIMUS draws the cloth away; a bronze lamp is seen on a tall tripod; afterwards he takes out a small silver jug and pours oil into the lamp's bowl. The lamp lights up by itself and burns with a strong, reddish glare.)

JULIAN: Is it time?

MAXIMUS: *(Without looking at him.)* Are your mind and your body pure?

JULIAN: I have fasted and anointed myself.

MAXIMUS: Then let the night's high ceremony begin! *(He gives a sign; dancing girls and flute players appear in the courtyard. The music and dance continue during what follows.)*

JULIAN: Maximus, what is this?

MAXIMUS: Roses in the hair! Sparkling wine. See, see, the beauty of the limbs in play.

JULIAN: And in all this riot of the senses you mean to—

MAXIMUS: There's sin only in the mind of the sinful.

JULIAN: Roses in the hair! Sparkling wine! *(He casts himself down onto one of the cushions at the table, empties a full glass, sets it down quickly and asks.)* Ah! What was in the wine?

MAXIMUS: A spark of the fire Prometheus stole. *(He reclines on the other side of the table.)*

JULIAN: My senses confuse their functions: I hear light and see sounds.

MAXIMUS: Wine is the soul of the grape. Freed yet willingly enslaved. Logos in Pan!

THE DANCING GIRLS: *(Singing in the courtyard.)*
> Break free, drink the welling
> Bacchus' blood.
> Rock on the swelling,
> Rhythmic flood.

JULIAN: *(Drinking.)* Yes, yes, in drunkenness there's freedom. Can you explain this ecstasy?

MAXIMUS: Intoxication is your union with the soul of nature.

JULIAN: A sweet enigma. Tempting. Enticing—! What was that? Why did you laugh?

MAXIMUS: I?

JULIAN: There's whispering on my left! The silk cushion is rustling—(*Pale, he half springs up.*) Maximus, we're not alone!

MAXIMUS: (*Cries out.*) We're five at table.

JULIAN: Symposium with the spirits!

MAXIMUS: With the shades.

JULIAN: Name my guests!

MAXIMUS: Not now. Listen, listen!

JULIAN: What is it? There's a rushing, like a storm through the house—

MAXIMUS: (*Shouting.*) Julian! Julian! Julian!

JULIAN: Speak, speak! What is happening to us?

MAXIMUS: The moment of annunciation is upon you!

JULIAN: (*Jumps up and shrinks back from the table.*) Ah!

(*The lamps on the table seem about to go out; over the great bronze lamp there arises a circle of bluish light.*)

MAXIMUS: (*Dropping to the floor.*) Look at the light!

JULIAN: There?

MAXIMUS: Yes, yes!

DANCING GIRLS: (*Singing softly in the courtyard.*)
All-seeing Night
Labors to spin
Her web of delight
Enticing you in.

JULIAN: (*Staring at the light.*) Maximus! Maximus!

MAXIMUS: (*Softly.*) Do you see anything?

JULIAN: Yes.

MAXIMUS: What do you see?

JULIAN: I see a face gleaming in the light.

MAXIMUS: Man or woman?

JULIAN: I don't know.

MAXIMUS: Speak to it.

JULIAN: Dare I?

MAXIMUS: Speak; speak!

JULIAN: (*Approaching.*) Why was I born?

A VOICE IN THE LIGHT: To serve the spirit.

MAXIMUS: Does it answer?

JULIAN: Yes, yes.

MAXIMUS: Ask more.

JULIAN: What is my mission?

VOICE: You shall establish the empire.

JULIAN: Which empire?

VOICE: The empire.

JULIAN: And by what path?

VOICE: That of freedom.

JULIAN: Speak more fully. What is the path of freedom?

VOICE: The path of necessity.

JULIAN: And by what power?

VOICE: By *willing* .

JULIAN: *What* should I will?

VOICE: What you must.

JULIAN: It's fading...vanishing—! *(Approaching.)* Speak; speak! What must I do?

VOICE: Julian!

(The circle of light fades; the lamps on the table burn as before.)

MAXIMUS: *(Looking up.)* Gone?

JULIAN: Gone.

MAXIMUS: Do you know, *now?*

JULIAN: Now, less than ever. I hover above a gaping abyss—midway between light and darkness. *(He lies down again.)* What is the empire?

MAXIMUS: There are three empires.

JULIAN: Three?

MAXIMUS: The first is that empire founded on the tree of knowledge; then that empire founded on the tree of the cross—

JULIAN: And the third?

MAXIMUS: The third is the empire of the great mystery, the empire to be founded on both the tree of knowledge and the tree of the cross, because it hates and loves them both and because it has its living-springs under Adam's grove and under Golgotha.

JULIAN: And that empire will come—?

MAXIMUS: It stands at the threshold. I have calculated and calculated—

JULIAN: *(Breaking off sharply.)* That whispering again! Who are my guests?

MAXIMUS: The three cornerstones beneath the wrath of necessity.

JULIAN: Who, who?

MAXIMUS: The three great helpers in denial.

JULIAN: Name them!

MAXIMUS: That I can't do. I don't know them; but I can show them to you—

JULIAN: Then show me them! Right now, Maximus!

MAXIMUS: Take care—!

JULIAN: Right now, right now! I must see them; I must speak with them, one by one.

MAXIMUS: You must take the consequence. *(He waves his staff and calls.)* Take shape, become visible, you—chosen as the first sacrificial lamb.

JULIAN: Ah!

MAXIMUS: *(His face covered.)* What do you see?

JULIAN: *(Subdued.)* He's lying there—in the corner. He is huge, like Hercules— and beautiful, yet no, not—*(Hesitant.)* If you can, speak to me!

VOICE: What would you know?

JULIAN: What was your mission in life?

VOICE: My transgression.

JULIAN: Why did you transgress?

VOICE: Why was I not my brother?

JULIAN: No evasions. Why did you transgress?

VOICE: Why was I myself?

JULIAN: And what did you *will*, as yourself?

VOICE: What I had to.

JULIAN: And why did you have to?

VOICE: I was myself.

JULIAN: You are spare with speech.

MAXIMUS: *(Not looking up.)* In vino veritas.

JULIAN: You're right, Maximus! *(He pours out a full glass in front of the empty seat.)* Bathe in the fumes of this, my pale guest! Refresh yourself. See, see it rises like the smoke of sacrifice.

VOICE: The sacrificial smoke doesn't always rise.

JULIAN: Why does that scar on your brow turn red? No, no—don't hide it under your hair. What is it?

VOICE: The sign.

JULIAN: Hm. Go no further with that. What fruit has your transgression borne?

VOICE: The most glorious.

JULIAN: What do you call the most glorious?

VOICE: Life.

JULIAN: And the ground of life?

VOICE: Death.

JULIAN: And that of death?

VOICE: *(Fading, in a sigh.)* Yes, *that* is the enigma.

JULIAN: Gone!

MAXIMUS: *(Looking up.)* Gone?

JULIAN: Yes.

MAXIMUS: Did you recognize him?

JULIAN: Yes.

MAXIMUS: Who was it?

JULIAN: Cain.

MAXIMUS: *That* path, then. Search no further!

JULIAN: *(With a dismissive gesture.)* The second, Maximus!

MAXIMUS: No, no no; I'll not proceed.

JULIAN: The next, I tell you! You've sworn I shall get to the bottom of these things. The second Maximus! I *will* see him; I *will* know who are my guests.

MAXIMUS: You demand this, not I. *(He waves his staff.)* Come forward and show yourself, willing slave, who helped turn the next great hinge of world history!

JULIAN: *(Staring a moment into the empty space; suddenly he stretches his hands as if defensively against the seat at his side and says, softly.)* No nearer!

MAXIMUS: *(Turning away.)* You see him?

JULIAN: Yes.

MAXIMUS: How does he appear?

JULIAN: I see him as a red-bearded man. With torn clothes and a rope round his neck. Speak to him, Maximus!

MAXIMUS: *You* must speak.

JULIAN: What were you in life?

VOICE: The world-chariot's twelfth wheel.

JULIAN: The twelfth? A fifth's considered superfluous.

VOICE: Where could the chariot have rolled without me?

JULIAN: Where did it roll with you?

VOICE: Into glory.

JULIAN: Why did you aid it?

VOICE: Because I *willed* it.

JULIAN: What did you will?

VOICE: What I *had* to will.

JULIAN: Who chose you?

VOICE: The Master.

JULIAN: Did the Master have foreknowledge when he chose you?

VOICE: Yes, there's the riddle.

    (Short silence.)

MAXIMUS: You are silent.

JULIAN: He's no longer here.

MAXIMUS: *(Looking up.)* Did you recognize him?

JULIAN: Yes.

MAXIMUS: What was he called in life?

JULIAN: Judas Iscariot.

MAXIMUS: *(Leaping up.)* The abyss heaves up blossoms. Night reveals itself!

JULIAN: *(Cries out to him.)* Summon the third!

MAXIMUS: He shall come! *(Waves his staff.)* Come forward, third cornerstone! Come forward, you third great one, liberated through necessity! *(He throws himself down on the cushion and turns away his face.)* What do you see?

JULIAN: I see nothing.

MAXIMUS: And yet he's here. *(Waves the staff again.)* By the seal of Solomon, by the eye in the triangle, I conjure you—become visible!—what do you see now?

JULIAN: Nothing, nothing.

MAXIMUS: *(Waving his staff.)* Come forward, you! *(Suddenly he stops, utters a cry and jumps up from the table.)* Ah, lightning in the darkness! I see it. All my art is useless.

JULIAN: *(Rising.)* Why? Speak, speak!

MAXIMUS: The third is not yet among the shades.

JULIAN: He is alive?

MAXIMUS: Yes, he lives.

JULIAN: And *here,* you said—!

MAXIMUS: Here, or elsewhere—or among the unborn; I do not know—

JULIAN: *(Confronting him.)* You're lying! You're deceiving me! *Here,* you said—!

MAXIMUS: Let go my cloak!

JULIAN: It must be either you or I. But which of us?

MAXIMUS: Let go my cloak, Julian!

JULIAN: Which of us? Which? Everything hinges on that!

MAXIMUS: You know more than I do. What did the voice in the light proclaim?

JULIAN: The voice in the light—? *(With a cry.)* The empire! The empire? Establish the empire—!

MAXIMUS: The third empire!

JULIAN: No, a thousand times no. Get away from me, you corrupt man! I tear myself from you and all your works—

MAXIMUS: From necessity?

JULIAN: I defy necessity! I'll not serve it. I am free, free, free!
(Tumult outside; the dancing girls and flute players flee.)

MAXIMUS: What's that shouting and screaming?

JULIAN: Some men are forcing their way into the house—

MAXIMUS: They're attacking your servants; they want to murder us.

JULIAN: Keep calm; no one can harm us.

EUTHERIUS: *(Enters, running across the courtyard.)* My lord, my lord!!

JULIAN: Who's making all that noise out there?

EUTHERIUS: Strangers have surrounded the house; they've posted guards at all the doors. They're breaking in—violently, almost. Here they come, my lord. There they are!

(LEONTES, a Quaestor, with a large and magnificent retinue, enters from the right.)

LEONTES: Forgive me, I beg you a hundred times, my gracious lord—

JULIAN: *(Takes a step back.)* What's this?

LEONTES: Your servants tried to prevent me entering; and as it's a most urgent matter—

JULIAN: You here in Ephesus, my worthy Leontes!

LEONTES: I've been riding night and day as the Emperor's emissary.

JULIAN: *(Pale.)* To me? What does the Emperor want with me? I'm not aware of any crime I've committed. I am sick, Leontes! This man *(Indicating MAXIMUS.)* is here as my doctor.

LEONTES: Allow me, gracious lord—

JULIAN: Why this violent breaking into my house? What does the Emperor want?

LEONTES: He wishes to overjoy you, my lord, with a great and important message.

JULIAN: Then I beg you, let me know what message you bring.

LEONTES: *(Kneeling.)* My most supreme lord—to your glory and to my good fortune, I hail you, Caesar.

LEONTES' MEN: Long live Julian Caesar!

MAXIMUS: Caesar!

JULIAN: *(Shrinking back with a cry.)* Caesar! Stand up, Leontes! What madness is this?

LEONTES: I bring you the words of the Emperor.

JULIAN: I—I Caesar! Ah, where is Gallus?

LEONTES: Oh, don't ask.

JULIAN: Where is Gallus? I implore you—where is Gallus?

LEONTES: *(Standing up.)* Gallus Caesar is with his beloved wife.

JULIAN: Dead!

LEONTES: In blessedness, with his wife.

JULIAN: Dead, dead! Gallus dead! While on his triumphal march! But when—and how?

LEONTES: Oh, beloved lord, spare me—

GREGORY: *(Struggling with the guards at the entrance.)* I *must* go in to him. Stand aside, I tell you. Julian!

JULIAN: Gregory, brother—so you've come back!

GREGORY: Is it true—this rumor that's fallen on the city like a shower of arrows?

JULIAN: I've been struck by those arrows, too. Dare I trust this mixture of good and bad fortune?

GREGORY: For the love of Christ, drive this tempter from you!

JULIAN: The Emperor's messenger, Gregory!

GREGORY: Would you trample on your brother's bloody corpse—

JULIAN: Bloody!

GREGORY: You don't know? Gallus Caesar was murdered.

JULIAN: *(With clasped hands.)* Murdered!

LEONTES: Ah, who is this meddlesome—?

JULIAN: Murdered, murdered! *(To LEONTES.)* He's lying, surely?

LEONTES: Gallus Caesar's crimes brought him down.

JULIAN: Murdered—who murdered him?

LEONTES: Whatever happened was from necessity, my noble lord! Gallus Caesar misused his power like a madman here in the eastern provinces. His position as Caesar no longer satisfied him. His behavior, both in Constantinople and other places along the route, showed only too well what his intentions were.

JULIAN: I didn't ask about his crimes; it's the other matter I want to know.

LEONTES: Oh, let me spare a brother's ears.

JULIAN: My brother's ears can bear what a son's ears have borne. Who killed him?

LEONTES: The tribune, Scudilo, who attended him, found it advisable to let him be executed.

JULIAN: Where? Surely not in Rome?

LEONTES: No, my lord, it happened on the way there, in a city called Pola in Illyrium.

JULIAN: *(Bowing.)* The Emperor is great and just. The last of my race, Gregory! The Emperor Constantius is great.

LEONTES: *(Takes a purple robe from one of the retinue.)* Noble Caesar, if you would do us the honor of wearing—

JULIAN: Red! Take it away! Was it this he wore in Pola—?

LEONTES: It's just now sent from Sidon.

JULIAN: *(With a glance at MAXIMUS.)* From Sidon! The purple robe—!

MAXIMUS: Apollinaris's vision!

GREGORY: Julian, Julian.

LEONTES: See, it was sent by your cousin, the Emperor. He permits himself to say that he, childless as he is, hopes you will heal this, his life's deepest wound.

He wishes to see you in Rome. After that, it's his will you go as Caesar to Gaul. The German border-tribes have crossed the Rhine and made dangerous inroads into the empire. He builds his trust on your success and progress against the barbarians. Certain things have been revealed to him in dreams, and his last word to me, before I set out, was that you, above all, would have the good fortune to establish the empire.

JULIAN: Establish the empire! The voice in the light, Maximus!

MAXIMUS: Sign against sign.

LEONTES: What is this, noble Caesar?

JULIAN: To me, too, certain things have been manifest; but this—

GREGORY: Say no, Julian! These are corrupt wings of destruction they want to fasten on your shoulders.

LEONTES: Who are you, defying the Emperor?

GREGORY: My name is Gregory; I am the son of the Bishop of Nazianzus—do what you want with me.

JULIAN: He's my friend and brother; no one shall harm him!

(Meanwhile, a large crowd has filled the courtyard.)

BASIL: (Pushing through the crowd.) Don't take the purple, Julian!

JULIAN: You too, my faithful Basil!

BASIL: Don't accept it! For the sake of the Lord God—

JULIAN: What is it appalls you?

BASIL: The terrors to come!

JULIAN: Through me the empire shall be established.

BASIL: Christ's empire?

JULIAN: The Emperor's great and beautiful empire.

BASIL: Was the Emperor's empire the light of your vision when, as a child, you proclaimed the faith from the graves of the Cappadocian martyrs? Was it the Emperor's empire you set out from Constantinople to establish here on earth? Was it the Emperor's empire—

JULIAN: Cloudy phantoms. That all lies behind me like a wild dream.

GREGORY: It were better you should lie at the bottom of the sea with a millstone round your neck, than abandon that dream to the past. Can't you recognize the work of the tempter? All the glory of the world lying at your feet.

MAXIMUS: Sign against sign, Caesar!

JULIAN: One word, Leontes! (Grasps his hand and draws him aside.) Where are you leading me?

JULIAN: To Rome, my lord!

JULIAN: That's not what I'm asking. Where are you leading me—to fortune and power, or to the slaughter bench?

LEONTES: Oh, my lord, such cynical mistrust—

JULIAN: Gallus's limbs have scarcely rotted yet.

LEONTES: I can dispel all doubts. *(Takes out a paper.)* This letter from the Emperor, which I would have preferred giving you in private—

JULIAN: A letter? What does he write? *(He opens the paper and reads.)* Ah, Helena! Oh, Leontes! Helena—Helena—for me!

LEONTES: The Emperor gives her to you, my lord! He gives you his beloved sister, for whom Gallus Caesar begged in vain.

JULIAN: Helena—for me! To have won the unattainable! But she, Leontes—

LEONTES: As I left he took the princess by the hand and led her to me. Her virgin blood rose to her lovely cheeks, she cast down her eyes and said: Greet my beloved cousin and tell him he has always been the man who—

JULIAN: Go on, Leontes!

LEONTES: With those words she fell silent, this chaste and pure woman.

JULIAN: The pure woman! It's all miraculously fulfilled! *(He calls loudly.)* The purple robe—put it on me!

MAXIMUS: You have chosen?

JULIAN: Chosen, Maximus!

MAXIMUS: Chosen, with sign against sign?

JULIAN: This is not sign against sign. Maximus, Maximus, you've been blind, you the seer! Put on the purple robe!

(LEONTES dresses him in the robe.)

BASIL: It is done!

MAXIMUS: *(Muttering to himself, with upstretched hands.)* Victory and light to the man who wills.

LEONTES: And now to the Governor's house; the people wish to greet Caesar.

JULIAN: Even in his elevation Caesar remains what he was—the poor philosopher who received everything through the Emperor's grace. To the Governor's house, honorable friends.

(All go out through he courtyard accompanied by the cheers of the crowd; only GREGORY and BASIL remain behind.)

BASIL: Gregory, whatever's in store, let's hold together.

GREGORY: Here's my hand on it.

END OF ACT THREE

ACT FOUR

Lutetia, in Gaul. A room in Caesar's palace, "The Warm Baths"outside the city. Main entrance door in the background; to the right another, smaller door; in the foreground on the left side is a curtained window. PRINCESS HELENA, richly dressed, with pearls in her hair, is sitting in an armchair, looking out through the window. A slave girl, MYRRHA, stands before her, holding the curtain to one side.

HELENA: What crowds! The whole city's streaming out to meet them. Hush, Myrrha—do you hear the flutes and drums?

MYRRHA: Yes, I really think—

HELENA: You're lying! The noise is too great: You can't hear a thing. *(Jumps up.)* Oh, it's agony, this uncertainty. Not knowing if he's coming back as conqueror or fugitive.

MYRRHA: You mustn't torture yourself, my lady. Caesar's always returned victorious.

HELENA: Yes, before; after all the smaller skirmishes. But this time, Myrrha! This fearfully huge battle. All the confusing rumors. If Caesar's returning victorious, why did he write that letter to the city magistrates forbidding them to welcome him outside the gates?

MYRRHA: Oh, but you know, my lady, how little your noble husband cares for such things.

HELENA: Yes, yes, that's true enough. And if he'd suffered defeat—they'd know about it in Rome—and then why would the emperor be sending his envoy, arriving today, whose messenger brought me all these splendid jewels and gifts. Ah, Eutherius! Well, any news?

EUTHERIUS: *(Entering from the back.)* Your highness, it's just about impossible to find out anything for certain—

HELENA: Impossible? You're concealing something. The soldiers, at least, must know something—

EUTHERIUS: They're nothing but barbarian auxiliaries who've straggled back—Batavians and suchlike—and they know nothing.

HELENA: *(Wringing her hands.)* Oh, do I deserve this agony! Sweet, blessed Christ, haven't I prayed to you night and day—*(Listens, then cries out.)* Ah, my Julian! I hear him! Julian, my darling!

JULIAN: *(In dusty armor, entering swiftly from the back.)* Helena! Close all the doors, Eutherius!

HELENA: Defeated! In flight!

JULIAN: Double the guards at the doors; don't let anyone slip in! Tell me, has any envoy arrived from the emperor?

EUTHERIUS: No my lord; one's on his way.

JULIAN: Go, go! *(To the slavegirl.)* Off with you.

(EUTHERIUS and MYRRHA go out through the back.)

HELENA: *(Sinking in the armchair.)* So it's all up with us.

JULIAN: *(Drawing the curtain.)* Who knows. With caution we might ride out the storm—

HELENA: After such a defeat—?

JULIAN: Defeat? My love, what are you talking about?

HELENA: Haven't the Alemanni defeated you?

JULIAN: If they'd defeated me, you wouldn't have seen me alive again.

HELENA: *(Jumping up.)* But then—god in heaven—what's happened?

JULIAN: *(Softly.)* The worst, Helena—an enormous victory.

HELENA: A victory, you say! An enormous victory? You've won, and yet—?

JULIAN: You've no idea how I stand. You only see the gilded surface of a Caesar's wretchedness.

HELENA: Julian!

JULIAN: Can you blame me for keeping all this from you? Both duty and shame made me—. Ah, but what's this? What a change—!

HELENA: What? What?

JULIAN: What a change in you in these last months! Helena, have you been ill?

HELENA: No, no; but tell me—?

JULIAN: Yes, you've been ill; you still must be ill—these feverish temples, the dark rings round your eyes—.

HELENA: Oh, it's nothing, my darling. Don't look at me, Julian! It's just all the worrying about you: sleepless nights; the fervent prayers to the Blessed One on the Cross—

JULIAN: Take care of yourself, dearest. It can't be good for you—all this devotional fervor.

HELENA: Really, that's a scandalous idea! But tell me about your own situation, Julian! I implore you, hide nothing from me!

JULIAN: There *can* be no hiding it any longer. Since the empress's death everything I do here in Gaul gets some bad construction put on it at Court. When I went cautiously against the Alemanni, they said I was timid and unadventurous. It was a standard joke to say the philosopher couldn't fit properly into the warrior's armor. When I won a victory over the barbarian, I had to listen to them saying I could have done more.

HELENA: But what about all your friends in the army—?

JULIAN: Who do you think are my friends in the army? No one, my dear

Helena! Yes, there's one—that Perusian knight, Sallust. At our wedding feast in Milan, I was forced to turn down what was a simple enough request by him. He approached me in the camp in the noblest manner, reminded me of our old friendship in Athens and asked to be allowed to follow me through all dangers. But what does Sallust count for at the Emperor's court? He's just one of those they term pagans, there. There's nothing he can do for me. And then, the others! The commander, Arbetio, who left me in the field to fend for myself when I found myself surrounded in Senones! Old Severus, weighed down by a sense of his own helplessness who can't take in my new battle strategy! Or do you think I can count on Florentius, the Praetorian Prefect? Let me tell you, that restless man's after the top position.

HELENA: Ah, Julian!

JULIAN: *(Pacing back and forth.)* If only I could keep track of their intrigues! Every week secret letters leave the camp for Rome. Everything I do is transmitted and distorted. No slave in the empire is as fettered as Caesar. Were you aware, Helena, the very menu my cook must prepare from is sent by the Emperor: I'm not permitted to change anything on it. Neither add nor take off a thing.

HELENA: And all this you've been secretly putting up with—

JULIAN: Everyone knows it, except you. They all laugh at Caesar's impotence. I can't bear it any longer. I won't bear it.

HELENA: But the great battle—? Describe it to me—has rumor exaggerated—?

JULIAN: Rumor couldn't exaggerate it—hush, what was that? *(Listens by the door.)* No, no, I just thought—I can truly say that in these months I've done all it rests in human power to do. Inch by inch, and despite all the hindrances from my own camp, I've driven the barbarians back to the eastern frontier. Before Argentoratum, with the Rhine at his back, King Knodomar brought up all his forces. Five kings and ten lesser princes backed him up. But before he was able to gather together all the boats he needed, I got my army to spring into attack.

HELENA: My hero, my Julian!

JULIAN: Lupicinus, with the spearmen and the light infantry, outflanked the enemy in the north; the veteran legions under Severus drove the barbarians farther and farther east toward the river; the Batavians, our allies, under that loyal leader, Bainabaudes, supported the legions heroically, and when Knodomar realized his situation was desperate, he attempted to escape to the south and get over to the islands. But, before he could, I sent on Florentius to confront him with the Praetorians and the cavalry. Helena, I flinch to say it out loud, but it's certain treachery or envy nearly robbed me of the fruits of victory. The Roman cavalry time and again retreated before the barbarians, who threw themselves to the ground and stabbed the horses in the belly. Defeat was right there, in front of my eyes—

HELENA: But the God of battles was with you!

JULIAN: I grabbed a standard, fired up the Imperial Guard with a battle cry, then swiftly harangued them with a speech worthy, maybe, of a more enlightened audience, and, encouraged by the cheers of the soldiers, threw myself into where the fighting was fiercest!

HELENA: Julian! Oh, you do not love me!

JULIAN: At that moment you weren't in my thoughts. I intended to die—I could see no other way out. But one appeared, my darling! It was as if, like lightning, terror flashed from the points of our lances. I saw Knodomar, that formidable fighter—yes, you've seen him yourself—I saw him flee from the battle on foot, and with him fled his brother Vestralp and King Hortar and King Suomar—all who had not fallen under our swords.

HELENA: Oh, I see it, I see it! Blessed Savior, it was Thou that once again sent forth the angels of death from the Milvian bridge![1]

JULIAN: Never have I heard such hideous screams: never seen such gaping wounds as on those we trampled as we waded through the fallen. The river did the rest; drowning men fought each other until they rolled over and sank to the bottom. Most of the princes fell into our hands alive; Knodomar himself tried to escape into a cluster of rushes; one of his own followers betrayed him; our men sent a shower of arrows into his hiding place without hitting him. Then he came out and surrendered of his own accord.

HELENA: And after a victory like that shouldn't you be feeling secure?

JULIAN: (Hesitantly.) After the victory, indeed that same evening, there was an incident, a thing of no consequence…

HELENA: An incident?

JULIAN: It's what I prefer to call it. In Athens we pondered a great deal on Nemesis. My victory was so overwhelmingly great, Helena; that my position's been thrown off balance; I don't know…

HELENA: Tell me. You frighten me.

JULIAN: It was something quite insignificant, I tell you. I had Knodomar, in chains, brought before me in full view of the army. Before the battle he'd vowed to have me flayed alive if I fell into his hands. Now he walked toward me on unsteady feet, his whole body trembling. Shattered by misfortune, in the manner of barbarians, he threw himself before me, clasped my knees, burst into tears and begged for his life.

HELENA: With terror shaking those powerful limbs. I can just see him lying there. So you killed him, my darling?

JULIAN: I couldn't kill that man. I granted him his safety and promised to send him as prisoner to Rome.

HELENA: Without torturing him?

JULIAN: Reason told me to use him gently. But then—I can't explain how it happened—in an outburst of joy and with a cry breaking from his lips, the barbarian sprang to his feet, raised his manacled hands in the air and then, little as he knew our language, called out in a loud voice: "Praise be to thee, Julian, thou mighty emperor!"

HELENA: Ah!

JULIAN: My companions wanted to laugh, but the barbarian king's cry exploded like a fierce fire through the ranks of the soldiers. "Long life emperor Julian" those closest to me shouted: and that cry spread out in wider and wider circles to the furthest distance—like a Titan had hurled a mountain into the sea—pardon the pagan image, dearest, but—

HELENA: Emperor Julian! He said: Emperor Julian!

JULIAN: What did the brutish German know of Constantius whom he'd never set eyes on? I was his conqueror so I was the greatest—

HELENA: Yes, yes; but the soldiers—?

JULIAN: I firmly set them right—because I clearly could see Florentius, Severus, and certain others—standing frozen still, white with fear and anger.

HELENA: Yes, yes, *them*. But not the soldiers.

JULIAN: Scarcely a night passed before my secret enemies had twisted the whole incident. "Caesar commanded Knodomar to proclaim him emperor" the story went, "and as a reward he spared the barbarian's life." And so, turned upside down, that's how it got reported in Rome.

HELENA: Are you sure of that? And by whom?

JULIAN: Yes, by whom? By whom? I wrote to the Emperor myself telling him the whole affair, but—

HELENA: Well—how did he answer?

JULIAN: As usual. You know that ominous silence of his when he's getting ready to strike someone.

HELENA: I think you're misinterpreting all of this. It's impossible otherwise. Just see—the envoy will soon bring you proof that—

JULIAN: I *have* proof, Helena! Here, on my breast, I keep hidden some intercepted letters, which—

HELENA: Oh, my God, let me see!

JULIAN: Later, later. *(He paces up and down.)* And this after all the service I've done him! Here I've broken the Alemmani's hold on the land for a long time to come, while he's been suffering defeat after defeat on the Danube, and while his army in Asia's not advanced an inch against the Persians. Disgrace and disaster on all fronts, except here, where they've put a reluctant philosopher in charge of things. And still they mock me at court. Yes, even after my latest great victory, they've written a satirical poem about me and called me Victorinus! This has got to end.

HELENA: Yes, I think so, too.

JULIAN: What is it worth being Caesar, living this way!

HELENA: No, you're right, Julian; we can't go on like this.

JULIAN: *(Stopping.)* Helena, could you dare to follow me?

HELENA: Don't fear for me—I'll not yield an inch.

JULIAN: Then let's get away from all this thankless servitude; away to that solitude I've sought so long for—!

HELENA: What's that you say? Solitude!

JULIAN: With you, my beloved, and with my precious books. I've scarcely had chance to open them, except for a few restless nights.

HELENA: *(Covering him with her glance.)* Oh, so that's what you mean!

JULIAN: Yes, what else?

HELENA: Exactly, what else?

JULIAN: That's what I'm asking—what else?

HELENA: *(Approaching.)* Julian—what was it the barbarian king called you?

JULIAN: *(Retreating.)* Helena!

HELENA: *(Closer still.)* What was the name that echoed through the soldiers' ranks?

JULIAN: Be careful: There might be someone listening at every door!

HELENA: Why be afraid of such spies? Isn't God's grace protecting you? Haven't you been blessed by fortune in every encounter? I see the beckoning Savior, the angel with the fiery sword who cleared the path for my father when he cast Maxentius into the Tiber.

JULIAN: And I should set myself up against the ruler of the empire?

HELENA: Only against those who stand against you. Go, go! Destroy them with the lightning of your anger! Have done with this wearying and joyless existence. Gaul is a wilderness. I'm freezing here, Julian! I want to return home, to the warm sun, to Rome and Greece.

JULIAN: Back home to your brother?

HELENA: *(Softly.)* Constantius is wasting away.

JULIAN: Helena!

HELENA: I can't stand it any longer, I tell you. Time passes. Eusebia is gone; her empty place stands there, beckoning me to honor and glory while I grow old.

JULIAN: You're not growing old; you're young and beautiful!

HELENA: No, no, no! Time passes; I can't just bear this patiently. Life is slipping away from me!

JULIAN: *(Looking at her.)* How alluringly beautiful, how divinely lovely you are!

HELENA: *(Clinging to him.)* Am I, Julian?

JULIAN: *(Embracing her.)* You're the only woman I've ever loved—the only one who's loved me.

HELENA: I'm older than you. I don't want to get any older. When all is over, I—

JULIAN: *(Tearing himself away.)* Stop! I won't hear any more.

HELENA: *(Following him.)* Constantius is dying a little every day; he's hanging by a thread over the grave. Oh, my dearest Julian, you have the soldiers on your side—

JULIAN: Enough, enough!

HELENA: He wouldn't be able to stand any shock. So what's there to hold you back? I'm not thinking of anything bloody—ugh, how could you imagine that? The fright will be enough; it will take him in its arms and lovingly end his sufferings.

JULIAN: Do you forget the invisible power that protects the anointed?

HELENA: Christ is good. Oh, believe in him, Julian, and what will he not forgive? I will help. Prayers shall be sent up for you. Praised be the saints. Praised be the martyrs! Trust me, we'll atone for everything afterward. Give me the Alemanni to convert. I'll send out our priests among them. They'll bow beneath the mercy of the Cross.

JULIAN: The Alemanni will not bow beneath it.

HELENA: Then they'll die! Like sweet incense their blood will rise up to Him on High, the Blessed One. We'll increase his glory; His praise will be sung by us. I'll join the ceremony. The Alemanni women shall be mine! If they do not submit, they'll be sacrificed. And then, my Julian, when you see me again—young again, renewed. Give me the Alemanni women, my love! Blood...it can't be called murder, and the remedy is said to be infallible, a bath in the blood of young virgins—

JULIAN: Helena, this is monstrous!

HELENA: Is it a sin to sin for your sake?

JULIAN: Oh, my beautiful, my only love!

HELENA: *(Bending over his hands.)* My lord before God and men! Don't flinch, this time, Julian! My hero, my emperor! I see heaven open. Priests shall sing Christ's praises; my women shall join in prayer. *(With upraised arms.)* Oh, you Blessed One. Oh, you God of Hosts—you who have mercy and victory in your hand—

JULIAN: *(With a glance at the door, crying out.)* Helena!

HELENA: Ah!

EUTHERIUS: *(In the background.)* My lord, the Emperor's envoy—

JULIAN: He's arrived?

EUTHERIUS: Yes, my lord.

JULIAN: His name? Who is he?

EUTHERIUS: The tribune Decentius.

HELENA: Really? The pious Decentius!

JULIAN: Who has he spoken with?

EUTHERIUS: With no one, my lord. He arrived this moment.

JULIAN: I'll see him at once. And listen: one thing more. Let the generals and commanders attend me here.

EUTHERIUS: Very well, most gracious lord! *(He goes out at the back.)*

JULIAN: Well, Helena, now it will be clear—

HELENA: *(Softly.)* Whatever happens, remember you can depend on the soldiers—

JULIAN: Ah, depend, depend—I'm not sure I can depend on anyone.

(DECENTIUS, the tribune, enters from the back.)

HELENA: *(Going to him.)* Welcome, noble Decentius! A Roman face—and above all, this face—oh, it brings a burst of sunshine to our gloom-ridden Gaul.

DECENTIUS: The Emperor meets your longing and your hopes halfway, noble Princess! We venture to think Gaul won't confine you much longer.

HELENA: You say so, you bringer of good news? The Emperor still thinks lovingly of me? How is his health?

JULIAN: Go, leave us, Helena dearest.

DECENTIUS: The Emperor's health has in no way got worse.

HELENA: Really, not so? That's just what I thought. All these distressing rumors; praise God they were only rumors! Thank him most lovingly, gentle Decentius. And to you, too, our thanks. With what rich gifts you announced your arrival. Imperial gifts; no, no, brotherly gifts in truth! Two gleaming black Nubians—you should see them, Julian! And pearls! I'm wearing them already. And fruits—sweet and ripe; ah! Peaches from Damascus, peaches in golden bowls! How they'll refresh me; fruit, fruit; I'm almost dying here in Gaul.

JULIAN: There'll be a joyful banquet to end the day; but business first. Leave us, dearest wife.

HELENA: I will go to church, to pray for my brother and for all our hopes. *(She goes out right.)*

JULIAN: *(After a brief pause.)* In speech, or in writing?

DECENTIUS: In writing. *(He hands him a scroll.)*

JULIAN: *(Reading, suppressing a smile and stretching out his hand.)* More!

DECENTIUS: Noble Caesar, that is about all.

JULIAN: Really? Has the Emperor sent his friend this long way only to—*(He breaks into a short laugh; then paces up and down.)* Had Knodomar, the Alemanni king, arrived in Rome before you left?

DECENTIUS: Yes, royal Caesar!

JULIAN: And how is he coping in that strange land—ignorant as he is of the language? Yes, he is quite ignorant of it, Decentius! He completely reduced my soldiers to laughter. Imagine, he confused such basic words as Emperor and Caesar.

DECENTIUS: *(Shrugging his shoulders.)* A barbarian. What can one say?

JULIAN: No, what can one say? But the Emperor has shown him mercy?

DECENTIUS: Knodomar is dead, my lord!

JULIAN: *(Halting.)* Knodomar dead?

DECENTIUS: In the enemy camp on the Caelian hill.

JULIAN: Dead? So? Yes, the air in Rome is unhealthy.

DECENTIUS: The King of the Alemanni died of homesickness, my lord! The longing for his family and freedom—

JULIAN:—is a wasting disease, Decentius. Yes, yes, I know that. I should never have sent him alive to Rome; I should have had him killed here.

DECENTIUS: Caesar's heart is merciful.

JULIAN: Hm—! Homesickness? Yes, well! *(To SINTULA master of the horse, entering from the back.)* So you're here, old faun? Don't tempt me any longer. *(To DECENTIUS.)* Ever since the battle of Argentoratum he talks to me of nothing but victory chariots and teams of white horses. *(To SINTULA.)* It would be like Phaeton's course with the Libyan horses of the sun. How did that end? Have you forgotten—have you forgotten your pagan heritage, I almost said. Forgive me, Decentius, if I wound your pious ear.

DECENTIUS: Caesar tickles his servant's ear: He does not wound it.

JULIAN: Yes, yes, bear with Caesar when he's joking. I don't know how to take it any other way. There they are.

(SEVERUS, a general, the Praetorian Prefect, Florentius, and many commanders and officers of Caesar's court enter from the back.)

JULIAN: *(Going to meet them.)* Good morning, friends and brothers-in-arms! Don't be too vexed I've summoned you here from your march, all battle-stained and weary; I ought to have allowed you some hours rest; but—

FLORENTIUS: Has something happened, my lord?

JULIAN: Yes, in truth it has. Can you tell me now, what was it still lacking for Caesar's happiness?

FLORENTIUS: What could still be lacking for Caesar's happiness?

JULIAN: Nothing, *now*. *(To DECENTIUS.)* The army has asked that I hold a victory celebration in the town. It's their wish I should enter the gates of Lutetia at the head of the legions. The captive barbarian leaders, their hands bound, would march next to the chariots; women and slaves from twenty conquered tribes would follow after, ranked tightly together, shoulder to shoulder—*(Suddenly breaks off.)* Rejoice, my valiant comrades; you see here the tribune Decentius, the Emperor's trusted friend and counselor. He arrived here this morning with gifts and greetings from Rome.

FLORENTIUS: Ah, then no more is needed for Caesar's happiness.

SEVERUS: *(Softly to FLORENTIUS.)* Incredible! So he's back in the Emperor's good graces!

FLORENTIUS: *(Softly.)* Oh, he's the Emperor of indecision!

JULIAN: You all look as if miraculously struck dumb. They think the emperor's gone too far, Decentius!

FLORENTIUS: How can Caesar even imagine such a thing?

SEVERUS: Too far, noble Caesar? In no way. The Emperor surely knows the proper limits of his generosity.

FLORENTIUS: Certainly this is a great and rare distinction.

SEVERUS: I'd say it was exceedingly great and rare.

FLORENTIUS: And especially provides a shining example of how our Emperor is free of all envy—

SEVERUS: An unparalleled example, I'd venture to say.

FLORENTIUS: But then, what hasn't Caesar accomplished these past few year in Gaul!

JULIAN: All one long dream, dear friends! I've accomplished nothing! Nothing, nothing!

FLORENTIUS: Your modesty reckons it as nothing? What was the army, when you took over? A disorderly mob—!

SEVERUS:—without organization, without discipline, with no leadership—

JULIAN: You exaggerate, Severus!

FLORENTIUS: And wasn't it with this mob you marched against the Alemanni; didn't you defeat them with this rabble which, through your victories, you transformed into a victorious army; didn't you recapture Colonia Agrippina—?

JULIAN: Ah, yes, but you see things with a friend's favorable eye, Florentius! Or is it really true? And true I drove the barbarians from the islands in the Rhine? That I built the fortifications of the city of Tres Tabernae, after its destruction, for the greater defense of the empire? Is that really so?

FLORENTIUS: My lord, can you question such great achievements?

JULIAN: No, in truth I think—and the battle of Argentoratum? Didn't I take part? I've the clear impression I defeated Knodomar. And after that victory—

Florentius, have I been dreaming, or did I rebuild Trajan's fortress when we crossed into German territory?

FLORENTIUS: Noble Caesar, is there any man so mad as to deny you these honors?

SEVERUS: *(To DECENTIUS.)* I thank the fates that blessed my old age to be following so successful a leader.

FLORENTIUS: *(Likewise to the Tribune.)* What turn this campaign against the Alemmani would have taken without Caesar's courage and shrewdness I hardly dare imagine.

SEVERAL COURTIERS: *(Pushing forward.)* Yes, my lord, Caesar is great!

OTHERS: *(Clapping their hands.)* Caesar has no equal!

JULIAN: *(Looks for a moment at DECENTIUS and the others then bursts into a shout of laughter.)* How blind is friendship, Decentius! How blind, blind! *(He turns to the others and strikes the roll of paper in his hand.)* For here is something altogether different! Listen, and drink it in like the refreshing dew of understanding. It's the Emperor's message to all the governors in the empire; our distinguished Decentius has brought us a copy. Here it states: I've done nothing in Gaul. It was a dream, as I just said. Here we have the Emperor's own words: It was under the Emperor's expert guidance the danger threatening the empire was averted.

FLORENTIUS: All affairs in the empire proceed under the Emperor's guidance.

JULIAN: There's more yet! Here it's reported it was the *Emperor* who fought and conquered on the Rhine; the Emperor who raised up the king of the Alemanni as he flung himself, begging humbly, before him. It's not my privilege to find my name anywhere in this document—nor yours, Florentius, nor yours either, Severus! And here, in the account of the battle of Argentoratum; where was it? Ah yes, here it is: It was the Emperor who commanded the battle; it was the Emperor himself who, at the risk of his life, fought through the enemy ranks, slashing until he blunted his sword; it was the Emperor, by the sheer terror of his presence, who sent the barbarians in headlong flight—here, read it, read it I say!

SEVERUS: Noble Caesar, your word is sufficient.

JULIAN: And what do you hope to gain then, with your flattering fantasies, my friends? In your overweening love for me would you render me a parasite, when you feed me on the leavings you pick from my cousin's table? What do you think, Decentius? What do you say to all this? You see, even in my own camp I must keep an eye on my followers who sometimes, in their blindness, come near to stumbling over the edge of insubordination.

FLORENTIUS: *(Quickly, to the Tribune.)* Indeed, my words have been grossly misinterpreted...

SEVERUS: *(Likewise to the Tribune.)* It could never occur to me to express such—

JULIAN: That's right, comrades: Let's all together swallow our pride. Earlier, I asked what was needed for Caesar's happiness. Now you know. Understanding the truth—that alone was needed for his happiness. Your silver helmet will not be covered with the dust of a triumph, brave Florentius! The Emperor's already held the triumph for us in Rome. So he finds all celebrations here to be superfluous. Go, Sintula, and see the parades we planned are canceled. The Emperor wishes to reward his soldiers with a good rest. It's his will they remain in camp outside the walls. *(SINTULA goes out the back.)*

Wasn't I once a philosopher? That's what they said, at least, in Athens and Ephesus. So weak is human nature in good fortune, I came near to being unfaithful to philosophy. The Emperor's reminded me. Thank him most humbly, Decentius! Have you more to report?

DECENTIUS: One thing more. After everything the Emperor's been able to gather, and from the letter you wrote him from Argentorum, it appears the great campaign's been favorably concluded, here in Gaul.

JULIAN: Certainly, the Emperor, through his courage and merciful magnanimity—

DECENTIUS: The Rhine border is secured.

JULIAN: By the Emperor, by the Emperor.

DECENTIUS: The country flanking the Danube is a totally different matter, and things are even worse in Asia; King Sapor is steadily gaining ground.

JULIAN: That presumptuous man! There's a rumor it was not the Emperor's pleasure, this summer either, to let his generals crush him.

DECENTIUS: The Emperor himself intends to crush him early the next year. *(Bringing out a paper scroll.)* Here he expresses his will, noble Caesar!

JULIAN: Let's see, let's see! *(Reading.)* Ah! *(He reads it again, with strong emotion; then he looks up.)* So it's the Emperor's will that—? Good, good, noble Decentius; the Emperor's will shall be carried out.

DECENTIUS: It is essential it be carried out this very day.

JULIAN: This very day; that's understood. Come here, Sintula! Now, where is he? Ah yes! Fetch Sintula back! *(A courtier goes out at the back; JULIAN goes over to the window and reads through the papers again.)*

FLORENTIUS: *(Quietly, to the Tribune.)* I beg you earnestly not to misconstrue what I said earlier. When I allowed Caesar the credit it was naturally with no intention of—

SEVERUS: *(Softly.)* It would never enter my mind to imply it wasn't the Emperor's wise leadership that—

A COURTIER: *(At the Tribune's other side.)* I implore you, noble lord, put in a word for me at Court and release me from this painful service with a Caesar who—yes, he is the Emperor's esteemed cousin but—

ANOTHER COURTIER: I'm afraid I could tell you of things that signify a great and boundless vanity and reckless ambition—

JULIAN: This very day! Let one thing be understood, Decentius! It's my highest wish to lay down this very responsible and dignified office.

DECENTIUS: The Emperor shall be informed.

JULIAN: I call Heaven to witness that I've never—Ah, here is Sintula; now we can—*(To the Tribune.)* You are going?

DECENTIUS: I've business to discuss with the generals, noble Caesar.

JULIAN: Without going through me?

DECENTIUS: The emperor has instructed me to spare his beloved kinsman. *(He leaves by the back, followed by the others with the exception of SINTULA, who remains standing by the door.)*

JULIAN: *(Looking at him awhile.)* Sintula!

SINTULA: Yes, my noble lord!

JULIAN: Come closer. Yes, truly, you look like an honest man. Forgive me, I never thought you could be so loyal to me.

SINTULA: How do you know I'm loyal, my lord?

JULIAN: Here, I read into this you are to desert me.

SINTULA: I, my lord?

JULIAN: The Emperor's disbanding the army in Gaul, Sintula.

SINTULA: Disbanding—?

JULIAN: Yes, what else is it but disbanding? The Emperor needs to strengthen his forces, both along the Danube and against the Persians. Our Batavian and Herulian auxiliaries are to depart as fast as possible to be in Asia by Spring.

SINTULA: But that's an impossibility, my lord. You most solemnly swore to just these allies there was no way they'd be used beyond the Alps.

JULIAN: Precisely, Sintula! The Emperor writes that I gave that assurance too hastily and without his consent. That's something I never suspected; but that's what it says. I shall be forced to break my word, discredit myself in the army's eyes, and turn the unbridled rage of the barbarians, and perhaps their deadly weapons, against myself.

SINTULA: That will never happen, my lord. The Roman legions will form a shield around you.

JULIAN: The Roman legions? Hm—my innocent friend! From each Roman legion three hundred men are to be detached and sent to the Emperor by the shortest route.

SINTULA: Ah! so that's—

JULIAN: Cleverly worked out, isn't it? All the divisions shall be arrayed against me so I can be rendered weaponless with the least possible risk.

SINTULA: And I tell you, my lord not a single general will let himself be used for that purpose.

JULIAN: My generals won't face that temptation. You're the man.

SINTULA: I, my Caesar!

JULIAN: It's written here. The Emperor delegates to you the job of organizing everything necessary and then leading the chosen detachments to Rome.

SINTULA: I'm delegated to do that? When men such as Florentius and old Severus—

JULIAN: You've no victories on your ledger to tell against you, Sintula!

SINTULA: No, that's true for certain. No one's ever given me opportunity to show—

JULIAN: I've been unjust to you. Thank you for your loyalty.

SINTULA: Such a great honor from the Emperor. My lord, may I see—

JULIAN: What do you want to see? You surely don't want to be a party to this?

SINTULA: God forbid that I should disobey the Emperor's command.

JULIAN: Sintula—you could take away your Caesar's power?

SINTULA: Caesar's always set little value on me. Caesar could never forgive my being foisted on him through the Emperor's choice.

JULIAN: The emperor is great and wise; he understands the art of choosing.

SINTULA: My lord, I am burning to perform my duty. May I know the Emperor's instructions?

JULIAN: (Handing him one of the scrolls.) Here are the Emperor's instructions. Go and do your duty.

MYRRHA: (Running frantically from the right.) Oh, merciful Savior!

JULIAN: Myrrha! What is it?

MYRRHA: Oh, heavens have pity, my mistress—

JULIAN: Your mistress, what about her?

MYRRHA: Sickness, or else madness—help, help!

JULIAN: Helena sick. The doctor! Find Oribases, Sintula. Fetch him!

(SINTULA goes out at the back. JULIAN is about to go out to the right but meets HELENA in the doorway surrounded by slave women. Her face is wild and distorted, her hair and clothes in disarray.)

HELENA: Loosen the comb! Loosen the comb, I tell you! It's red hot. My hair's on fire; I'm burning, burning!

JULIAN: Helena! For merciful God's sake—

HELENA: Will no one help me? These piercing needles, they're murdering me!

JULIAN: Helena, my dearest! What has happened to you?

HELENA: Myrrha, Myrrha! Save me from these women, Myrrha!

ORIBASES: *(Entering from the back.)* What terrible news is this—? Is it true? Ah!

JULIAN: Helena! My love, light of my life—

HELENA: Get away from me! O, sweet Jesus, help me. *(Half-collapsing among the slave women.)*

JULIAN: She's beside herself. What can it be, Oribases? See, see her eyes, how huge they are—!

ORIBASES: *(To MYRRHA.)* What has the Princess taken? What did she eat or drink?

JULIAN: Ah, you think—?

ORIBASES: Answer me, women; what have you given the Princess?

MYRRHA: We? Nothing, believe me; she herself—

ORIBASES: Yes, yes?

MYRRHA: Some fruit; there were peaches, I think—oh, I don't know—

JULIAN: Fruit! Peaches? From those which—

MYRRHA: Yes…no…yes; I don't know, my lord—it was the two Nubians—

JULIAN: Help, help, Oribases!

ORIBASES: Unfortunately, I fear—

JULIAN: No, no no!

ORIBASES: Hush, my lord. She's coming round.

HELENA: *(Whispering.)* Why did the sun go down? Oh, blessed, secretive darkness!

JULIAN: Helena! Listen, gather your thoughts—

ORIBASES: My noble Princess—

JULIAN: It's the doctor, Helena! *(Taking her hand.)* No, here—here I am.

HELENA: *(Tearing free.)* Ugh, there he is again!

JULIAN: She doesn't see me. I'm here, here, Helena!

HELENA: Disgusting man—he's always about me.

JULIAN: What does she mean?

ORIBASES: Step to one side, gracious lord—!

HELENA: Sweet, restful peace! He doesn't suspect; oh, my Gallus!

JULIAN: Gallus!

ORIBASES: Leave, noble Caesar; this will not help—

HELENA: How proudly your thick hair curls round your neck. This strong, sensuous neck—

JULIAN: Abyss of all abysses—!

ORIBASES: Her delirium gets worse—

JULIAN: I see it, I see it! We must investigate further, Oribases!

HELENA: *(Laughing softly.)* Now he wants to investigate again. Ink on his fingers; book dust in his hair—unwashed; ugh, ugh, how he stinks.

MYRRHA: My lord, would you prefer that I—

JULIAN: Away with you, woman!

HELENA: How could you let him vanquish you, you strong, suntanned barbarian? He can't vanquish women. How I detest this virtuous impotence!

JULIAN: Stand aside, all of you! Not so near, Oribases! I will tend the Princess myself.

HELENA: Are you angry with me, Lord? Gallus is dead, isn't he? Beheaded. What a blow that must have been! Don't be jealous, Thou, my first and last. Let Gallus burn in hellfire—there was only You, You, You—!

JULIAN: No closer, Oribases!

HELENA: Kill the priest, too! I'll not see him after this. You well know our sweet secret. Oh You, my days' longing, the ecstasy of my nights! It was always just You—in your servant's guise—in the chapel; yes, yes, you were there, in the darkness, in the air, in the veiling clouds of incense, that night when the new Caesar stirred under my heart—

JULIAN: *(With a cry.)* Ah!

HELENA: *(With outstretched arms.)* My lover and my lord! My, my—*(She falls to the floor; the slave women run to her, flocking round her.)*

JULIAN: *(Stands motionless for a moment; then clenches and raises his fists and cries.)* Galilean!
(The slave women carry the Princess out, right; at the same moment SALLUST rushes in through the main door in the back.)

SALLUST: The Princess has fainted. Ah, so it's true?

JULIAN: *(Grips the doctor by the arm and leads him to one side.)* Tell the truth! Did you know, before today, that—well, you understand me; did you know before today anything about—about the Princess's condition?

ORIBASES: I, like everyone else, my lord!

JULIAN: And you said nothing to me, Oribases!

ORIBASES: Said what, my Caesar?

JULIAN: How could you keep silent about such a thing?

ORIBASES: My lord, there was *one* thing none of us knew.

JULIAN: And that was?

ORIBASES: That Caesar knew nothing. *(About to leave.)*

CAESAR: Where are you going?

ORIBASES: To try what medicines my skill can—

JULIAN: I believe your skill will prove useless.

ORIBASES: My lord, it is still possible—

JULIAN: Useless, I tell you.

ORIBASES: *(Back a step.)* Noble Caesar, it is my duty to disobey you in this matter.

JULIAN: What did you think I meant? Go, go, try what your skill can do; save the Emperor's sister. The Emperor would be inconsolable if his loving care should cause any misfortune. Of course you're aware the fruit was a gift from the Emperor?

ORIBASES: Ah!

JULIAN: Go, go, man—and see what your skill—

ORIBASES: *(Bowing respectfully.)* I believe my skills are useless, my lord! *(He goes out to the right.)*

JULIAN: Ah, Sallust, there you are! What do you think? They're beginning again—the waves of destiny rolling over our family.

SALLUST: Oh, but there's still hope. Oribases will—

JULIAN: *(Curtly, dismissive.)* The Princess is dying.

SALLUST: If only I dared to speak. If I dared trace the secret threads in this web of disaster!

JULIAN: Rest assured, my friend; all the threads will come to light one day. And then—

DECENTIUS: *(Entering from the back.)* How shall I approach in sight of my Caesar! How inscrutable are the ways of God! I'm devastated! If you only knew how I feel it, here, inside me! To be the messenger of such misery and suffering.

JULIAN: Yes, you may well say that again, Decentius! And how shall I find words tender and tactful enough to convey this appropriately to the Emperor's brotherly ears?

DECENTIUS: So unfortunate that something like this should happen almost simultaneously with my mission! And just now! A sudden bolt from a blue sky bright with our hopes.

JULIAN: Yes, this tempest of destiny drowns and devours our ship just as it seemed to be entering its long-sought harbor; this, this—sorrow makes us eloquent, Decentius, you, as well as me. But first to business. The two Nubians must be arrested and tried!

DECENTIUS: The Nubians, my lord? Do you imagine my indignant rage could allow those two negligent servants for a moment to—

JULIAN: How is this? Surely you never—

DECENTIUS: Call me an impetuous man, noble Caesar, but my love for the Emperor and his grief-stricken house would truly be feebler than it is if, at a moment like this, I'd been capable of calm deliberation.

JULIAN: You've had both slaves put to death?

DECENTIUS: Didn't they deserve death seven times over as a consequence.

They were two heathen savages, my lord! Their evidence would have served no purpose. It was impossible to get anything out of them except that they'd left the objects of their important watch unguarded in the antechamber a considerable time, accessible to each and every—

JULIAN: Aha! So that's it, Decentius!

DECENTIUS: I accuse no one. Oh, but beloved Caesar, I must warn you; you are surrounded by disloyal servants. Your court—through some unfortunate misunderstanding—imagined they detected some kind of displeasure in the measures the Emperor, out of necessity, has seen fit to adopt here; in brief—

SINTULA: *(Entering from the back.)* My lord, you have given me a task I can in no way carry out.

JULIAN: It's the Emperor gave you that task, good Sintula.

SINTULA: Relieve me of it, my lord. I'm truly not equal to it.

DECENTIUS: What has happened?

SINTULA: The camp's in wild uproar. The legionaries and allies have joined in revolt.

DECENTIUS: In defiance of the Emperor's will!

SINTULA: The soldiers are shouting they will hold Caesar to his promises.

JULIAN: Listen, listen; hear that row outside—!

SINTULA: The mob's storming this way—

DECENTIUS: Let no one get in!

SALLUST: *(By the window.)* It's too late; the whole square's full of rebellious troops.

DECENTIUS: Caesar's precious life's in danger! Where is Florentius?

SINTULA: Fled.

DECENTIUS: That big-mouthed braggart. But Severus, then?

SINTULA: Severus has reported sick; he's taken himself off to his estate.

JULIAN: I'll talk to the madmen myself.

DECENTIUS: Stay where you are, noble Caesar!

JULIAN: Now what?

DECENTIUS: It is my duty, most gracious lord; the Emperor's command...his beloved cousin's life—Caesar's my prisoner.

SALLUST: Ah!

JULIAN: It's out at last!

DECENTIUS: The household guard, Sintula! You have the duty of taking Caesar safely to Rome.

JULIAN: To Rome!

SINTULA: What do you say, my lord!

DECENTIUS: To Rome, I tell you!

JULIAN: Like Gallus! *(Shouts through the window.)* Help! Help!

SALLUST: Fly, my Caesar! Fly, fly!

(Wild clamor heard outside. Roman legionaries, Batavian auxiliaries, and other allies, climb in through the windows. At the same time other soldiers swarm in through the door upstage. Among the leaders is the standard bearer MAUROS; women, some of them with children, follow the intruders.)

CRIES OF SOLDIERS: Caesar, Caesar!

OTHER VOICES: Caesar, why have you betrayed us?

STILL OTHERS: Down with Caesar, the traitor!

JULIAN: *(Throwing himself with outstretched arms into the midst of the soldiers, crying.)* Comrades, companions in arms, save me from my enemies!

DECENTIUS: Ah, what's that—!

WILD SHOUTS: Down with Caesar. Strike him down!

JULIAN: Make a circle round me, draw your swords!

MAUROS: They're drawn already!

WOMEN: Strike him! Strike him!

JULIAN: Thank God that you came, Mauros! Honest Mauros! Yes, yes, I can rely on you.

BATAVIAN SOLDIER: How dare you send us to the ends of the earth. Was that what you swore to us?

OTHER ALLIES: Not beyond the Alps! That's not our duty!

JULIAN: Not to Rome! I will not go! They intend to murder me as they murdered my brother, Gallus!

MAUROS: What's that you're saying, my lord?

DECENTIUS: Don't believe him!

JULIAN: Don't touch the noble Decentius; he is not to blame.

LAIPSO, A CENTURION: That's true; it's Caesar who's to blame.

JULIAN: Ah, is it you, Laipso, brave friend. You fought well at Argentoratum.

LAIPSO: You remember, Caesar?

VARRO, A CENTURION: It's his promises he doesn't remember.

JULIAN: Wasn't that the voice of our fearless Varro? Yes, there he is! Your wound's healed, I see. Oh, you well-deserving warrior—to think they'd not allow me make you captain!

VARRO: That's what you really wanted?

JULIAN: Don't hold it against the Emperor that he rejected my request. The Emperor doesn't know any of you as I know you.

DECENTIUS: Soldiers, listen to me—!

MANY VOICES: We've got nothing to do with the Emperor.

OTHERS: *(Pushing menacingly forward.)* Caesar must answer to us!

JULIAN: What power has your unhappy Caesar, my friends? They intend taking me to Rome. They refuse me control even over my own affairs. They are confiscating my share of the spoils. Five gold pieces and one pound of silver—that's what I intended giving every soldier, but—

SOLDIERS: What's he saying?

JULIAN: It's not the Emperor who forbids it; it's his wicked and envious advisers. The Emperor is good, dear friends! Ah, but the Emperor's sick; he can't manage—

MANY SOLDIERS: Five gold pieces and a pound of silver!

OTHERS: And they refuse to give it us!

STILL OTHERS: Who dares refuse Caesar anything?

MAUROS: And that's how they deal with Caesar, the soldiers' father!

LAIPSO: With Caesar, who's been more a friend to us than master. Or isn't that true?

MANY VOICES: Yes, yes, it's true, he has!

VARRO: Shouldn't Caesar, after his victories, be able to choose his own captains?

MAUROS: Shouldn't he have a free hand to do as he wants with the spoils that fell to him?

LOUD VOICES: Yes, yes yes!

JULIAN: Ah, what good would such riches do you? What use would you have with earthly goods, you, who are to be sent to distant lands to meet an uncertain fate—

SOLDIERS: We won't go!

JULIAN: Don't look at me; I am ashamed; I'm almost ready to weep a flood of tears, when I think that in a few months you'll be exposed to disease, hunger, and the weapons of a bloodthirsty enemy.

MANY SOLDIERS: *(Crowding round him.)* Caesar! Kind Caesar!

JULIAN: And then your defenseless wives and children you must abandon to their scattered homes! Who'll protect these pitiful ones, these future widows and orphans, who'll soon enough suffer the Alemanni's vindictive attacks.

WOMEN: *(Weeping.)* Caesar, Caesar, protect us!

JULIAN: *(Also in tears.)* What is Caesar? What can the fallen Caesar do?

LAIPSO: Write to the Emperor and let him know—

JULIAN: Ah, what is the Emperor? The Emperor's sick in mind and body; he's broken down with caring for the empire's well-being. Isn't that true, Decentius?

DECENTIUS: Yes, certainly—but—

JULIAN: How it pierced my heart when I learned—*(Pressing the hands of those around him.)* Pray for his soul, all of you who worship the good Christ! Offer sacrifices for his health, you who've remained loyal to the gods of your fathers!…Did you know the Emperor's held a triumphal march in Rome?

MAUROS: The Emperor has?

VARRO: What? With the defeat he suffered on the Danube?

JULIAN: After the Danube debacle he held a triumph to celebrate our victories—

DECENTIUS: *(Menacingly.)* Your Highness, consider—!

JULIAN: Yes, what the Tribune says is true; consider how the Emperor's mind must be clouded when such a thing can happen? Oh, my sorely afflicted kinsman! In Rome, when he rode through the mighty arch of Constantine he believed himself so big he bowed his back so his head touched his saddlebow.

MAUROS: Like a cock in a doorway.

(Laughter among the soldiers.)

SEVERAL VOICES: Is *that* an Emperor?

VARRO: And we're to obey him?

LAIPSO: Away with him!

MAUROS: Caesar, you take command!

DECENTIUS: Mutiny—!

MANY VOICES: Seize power, seize power, Caesar!

JULIAN: Madmen! Is this to speak like Romans? Do you want to echo the Alemannian barbarians? What was it Knodomar shouted at Argentoratum? Tell me, good Mauros, what was that he cried out?

MAUROS: He cried: Long live Emperor Julian!

JULIAN: Ah, shh, shh, shh. What are you saying?

MAUROS: Long live Emperor Julian!

THOSE STANDING BEHIND: What's happening?

VARRO: They're proclaiming Julian Caesar Emperor!

LOUD SHOUTS: Long live the Emperor! Long live Emperor Julian!

(The shout spreads in wider and wider circles outside and beyond. All are talking at the same time; it is some time before JULIAN can be heard.)

JULIAN: Oh, I beseech you—! Soldiers, friends, comrades in arms—see, I stretch out my trembling arms—! Don't be alarmed, good Decentius! Oh, that it should come to this! I lay no blame on you, loyal friends. Despair's driven you to it. It's your will. Good, I submit to the army's will. Sintula, tell my generals to assemble. You, Tribune, can bear witness to Constantius I'd no alternative. *(Turns to VARRO.)* Go, captain, and announce to the camp this unexpected development. I'll be writing to Rome without delay.

SALLUST: My lord, the soldiers wish to see you.

MAUROS: A golden circle on your head, my Emperor!

JULIAN: I've never owned such an ornament.

MAUROS: This will do. *(He removes his neck-chain and winds it many times round Caesar's forehead.)*

SHOUTING OUTSIDE: The Emperor! The Emperor! We want to see the
    Emperor!
SOLDIERS: On to the shield with him! Up, up!
    *(The soldiers near JULIAN lift him high in the air on a shield and show him to
    the crowd outside amid continued cheering.)*
JULIAN: The army's will be done! I bow to the inevitable and renew all
    promises...
LEGIONARIES: Five gold pieces and a pound of silver!
BATAVIANS: Not beyond the Alps!
JULIAN: We'll set up headquarters in Vienne. It's Gaul's strongest city and richly
    supplied with everything we need. There it will be my intention to wait until
    we see if my enfeebled kinsman approves of what, in the interests of the
    empire, we've undertaken here.
SALLUST: He'll not do that, my lord!
JULIAN: *(With raised hands.)* Divine wisdom bring light to his darkened soul and
    lead him to act wisely. Stay with me, Fortune, you who've never yet deserted
    me!
MYRRHA AND THE WOMEN: *(Wailing outside to the right.)* Dead, dead,
    dead!

END OF ACT FOUR

PAGE 58
[1] Constantine won the battle of the Milvian bridge, established his imperial
    claims, and created the spiritual hegemony of Christianity in the ancient
    world.

ACT FIVE

In Vienne. A vaulted space in the catacombs. To the left a winding passage leads upwards. Into the rockface in the back is cut a flight of stairs that ends at a closed door. Downstage, right, many steps lead down to the passages far below. The room is dimly lit by a hanging lamp. JULIAN, with unshaven beard and in dirty clothes, stands leaning over the opening on the right. The muffled sound of psalm singing can be heard from the door on the right leading to the church that is built just beyond.

JULIAN: *(Calling down.)* Still no sign?

A VOICE: *(From deep below.)* Nothing.

JULIAN: Not yes or no? Neither for nor against?

VOICE: Both.

JULIAN: That's the same as nothing.

VOICE: Wait, wait.

JULIAN: I've waited five days; you asked only for three. I tell you—I'm not in the mood to—*(He listens toward the exit and calls softly down.)* Don't speak!

SALLUST: *(Enters from up in the passage, left.)* My lord! My lord!

JULIAN: Is it you, Sallust? What do you want down here?

SALLUST: All this darkness—ah, now I can see you.

JULIAN: What do you want?

SALLUST: To serve you however I can. To lead you out to the living again.

JULIAN: What's the news from the world above?

SALLUST: The soldiers are restless. There are signs everywhere they're losing patience.

JULIAN: The sun must be shining up there now.

SALLUST: Yes, my lord.

JULIAN: The sky arches like a sea of glittering light. Perhaps it's high noon. It's warm; the air quivers along the walls of houses. The river, shrunken, ripples over white flintstones. Beautiful life, beautiful world!

SALLUST: Come, come my lord! Your lingering in the catacombs like this is causing people to speak against you

JULIAN: What are they saying?

SALLUST: Dare I tell you?

JULIAN: You may dare, and you shall. What are they saying?

SALLUST: Many believe it's not so much grief as repentance driving you underground like this.

JULIAN: They believe I killed her?

SALLUST: The mysteriousness of the circumstances should excuse them, when—

JULIAN: No one murdered her, Sallust! She was too pure for this sinful world; that's why an angel from heaven descended each night into her bedchamber and called to her. Or don't you think so? Don't you know the priests in Lutetia explain her death in this way? And the priests should know. Hasn't her funeral procession here been treated like a triumphal march throughout the land? Didn't the women from Vienne stream out to meet her coffin outside the gates, greeting her with green branches in their hands, spreading carpets on the road and singing songs of praise in honor of the bride of heaven who was being led to her bridegroom's house? What are you laughing at?

SALLUST: I, my lord?

JULIAN: Night and day ever since, I've listened to the bridal songs. Hear that! They're lifting her into glory. Yes, in truth she was a genuine Christian woman. She kept the commandment rigidly, rendering unto Caesar's what was Caesar's, and to the other she rendered—but *that's* not what we should be talking about; you are not initiated into the mysteries of the faith, Sallust! What's the news, I asked you.

SALLUST: The most important I know is that the Emperor, hearing what happened in Lutetia, fled to Antioch.

JULIAN: I know that news. Constantius imagined us already at the gates of Rome.

SALLUST: The friends who dared to join you in this dangerous venture, imagined the same.

JULIAN: The time's not favorable, Sallust! Didn't you know that in the games before we set out from Lutetia, my shield broke in pieces, so all I held was the handle? And didn't you know that when I was about to mount my horse, the servant stumbled as I swung up on his folded hands?

SALLUST: Yet you got into the saddle, my lord!

JULIAN: But the man fell.

SALLUST: Better men will fall if Caesar hesitates.

JULIAN: The Emperor's dying.

SALLUST: The Emperor lives. The letters you wrote him about your proclamation—

JULIAN: About my unwilling proclamation. It was forced on me; I'd no choice.

SALLUST: The Emperor's not likely to be impressed by that explanation. It's his intention, when his army's assembled in the eastern provinces, to invade Gaul.

JULIAN: How do you know?

SALLUST: Through chance, my lord! But I beg you to believe me—!

JULIAN: All right, all right then. When that happens, I'll go meet him in Constantinople—but not with sword in hand.

SALLUST: No? In what manner do you think you'll be meeting him?

JULIAN: I will render unto the Emperor what is the Emperor's.

SALLUST: Do you mean by that you intend to stand down?

JULIAN: The Emperor's dying.

SALLUST: Oh, that futile hope! *(Drops to one knee.)* Then take my life, my lord!

JULIAN: What now?

SALLUST: Caesar, take my life; I'd rather die by your command than by the Emperor's.

JULIAN: Stand up, my friend.

SALLUST: No, let me lie here at my Caesar's feet and confess everything. Oh, my beloved lord—to have to tell you this! When I sought you out in the camp on the Rhine—reminding you of our earlier friendship in Greece—when I begged to be allowed to share the dangers of war with you, oh, Caesar, I then came as a secret agent in the pay of the Emperor—

JULIAN: You—!

SALLUST: For some time my mind had been filled with resentment toward you. You remember that trivial quarrel in Milan—not trivial to me, however—for I'd hoped Caesar would help me get my battered fortune back on its feet again. They took advantage of that in Rome and decided I was the ideal man to keep track of your actions.

JULIAN: And you could go along with that? With such black treachery?

SALLUST: I was ruined, my lord; and I felt Caesar had washed his hands of me. Yes, my Caesar, I betrayed you—in the first few months, not after. Your friendliness, your generous spirit, all the favors you showed me; I became what I'd only seemed to be, you loyal follower, and in my secret dispatches to Rome I deceived those who'd sent me.

JULIAN: Those letters were from *you?* Oh, Sallust!

SALLUST: They contained nothing to harm you, my lord! What others may have written, I can't say. I only know I suffered agonies from my enforced and hateful silence. I worked as much as I dared to make amends. That letter, addressed to an unknown man in your camp, describing the Emperor's victory march into Rome, which, one morning on your way to Lutetia, you found smuggled into your tent—you did find it, my lord?

JULIAN: Yes, yes—

SALLUST: It was written by me and by a stroke of luck I was able to make sure it fell into your hands. I dared not say anything. I *wanted* to speak; but I couldn't; day after day I put off revealing my treachery. Oh, punish me, my lord; see, here I lie!

JULIAN: Stand up; you are all the more dear to me because of this—victory against my will and your own. Stand up, my soul's friend; no one shall harm a hair of your head.

SALLUST: It were better you took a life you no longer have the power to protect. You say the Emperor is dying. *(Gets up.)* My Caesar, I'll now reveal to you something I've sworn to keep concealed. Build no hope on the Emperor's failing health. The Emperor's taken a new wife.

JULIAN: Ah, what insanity! How can you think—

SALLUST: Taken a new wife, my lord! *(Hands over some papers.)* Read, read, noble Caesar. These letters will leave you in no doubt.

JULIAN: *(Taking the papers and reading.)* Yes, by the sun's light and strength—!

SALLUST: Oh, if I'd only dared speak earlier!

JULIAN: *(Continuing to read.)* He's taken a wife. Constantius—that feeble shadow of a man—! Faustina, what does it say? young—scarcely nineteen years old—a daughter of—ah! A daughter of that arrogant family. An ardent Christian, at the same time. *(Folds the letter up.)* You're right, Sallust; his failing health gives no room for hope. As for his weakening, his dying, what can one say? Isn't Faustina pious? An angel of annunciation will appear to her—or else—ha-ha! in short, in one way or another—behold, a young Caesar's on its way, and then—

SALLUST: To hesitate is to lose everything.

JULIAN: This has been planned for a long time—and in secrecy, Sallust. Yes, now I see, this clears up all the enigmas. Helena—it wasn't what I thought, her thoughtless tongue, that killed her—

SALLUST: No, my lord!

JULIAN: It was thought—they believed—oh, unfathomable, inexorable justice! That's why she had to be got rid of.

SALLUST: Yes, that's why: I was the man they first cast their eyes on in Rome. Oh, my lord, you can't doubt I turned it down. I pleaded the impossibility of finding an opportunity; they assured me the wicked scheme had been abandoned, and then—

JULIAN: They won't stop at—at the double corpse in the sarcophagus up there. Constantius is taking a wife. That's why I was to be rendered powerless in Lutetia.

SALLUST: Only one thing can save you, Caesar; you must take control before the Emperor gathers his strength.

JULIAN: If, of my own free will, I retired into solitude, devoted myself to that wisdom I've been forced to neglect? Would the new people in power permit such an existence? Wouldn't simply knowing I was still alive be like a sword hanging over their heads?

SALLUST: In the future Empress's family are the same men who attended Gallus Caesar in his last hours.

JULIAN: The Tribune Scudilo. Believe me, friend—I've not forgotten that. And for such a bloody Emperor I'm supposed to give way and fall! To spare him, who for long years has trampled upon the corpses of my closest kinsmen!

SALLUST: Spare him—and in three months he will be trampling on the corpses of your followers.

JULIAN: Yes, yes, you're right in that. It's almost my bounden duty to rise against him. If I do, it won't be for my sake alone, for isn't the well-being of thousands also involved? Was it in my power to avoid this extreme? You are more guilty than I, Sallust. Why didn't you speak before?

SALLUST: In Rome they made me swear a solemn oath to keep silent.

JULIAN: An oath. So. By the gods of your ancestors?

SALLUST: Yes, my lord, by Zeus and Apollo.

JULIAN: And you've broken your oath?

SALLUST: I wish to live.

JULIAN: But the gods?

SALLUST: The gods—they're far away.

JULIAN: Yes, your gods are far away; they don't constrain you; they don't oppress you; they leave a man space to act in. Oh, this Greek happiness, to feel so free! You said the Emperor, vindictive as he is, will shed the blood of my loyal followers. Yes, who can doubt that's what will happen? Was Knodomar spared? Didn't that harmless prisoner pay with his life for a slip of his tongue. Oh yes, I know, Sallust—they murdered him; it was a lie—all that about the barbarian's home sickness. Can you imagine the light in which Decentius, back in Rome, got them to see what occurred?

SALLUST: It best explains the Court's rapid flight to Antioch.

JULIAN: Am I not the army's father, Sallust?

SALLUST: The soldiers' father, the shield and protector of their wives and children.

JULIAN: What would be the fate of the empire if I weakened now? A dying Emperor and after him a helpless baby on the throne; division and rebellion; each man's hand raised against all others in a scramble for power. Not many nights ago I had a vision. A figure appeared before me with a halo around its head; it looked at me angrily and said, "Choose!" Then it melted away like morning mist. Until now I've interpreted this vision as signifying something quite different; but now, when I hear of the Emperor's approaching marriage—yes, in all truth, I must choose before disaster overwhelms the empire. I'm not thinking of my own advantage; but dare I refuse the choice, Sallust? Isn't my duty to the Emperor to protect my life?

Would I be right to stand idly by, waiting for the murderers his fear prompts him to pay to strike me down? Have I the right to give our unfortunate Constantius the chance to add a new debt of blood on his sinful head. Surely it's better for him—as it says in the Scriptures—that he should suffer wrong rather than do wrong? Even if what I do to my cousin can be called a wrong, then this wrong is cancelled by preventing him doing *me* a wrong. I imagine both Plato and Marcus Aurelius, the crowned bridegroom of Sophia, would support me in this. Not a bad subject for the philosophers, at any rate, Sallust.

SALLUST: My lord, you yourself are enough of a philosopher...

JULIAN: True, true, but I'd still like to hear other views. Not because I'm wavering, don't think that! Nor do I find any grounds for doubting our complete success. Nor should we be daunted at all by ominous events. That incident when I was left holding only the handle when my shield was shattered in the tournament, could, I think, be interpreted that I'll keep whatever my hand seizes. And when I swung onto my horse and knocked to the ground the man helping me into the saddle, why that seems to predict a sudden fall for Constantius who elevated me! Whatever the case, I'll write a tract quite clearly justifying—

SALLUST: All very well, gracious lord, but the soldiers are impatient; they wish to see you and hear their fate from your own lips.

JULIAN: Go, go and put them at ease—tell them Caesar will soon show himself.

SALLUST: My lord, it isn't Caesar, it's the Emperor they wish to see.

JULIAN: The Emperor is coming.

SALLUST: Then he's coming—empty-handed—yet with thousands of lives in his hand!

JULIAN: A fair deal, Sallust, thousands of lives as against thousands of dead.

SALLUST: Do your enemies have the right to live?

JULIAN: You're lucky your gods are so far away. To possess a will always armed for battle—!

A VOICE: (*Calling from deep down in the catacombs.*) Julian! Julian!

SALLUST: Ah, what was that?

JULIAN: Leave, dear friend; go away quickly!

VOICE: Silence the hymn singing, Julian!

SALLUST: There it calls again. Oh, then it's true!

JULIAN: What's supposed to be true?

SALLUST: That you live down here with a mysterious stranger—a prophet or magician—who came to you at night.

JULIAN: Ha! ha! Is that what they're saying. Go, go!

SALLUST: I beg you, my lord—leave all this frantic dreaming. Come with me—come up into the day.

VOICE: *(Closer, below.)* All my labor's wasted.

JULIAN: *(At the stairway, right.)* No sign, my brother?

VOICE: Waste and emptiness.

JULIAN: Oh, Maximus!

SALLUST: Maximus!

JULIAN: Leave, I tell you. If I ever walk out of this charnel house, it will be as Emperor.

SALLUST: Please, I implore you—what do you seek here in the darkness?

JULIAN: Light! Go, go!

SALLUST: If Caesar hesitates, I fear he'll find the path blocked.

(He leaves through the passage, left. Soon after MAXIMUS climbs up the steps; he wears a white sacrificial band round his forehead; in his hand he carries a blood-stained knife.)

JULIAN: Speak, my Maximus!

MAXIMUS: All my labor's wasted, I tell you. Why couldn't you silence that church hymn? It smothered all the omens; they wished to speak but couldn't utter the words.

JULIAN: Silence, darkness—and I can wait no longer! What should I do?

MAXIMUS: Go forth in blindness, Julian; the light will seek you out.

JULIAN: Yes, yes, yes. I think so too. I hardly needed to send for you all this way. Do you know what I've just learned—?

MAXIMUS: I don't wish to know what you've learned. Take your fate into your own hands.

JULIAN: *(Paces uneasily up and down.)* In all truth, just what is he, this sinner pursued by furies, this crumbling ruin of what was once a man?

MAXIMUS: Be his tomb, Emperor Julian!

JULIAN: In all his actions against me hasn't he been like a shipwreck without a rudder—now driven to the left by a current of mistrust, and then driven to the right by a blast of remorse? Didn't he reel onto the throne, terror-stricken, with his purple robe dripping with my father's blood? Perhaps with my mother's too. Didn't all my family have to perish so he could sit securely on his throne? No, not quite all. Gallus was spared, and I—a couple of lives had to continue—to bribe a little forgiveness. Then he drifted again, on the current of mistrust. Remorse forced from him the title of Caesar for Gallus; then fear forced from him Caesar's death-warrant. And I? Should I thank him for the life he's granted me till now? One by one, first Gallus and then—every night I've lain sweating in terror that the day just passed should prove my last.

MAXIMUS: Were Constantius and death your worst terrors? Think on that!

JULIAN: Yes, you are right. Priests—! All my youth's been a long, dual dread of the Emperor and of Christ. Oh, he's terrible, this mysterious—this merciless god-man! Every path I wanted to take he always rose up, great and powerful, barring my way with his uncompromising and implacable demands.

MAXIMUS: And these demands—did they come from within you?

JULIAN: Always from without. "Thou shalt!" Even when my soul was eaten up with hatred for my family's murderer, still the commandment told me, "Love thine enemy!" When I was thrilled by beauty and thirsted for the life and the lovely images of the lost Greek world, then the Christian demand, "Seek the one thing needful!" broke my spirit.

When I felt the sweet desires and longings of the body in so many ways, it was then the Prince of self-denial cowed me with his, "Die unto this life to live in the life beyond." To be fully human has been forbidden from the day the seer of Galilee gained control of the world. With him, to live is to die. To love or to hate, each is a sin. Has he then changed man's flesh and blood? Hasn't earthbound man remained what he always was? All that's healthy within our souls rises against this; and yet we are to will against our own will! Thou shalt! Thou halt! Thou shalt!

MAXIMUS: And you've got no further than that? Shame on you!

JULIAN: On me?

MAXIMUS: Yes, you the man from Athens and from Ephesus.

JULIAN: Ah, those days are gone, Maximus! At that time it was so easy to choose. What was it we sought to create so ardently? A system of philosophy. Nothing more nor less.

MAXIMUS: Doesn't it say someplace in your Scripture: "Either for us or against us?"

JULIAN: Didn't Libanius remain the man he was in a debate, whether he stood on the side of the prosecution or the defense? This lies deeper. It's something I must put in practice. "Render unto the Emperor that which is the Emperor's." In Athens we made a game of it; but it goes deeper than that. You can't fathom it, you who've never been in this god-man's power. It's more than a teaching he's spread over the world: It is a witchcraft that takes the soul prisoner. Those who've once come under his spell, I believe, can never break free.

MAXIMUS: Because you do not will it absolutely.

JULIAN: How can I will what is impossible?

MAXIMUS: Is it worth willing anything but the impossible?

JULIAN: That's just the chatter of the schoolroom. You can't satisfy me with that stuff anymore. And yet—oh, no no, Maximus! You just can't fathom how it is with us. We're like a vine planted in strange new soil; plant us back again and we'd die; but in the new soil we can't thrive.

MAXIMUS: We? Who do you call we?

JULIAN: All those who live under fear of the revelation.

MAXIMUS: Phantom fears!

JULIAN: Whatever they are. But don't you see how this paralyzing fear's solidified to build a towering wall around the Emperor? Oh, I understand why the great Constantine would impel such an emasculating doctrine to victory and power over his empire. No bodyguard with spears and shields so effectively protects the imperial throne as this enthralling faith which all the time points beyond earthly life. Have you looked closely at them, these Christians? Hollow-eyed, pale-cheeked, flat-chested, all of them; they are like the linen-weavers of Byssos. No noble ambition is allowed to stir in this brooding atmosphere; the sun shines for them, and they don't see it; the earth offers its abundance, and they've no desire for it. Their only desire is to renounce and suffer so that they may die.

MAXIMUS: Then make use of them as they are; but you must stand aloof. Emperor or Galilean—*that* is the choice. Be a slave to fear or rule in the land of daylight and joy. You can't will an agreement of two opposites; but that's just what you want. You wish the union of what can't be united, to reconcile what won't be reconciled; and so you lie here rotting in the dark.

JULIAN: If you can, show me the light!

MAXIMUS: Are you the Achilles your mother dreamt she was to give to the world? It's not the vulnerable heel that makes a man an Achilles. Rise up, my lord! Ready for victory, like a rider on his spirited horse, you must overthrow the Galilean if you intend to gain the imperial throne—

JULIAN: Maximus!

MAXIMUS: My beloved Julian, look at the world around you! Those Christians you describe as longing for death are few. But how does it stand with all the others? Aren't they deserting the Master in their hearts, one by one? Yes, answer me—what's become of this strange gospel of love? Doesn't one sect furiously rage against another? And the bishops, those lords of the gold coffers who call themselves chief shepherds of the Church! Do even the grandees of the Court outdo them in greed, in lust for power, and in groveling before the great?

JULIAN: They are not all like that; think of the admirable Athanasius of Alexandria—

MAXIMUS: He was the only one. And where's Athanasius now? Hounded out because he wouldn't be bought at the Emperor's bidding. Wasn't he forced to flee to the Libyan desert where lions devoured him? Can you name me *one* more like Athanasius. Look at Bishop Maris of Chalcedon who's switched his mind three times on the Arian controversy. Or Bishop Marcus in Arethusa: You know him from your boyhood. Didn't he recently, against law and justice, confiscate all municipal property and hand it over to the church? And think of that feeble, spineless Bishop of Nazianzus, who's become the joke of his own congregation because he swears both yes and no on any issue, hoping to avoid all controversy.

JULIAN: True, true true!

MAXIMUS: These are your brothers-in-arms, my dear Julian; you won't find any better. Or perhaps you're pinning your hopes on that great pair of pampered Galileans from Cappadocia? Ha-ha, Gregory the Bishop's son pursues law in his hometown, and Basil's studying secular philosophy on his estate in the eastern provinces.

JULIAN: Yes, I know only too well. Desertions on all sides. Hecebolius, my old tutor, becomes a wealthy man for his zeal in the faith and his interpretation of the Scriptures, and since that time—! Maximus, soon I'll be standing alone in steadfastness.

MAXIMUS: You *are* standing alone. Your whole army's flown in panic or lies dead around you. Sound the charge—no one will hear you; advance, no one will follow you. You think you can promote a cause that's already lost faith in itself? You'll go under, I tell you! And then where will you go? Repudiated by Constantius, you will be repudiated by every power on earth—and above the earth. Or will you seek refuge in the embrace of the Galilean? How do things stand between you and him? Haven't you just said you're in terror of him? Are his commands alive in you? Do you love your enemy, Constantius, even though you don't strike at him? Do you hate the cravings of the flesh and the earth's seductive joys even though you don't plunge into them like an ardent swimmer? Do you forsake the world, even though you lack the courage to possess it? And are you so sure that—when you die here—you'll live in a beyond?

JULIAN: *(Pacing up and down.)* What has he done for me, this great taskmaster? If he holds the reins of the world chariot in his hands, then he surely could have—*(The hymn singing rises louder from above in the church.)* Listen, listen! That's what they call serving him. Which he accepts as the sweet smoke of sacrifice. Hymns in his praise—and hymns to her in the coffin. If he knows all things, then how can he—

EUTHERIUS: *(Hurrying in through the passage, left.)* Caesar! My lord, where are you?

JULIAN: Here, Eutherius! What do you want with me?

EUTHERIUS: You must come up, my lord; you must see with your own eyes;—the Princess's body's performing miracles.

JULIAN: You're lying!

EUTHERIUS: I'm not lying, my lord! I'm no follower of this strange faith; but what I've seen I cannot doubt.

JULIAN: What have you seen?

EUTHERIUS: The whole town's in an uproar. The sick and crippled are carried to the Princess's coffin; the priests let them touch it, and they go away healed.

JULIAN: And you've seen this yourself?

EUTHERIUS: Yes, my lord, I saw a woman with epilepsy go out of the church healed and praising the god of the Galileans.

JULIAN: Ah, Maximus, Maximus!

EUTHERIUS: Hear how the Christians are rejoicing—that must be another miracle.

ORIBASES: *(Calling from up in the passage, left.)* Eutherius, have you found him?

JULIAN: *(Going toward him.)* Here, here—is it true, Oribases?

ORIBASES: *(Coming forward.)* Incredible, inexplicable—and yet true; they touch the coffin, the priests read and pray over them, and they depart cured. A voice proclaims from time to time: "Holy, holy is the pure woman."

JULIAN: A voice!

ORIBASES: A voice from an invisible presence, Caesar; a voice high up in the church's vaulting—no one knows where it comes from.

JULIAN: *(Stands uncertainly for a moment, then turns quickly to MAXIMUS and shouts.)* Life or the Lie!

MAXIMUS: Choose!

ORIBASES: Come, come, my lord; the soldiers are terrified and are threatening you—

JULIAN: Let them threaten!

ORIBASES: They hold you and I guilty of the Princess's death—

JULIAN: I will come; I'll calm them down.

ORIBASES: There's only one way to do it; you must turn their thoughts in another direction, my lord; they're wild with despair over their fate if you hesitate any longer.

MAXIMUS: Ascend to heaven, you fool; now you can die for your lord and master!

JULIAN: *(Gripping his arm.)* The Emperor's realm for me!

MAXIMUS: Achilles!

JULIAN: How do I break loose from the bond?

MAXIMUS: *(Handing him the sacrificial knife.)* With this.

JULIAN: How wash away the baptism?

MAXIMUS: The blood of the victim. *(He tears away the sacrificial bandage from his forehead and binds it round Caesar's.)*

ORIBASES: What are you thinking of, my lord?

JULIAN: Do not question.

EUTHERIUS: Listen to the noise. Come up, come up, my Caesar!

JULIAN: First down—and then up. *(To MAXIMUS.)* To the sanctuary, my beloved brother—?

MAXIMUS: Immediately below, in the second chamber.

ORIBASES: Caesar, Caesar, where are you going?

MAXIMUS: To freedom.

JULIAN: Through darkness to light. Ah—! *(He goes down into the catacombs.)*

MAXIMUS: *(Softly, watching him.)* So it has come!

EUTHERIUS: Speak, speak! What's the meaning of these secret arts?

ORIBASES: And now, when every second is precious—!

MAXIMUS: *(Whispering uneasily as he shifts his position.)* These dank, gliding shadows! Ugh! these slimy forms creeping round my feet—!

ORIBASES: *(Listening.)* The noise is getting louder, Eutherius! It's the soldiers, listen!

EUTHERIUS: It's the singing from the church.

ORIBASES: No, it's the soldiers. Here they come!

(SALLUST appears above in the passage surrounded by a large group of excited soldiers. MAURUS, the standard-bearer is among them.)

SALLUST: Be patient, I beg you—!

SOLDIERS: Caesar has betrayed us! Caesar shall die!

SALLUST: And then what, you madmen!

MAURUS: Then what? With Caesar's head we can buy our pardon—

SOLDIERS: Come out, come out, Caesar!

SALLUST: Caesar—my Caesar, where are you?

JULIAN: *(Calling out in the chamber below.)* Helios! Helios!

MAXIMUS: Liberated!

CHOIR: *(In the church, singing.)* Our Father, which art in heaven!

SALLUST: Where is he? Eutherius, Oribases, what's happening here?

CHOIR: *(In the church.)* Hallowed be thy name!

JULIAN: *(Climbing up the stairs; he has blood on his forehead and his breast and hands.)* It is fulfilled!

SOLDIERS: Caesar!

SALLUST: Blood—! What have you done?

JULIAN: Torn away the mists of fear.

MAXIMUS: Creation's in your hands.

CHOIR: *(In the church.)* Thy will be done, on earth as it is in heaven! *(The singing will continue during the following.)*

JULIAN: There's no power protecting Constantius now.

MAUROS: What are you saying, my lord!

JULIAN: Ah, my loyal comrades! Up into the light of day, to Rome and to Greece!

SOLDIERS: Long live Emperor Julian!

JULIAN: We'll not look back; all ways lie open to us. Up into the daylight. Through the church! The liars shall be silenced—! *(He dashes up the steps in the background.)* My army, my treasure, my imperial throne!

CHOIR: *(In the church.)* Lead us not into temptation, but deliver us from evil! *(JULIAN throws the door wide open. The brilliantly lit church is revealed. Priests are standing at the high altar. Worshippers kneel solemnly round the Princess's coffin.)*

JULIAN: Free, free! Mine is the kingdom.

SALLUST: *(Calling to him.)* And the power and the glory!

CHOIR: *(In the church.)* Thine is the Kingdom and the power and the glory—

JULIAN: *(Blinded by the light.)* Ah!

MAXIMUS: Victory!

CHOIR: *(In the church.)* For ever and ever, amen!

END OF ACT FIVE

AND OF

EMPEROR AND GALILEAN

PART ONE: CAESAR'S APOSTASY

Emperor and Galilean

PART TWO

THE EMPEROR JULIAN

"KEJSER JULIAN"

A Drama in Five Acts

CHARACTERS

EMPEROR JULIAN

NEVITA, a general

POTOMAN, a goldsmith

CAESURIUS from Nazianzus, physician to Julian

THEMISTEUS, Orator

MAMERTINUS, Orator

URSULUS, The Emperor's Chancellor

EUNAPIUS, a barber

BARBARA

HECEBOLIUS, theologian

Courtiers and civil servants

Citizens of Constantinople

Participants in the procession of Dionysos, flute players, dancers, acrobats, and
 women

Envoys from the Eastern monarchs

EUTHERIUS, a chamberlain

Servants in the palace

Judges, orators, teachers, and citizens of Antioch.

MEDON, a corn merchant

MALKOS, a tax-collector.

GREGORY of Nazianzus, brother of Canarius

PHOKION, a dyer

PUBLIA

HILARION, her son

AGATHON from Cappadocia

BISHOP MARIS of Chalcedon

Participants in the procession of Apollo, priests, temple servants, harpists, and city
 guards

Agathon's younger brother

Procession of Christian prisoners

HERAKLEOS, a poet

ORIBASES, the emperor's physician

LIBANIUS, orator and chief magistrate in Antioch

APOLLINARIS, a hymn writer

CYRILLUS, a teacher

An old priest in the sanctuary of Kybele

Female psalm singers of Antioch

FROMENTINUS, a captain

JOVIAN, a general
MAXIMUS, a mystic
NUMA, a soothsayer
Two other Etruscan soothsayers
PRINCE HORMISDAS, in exile from Persia
ANATALUS, captain of the bodyguard
PRISKUS, a philosopher
CHYTRON, a philosopher
AMMIAN, a captain
BASIL of Caesarea
MACRINA, his sister
A Persian deserter
Roman and Greek soldiers
Persian warriors

SETTING

The events occur between December A.D. 361 and the end of June A.D. 363.

ACT ONE

The harbor in Constantinople. In the foreground to the right a superbly decorated and carpeted landing stage. On the shore, high up, near the landing stage, is a veiled stone surrounded by guards. Far out on the Bosphorus the imperial fleet is lying, hung with flags of mourning.

Huge crowds in boats and on the shore. At the end of the landing stage stands EMPEROR JULIAN, dressed in purple, with gold decorations. He is surrounded by COURTIERS and HIGH RANKING OFFICIALS. Among those closest to him are NEVITA, the General, and the court physician, CAESARIUS, accompanied by the orators, THEMISTIUS and MAMERTINUS.

JULIAN: *(Gazing across the water.)* What an encounter! The dead emperor and the living. To think he'd draw his last breath so far from home! And that I, for all my haste, have lost the sweet joy of clasping my cousin for the last time! For both of us, a bitter fate—. In which ship is the corpse?

NEVITA: There it comes.

JULIAN: The long boat?

NEVITA: Yes, gracious Emperor!

JULIAN: Poor cousin. In life so high and mighty, and now must make do with a roof so low. You'll not be butting your brow on the coffin lid, who bowed your head riding beneath the Arch of Constantine.

A MAN: *(To POTAMON the goldsmith.)* How young he looks, our new Emperor!

POTAMON: Still, he looks stronger than before. When I last saw him some nine or ten years ago, he was much more slightly built.

ANOTHER MAN: Ah yes, he's done great things these last years.

A WOMAN: And then all the dangers he's endured from childhood on.

A PRIEST: Miraculously preserved from all of them; providence protects him.

POTAMON: Though there's a rumor he relied on protection of a different kind in Gaul.

PRIEST: Lies, lies—you can be sure of it.

JULIAN: Here he comes. The Sun whom I invoke, and the great god of lightning know I did not wish for Constantinus's death. Truly, that's been far from my thoughts. I've sent up prayers for his life. Tell me Caesarius— you must know best—was the Emperor's body on its journey here given all due honor?

CAESARIUS: The funeral procession was like the procession of a conqueror all through Asia Minor. In every city we passed through the faithful multitudes flocked into the streets; all through the night churches echoed with prayers and hymns; darkness was made day from the thousands of candles—

JULIAN: Good, good, good! I'm seized with indescribable anxiety just thinking of taking the helm from so great and worthy and much beloved an Emperor. Why wasn't it granted me to live in peaceful obscurity?

MAMERTINUS: Who more capable of taking on this formidable destiny than you, most supreme lord? I boldly challenge any who have a mind to the throne: Come forward and take charge of the ship of state: but take charge of it the way Julian does. Watch night and day over the welfare of all. Be masters in name yet servants in fact of the people's liberty. Choose your place in the front ranks of warriors in battle, not at the banquet tables. Take nothing for yourselves, but give freely to all. Let your rule of justice be equally far from laxity as from cruelty. Live in such a way no virgin in the wide world need wring her hands in anguish over your actions. Master of the impassable wilderness of Gaul and the cold of Germany. How will they answer? Frightened by such fearful demands, they'd stop up their delicate ears and shout: Only a Julian is equal to all that!

JULIAN: He who controls all things grant such great hopes are not misplaced. Yet how far short I fall from fulfilling them! I shudder to be compared with Alexander, with Marcus Aurelius, and with so many other unmatchable men! Didn't Plato say only a god can rule over men? Oh, pray with me that I may free myself from ambition's snares and the temptations of power. Athens! Athens! It's there I long to be! I was like a man exercising for his body's health, and it's as if one now came to me and said: "Leave the playground and go and win the Olympic Games. All Greece will be your audience." Mustn't my soul be filled with terror before I even begin the contest?

THEMISTEUS: Why terror, oh Emperor? You've already the applause of all Greeks before the contest begins? Haven't you already restored to all the banished virtues their former rights? Isn't there gathered in you all those heroic powers that Herakles, Dionysos, Solon, that…?

JULIAN: Quiet! Nothing but the dead man's praise is to be heard today. They are pulling in to land. Take my crown and chains. I won't wear the imperial ornaments at a time like this.

(He gives the ornaments to one of his attendants. The funeral procession comes up the landing stage with great ceremony, led by priests with lighted candles. The coffin is drawn on a low carriage with church banners drawn before and after it. Choirboys swing censers; crowds of Christians follow after.)

JULIAN: *(Laying his hand on the coffin and audibly sighing.)* Ah!

AN ONLOOKER: Did he make the sign of the Cross?

A SECOND: *(In the crowd.)* No.

THE FIRST: You see! You see!

A THIRD ONLOOKER: He didn't bow before the host, either!

THE FIRST ONLOOKER: *(To the SECOND.)* Did you see! What did I tell you?

JULIAN: Return home in splendor and honor, soulless body of my cousin. I won't hold this dust guilty for what your spirit worked against me. What am I saying? Was it your spirit that acted so harshly against my family that I alone am its survivor? Was it your spirit that caused my childhood to be blighted by a thousand terrors? Was it your spirit that caused the noble Caesar's head to fall? Was it you who assigned me, an inexperienced youth, to so hazardous a post in inhospitable Gaul and then after, when adversity and misfortune failed to break me, fought to deny me the honor of my victories? Oh, Constantius, my cousin, all this didn't have its origin in your great heart. Why did you writhe in anguish and torment, seeing blood-soaked shades crowd about the agony of your deathbed? Evil counselors embittered your life and your hour of death. I know them well, these counselors, who could create dark evil from the sunshine of your bounty. I know them, these men so eager to clothe themselves in the latest fashion of court doctrine.

PAGAN CITIZENS: *(Among the onlookers.)* Long live Emperor Julian!

CAESARIUS: Gracious Lord, the procession is waiting…

JULIAN: *(To the priests.)* Don't stop your pious hymns for my sake. Forward, my friends! *(The procession moves slowly to the left.)* What am I? Emperor. Does that say all? Name one imperial office that hasn't been rendered contemptible in reputation in recent years. What was philosopher, Marcus Aurelius? Emperor? Only Emperor? I nearly asked: Wasn't he somewhat more than Emperor? Was he not Chief Priest at the same time?

VOICES IN THE CROWD: What's the Emperor saying? What was it he said?

THEMISTEUS: Oh, Emperor, is it truly in your mind to—?

JULIAN: Not even my uncle, great Constantine, dared set aside this dignity. Though he'd permitted a certain new doctrine quite extraordinary privileges, still he continued to be called Chief Priest over all who kept true to the ancient gods of the Greeks. That this office has been sadly neglected in recent years, I will pass over, except to mention that not one of my illustrious predecessors, not even he to whom we now offer our final, grief-stricken farewell, dared relinquish it. Should I then presume to do what such wise and upright emperors did not find right or proper to perform? Let no such thought come near me!

THEMISTEUS: Oh, great Emperor, then you intend—?

JULIAN: I intend to proclaim full freedom for all citizens. Hold fast to the Christians' god, those who need to for their peace of mind. Where I'm concerned, I'll not risk building hopes on a god who up to now how has been the enemy of my every venture. I'm convinced by certain signs and omens that I owed all my victories on the frontier of Gaul to those other gods who favored Alexander in a similar way. Protected by these I prospered through all dangers; it was they especially who led me forward on my journey here with such miraculous speed and success that in these streets I've heard the cry I must somehow be divine: a wild exaggeration, my friends! One thing is sure, however: I dare not be ungrateful to such constant proofs of favor.

VOICES IN THE CROWD: *(Subdued.)* What's he going to do?

JULIAN: Therefore to the venerable gods of our forefathers I restore their ancient rights. But let no insult be offered to the Galileans' god, nor to that of the Jews. The temples built by our former rulers with such exquisite art shall rise again in renewed splendor, with altars and statues, each for its special gods, so that proper worship can find its place once more. I'll in no way permit the Christian churches to be subject to malicious attacks; nor any injury be offered to their graveyards, nor those other places a peculiar delusion leads them to consider sacred. We will be tolerant of the illusions of others; I myself was once ensnared in error; however, over that I cast a veil. I won't dwell on what I've thought about divine matters since my twenty-first year. All I'll say is I congratulate those who follow me...I smile at those who don't wish to tread in my footsteps...I'll seek to persuade, but will coerce no one. *(He pauses a moment expectantly; faint applause is heard here and there in the crowd. He continues, forcefully.)* I'd the right to expect more grateful applause but all I hear is puzzled curiosity. However, I should have known; only a pitiable apathy exists among those claiming to have held fast to our ancient faith. Repression and mockery have brought our ancestors' beliefs into oblivion. I've already searched, high and low; but hardly anyone could give me a convincing account of how a sacrifice to Apollo or Fortuna should be conducted. So I must lead the way in this as in other matters. I've lost many a night's sleep discovering from ancient books how these things previously were done. Yet I don't begrudge that labor when I remember what a great debt of gratitude we owe these deities. Nor am I ashamed to officiate in this myself—where are you off to, Caesarius?

CAESARIUS: To church, gracious Emperor; I want to pray for the soul of my departed master.

JULIAN: Go, go. Everyone is free in such matters. *(CAESARIUS and several other OLDER COURTIERS go out left.)* But that freedom I grant to the humblest citizen I claim also for myself. So I announce to you, Greeks and Romans, I'm returning with all my heart to the teachings and customs our ancestors held sacred. These shall be freely promulgated and observed alongside all new and alien doctrines; and, as a child of this city, it's all the more dear to me to proclaim this in the name of the gods who protect it. *(He gives a sign; servants unveil the stone; an altar can be seen and at its base a wine flagon, an oil jar, and a little pile of wood and other accessories. A strong but silent movement stirs the crowd as JULIAN goes up to the altar and prepares the sacrifice.)*

THEMISTEUS: Oh, how can I, as a Greek, not melt in tears to see such humility and gentle reverence!

A CITIZEN: See, he's breaking the firewood himself.

A SECOND CITIZEN: Over his left thigh. Is that how it's done?

MAMERTINUS: The fire you kindle here, oh mighty Emperor, will ignite learning and inquiry from which shall rise renewed, like that miraculous bird—

NEVITA: This fire will harden the Greeks' weapons. I don't know much about Galilean notions; but I've noticed all those who hold to them are faint-hearted and unfit for greater deeds.

THEMISTEUS: In this fire, incomparable one, I see philosophy purified of every libel and accusation The wine you pour out is the purple you adorn the truth with and set on a royal throne. Now, as you lift up your hands—

MAMERTINUS: Now, as you lift up your hands, it's as if you honor the brow of wisdom with a wreath of gold; and the tears you shed—

THEMISTEUS: *(Drawing closer.)* Yes, yes, the tears I see you now let fall, these are like pearls of great price with which eloquence once more shall be royally rewarded. At last the Greeks are free to raise their eyes again to the heavens and follow the course of the eternal stars! How long since this was granted us! Were we not compelled, out of fear of informers, to tremble and bow our heads to the earth, like beasts? Who among us dared boldly observe the rising and setting of the sun? *(Turning to the crowd.)* Even you farmers of the land who've flocked here today in such numbers, even you dared not mark the movements of the heavenly bodies that should have guided your labors—

MAMERTINUS: And you seamen—did you or your fathers dare utter the names of the constellations you steered your courses by? Now you may dare; now none shall forbid you—

THEMISTEUS: No Greek need any longer live on sea or land without guidance from the immutable laws of the heavens; no longer need he be tossed like a ball for chance and accident to sport with—

MAMERTINUS: Oh, what a man is this Emperor to whom we owe such great blessings!

JULIAN: *(Before the altar, with upraised arms.)* There, openly and humbly, I've poured oil and wine for you, benevolent gods, who for so long lacked those pious acts that are your due. I've sent up my thanks to you, Apollo, who some wise men, above all those from the east, have named Sun King, because you bring and renew that light from which all life has its ground and origin. I've brought my sacrifice to you, Dionysos, god of Ecstasy, who lifts the souls of men from baseness, raising them to a mystical communion with higher spirits. And, though I call on you last, I don't think of you least, Fortuna! Would I be standing here without your help? I know full well you no longer reveal yourselves to us as in that golden past described by the incomparable blind poet. Yet I know—and all lovers of wisdom know with me—it's you who truly act to choose those attendant spirits, good or harmful, that shall accompany every man on his life's journey. I've no cause to complain of you, Fortuna! Rather I've the strongest reason to render you all honor and praise. This most precious duty of my heart is what I've taken upon myself today. I've not shunned even the most menial task. Here I stand, in the bright light of day; the eyes of all the Greeks are upon me; I expect the voice of every Greek to join me in praise of you, immortal gods!

(During the ceremony of sacrifice most of the Christian onlookers gradually have drifted away; only a little group remains behind. When JULIAN stops speaking, faint cheers are heard, blended with soft laughter and astonished whispering.)

JULIAN: *(Looking around.)* Aha! What's become of them all? Have they sneaked away?

THEMISTEUS: Yes, blushing with shame over so many years of ingratitude.

MAMERTINUS: No, that was joy flushing their cheeks. They left to spread the great tidings throughout the city.

JULIAN: *(Leaving the altar.)* The ignorant mob can never adapt to the unfamiliar. I've a difficult job to do, but I'll let no obstacle dishearten me. What's more suitable for a philosopher than to root out error? In this endeavor I count on you, my enlightened friends! However, we must set all that aside for a while. Come with me; I've now got other matters to see to. *(He quickly departs without acknowledging the citizens' greetings. The COURTIERS and the rest of his entourage follow him.)*

(A great hall in the Imperial Palace. Doors on both sides and in the rear; on a dais by the left wall, in the foreground, is the imperial throne. JULIAN is surrounded by his Court and high officials, among them the Chancellor, URSULUS, and the Orators, THEMISTEUS and MAMERTINUS.)

JULIAN: So far, the gods have helped us. Now our work will surge forward like the waves of a floodtide. The silent resentment I detect from certain quarters where I'd least expected it, is not going to disturb my mind. Indeed, the truest test of wisdom is to show patience at such times. We all know how the body's ills can be cured by proper medicines; but can we use fire and sword against delusions in divine affairs? What use to me if your hands should sacrifice while your souls condemned the actions of your hands? In this way we'll live in harmony together. My court shall be hospitable to all distinguished men, whatever their opinions. Let's show the world the rare and inspiring spectacle of a court free of hypocrisy—in truth the only court of its kind—a court in which flattery is deemed the most dangerous foe. We'll condemn and criticize each other whenever appropriate without loving one another any the less. *(To NEVITA who enters from the back.)* Your face is radiant, Nevita; what good news are you bringing?

NEVITA: Truly the best and happiest. A great crowd of envoys from princes of distant India have arrived to bring you gifts and beg your friendship.

JULIAN: Ah, but tell me—from which nations?

NEVITA: From the Armenians, and from others beyond the Tigris. Some visitors even claim to come from the islands of Diu and Serandib.

JULIAN: From the furthest ends of the earth, then, my friends!

THEMISTEUS: Even so far has report borne your name and your glory!

MAMERTINUS: Even in unknown regions your sword strikes fear in princes and their peoples.

THEMISTEUS: Diu and Serandib! Far east in the Indian Ocean…

MAMERTINUS: I don't hesitate to say: beyond the earthly globe…

JULIAN: Let my barber appear! *(A COURTIER goes out to the right.)* I'll receive the envoys in appropriate style—but without pomp or ostentation. That's how the sublime Marcus Aurelius would have greeted them; and I choose him for my model rather than the Emperor who recently departed us. No more display of transient earthly things! Even the barbarians shall observe that wisdom—though in the person of her humblest servant—has again taken her place on the imperial throne.

(The COURTIER returns with EUNAPIUS, the barber, who is magnificently dressed.)

JULIAN: *(Regarding him with wonder, goes to him and addresses him.)* What do you want here, my lord?

EUNAPIUS: Gracious majesty, you have sent for me…

JULIAN: You're mistaken, my friend; I've not sent for any of my councilors.

EUNAPIUS: Most gracious Majesty…

URSULUS: Excuse me, my lord, this man's the imperial barber.

JULIAN: What are you saying? Honestly? This fellow…no, you're joking…this fellow in silk, with gold embroidered shoes, he's…Well, well! So you're the barber! *(Bowing to him.)* I could never presume to be served by such delicate hands.

EUNAPIUS: Most gracious Majesty—I beg you, for God and our Savior's sake—

JULIAN: Oho! A Galilean! Yes, I thought as much. So this is the self-denial you all boast about? But I know you well. Which god's temple have you plundered? How many times dipped into the Emperor's coffers in order to get yourself up like this? You can go; I've no need of you. *(EUNAPIUS goes out to the right.)* Tell me, Ursulus, what's that fellow's salary?

URSULUS: Most gracious Majesty, following your illustrious predecessor's order, he's allotted the maintenance of twenty men—

JULIAN: I see. Anything more?

URSULUS: Yes, my lord, most recently he's been given free use of the imperial stables, together with a considerable sum in cash and a gold piece for each time he—

JULIAN: And all that for a barber. Then what must the others...? We'll put a quick stop to all that...Let the foreign envoys enter. *(NEVITA goes out at the back.)* I'll have to receive them without a haircut. That's as it should be. Though I'm well aware it's not the unkempt hair nor the tattered tunic makes the true philosopher, I think the example both Antisthenes and Diogenes have set might be followed by the man who, even on the imperial throne, intends following those great teachers' footsteps.

(He climbs the dais on which the throne stands. The courtiers position themselves below. The envoys, led in by NEVITA and EUTHERIUS enter in magnificent procession, followed by slaves bearing all kinds of gifts.)

NEVITA: Great emperor and lord! Not being fluent in that noble tongue which so many eloquent men, not least yourself, have brought to a perfection beyond all other tongues—and mindful, moreover, that barbarian sounds might grate on your ears, these envoys of the eastern princes elect me as their spokesman.

JULIAN: *(Seated on the throne.)* I'm ready to hear you.

NEVITA: First, the King of Armenia lays at your feet his armor which he asks you to wear in battle against the enemies of the empire even though he's well aware that you, invincible hero, stand under the protection of the gods who'll not permit any mortal's weapon to injure you. Receive also precious carpets, tents, and saddlery from the princes beyond the Tigris. With these they acknowledge that when the gods blessed their land with such inordinate riches, they did so for the benefit of their favorite. The King of Serandib and likewise the King of Diu, send you these weapons; sword, spear, and shield, together with bows and arrows; for, they say. "We think it wise to stand weaponless before a conqueror who, like a god, shows himself powerful enough to smash down all resistance."…In return, they all beg the highest favor of your friendship, and especially if, as rumored, you plan to crush the presumptuous Persian King, you will spare their lands from any incursions.

JULIAN: This mission wasn't entirely unexpected. The gifts they've brought shall be deposited in my treasury. Through you, let me inform your rulers it's my intention to maintain friendly relations with all peoples who don't oppose me, either by arms or treachery. The fact that in your distant lands, you've been led to believe there's something divine about me and my lucky victories—that's a matter I won't go into any further. I think too highly of the gods to claim an unmerited place among them—even though I'm well aware heroes and rulers once were so marked out for the love and favor of the gods it was hard to tell if they should rightly be reckoned mortal or immortal. In matters like this, though, it's always risky to decide, even for us Greeks. How much more so, then, for you? But, enough of that. Eutherius, let the visitors get some rest and see they've all they need.

(The envoys and their followers are led from the hall by EUTHERIUS. JULIAN steps down from the dais. Courtiers and orators surround and congratulate him.)

THEMISTEUS: So young…and already so highly honored above all other emperors!

MAMERTINUS: I'd ask: Won't Fame lack lungs to sing your praises should the gods, as I fervently hope, grant you a long life?

THEMISTEUS: The cry of terror uttered by the Alemanni as they fled from the furthest banks of the Rhine has rebounded back to strike against the Taurus and the Caucasus.

MAMERTINUS: —and now it echoes, in rolling waves, over the whole of Asia.

NEVITA: What has terrified the Indians is the likeness between our Greek Julian and the Macedonian Alexander—

MAMERTINUS: What likeness? Did King Alexander have secret enemies in his own camp? Did he have to overcome the envious slanders of the Imperial Court?

NEVITA: True, true; nor were there incompetent generals getting in the way of Alexander's progress.

JULIAN: Ursulus, I wish these envoys' arrival to be made known in the city and throughout the empire. It should be reported fully—where they come from and what gifts they've brought. I'll not keep back from the people anything to do with my government. It won't harm to include a few words about that strange belief among the Indians that Alexander's returned in person.

URSULUS: Forgive me, gracious majesty, but—

JULIAN: Well?

URSULUS: You said yourself no flattery's to be tolerated in your court.

JULIAN: That's right, my friend!

URSULUS: Then permit me in all frankness to point out these envoys came to seek out your predecessor, not you.

JULIAN: What are you presuming to tell me!

THEMISTEUS: Ha! What a ridiculous notion!

MAMERTINUS: What a fabrication!

URSULUS: It's true! I've known for some time these men were on their way— well before Emperor Constantinos closed his eyes. Oh, my esteemed lord, don't let false vanity worm its way into your young mind—

JULIAN: Enough! enough! Then you mean that—

URSULUS: Work it out for yourself. In what way could your victories in Gaul, however glorious they might have been, so quickly have reached the ears of those distant peoples? When the envoys spoke of the Emperor's heroic victories, they were thinking of the Persian Wars.

NEVITA: I can't imagine the war against King Sapor was likely to spread terror to the ends of the earth!

URSULUS: True, Fortune did not advance our arms in those regions. It was rumors of the huge forces the Emperor was assembling for a Spring offensive, however, that alarmed the Armenians and other nations. Just consider the time involved my lord; reckon the number of days, and say how it could be otherwise. Your company marched here with extraordinary speed; but these men had to travel from the Indian islands; it would have been ten times more incredible, if…just ask them and you'll hear—

JULIAN: (Pale with rage.) Why are you telling me all this?

URSULUS: Because it's the truth, and because I can't bear seeing your young and splendid glory sullied with borrowed achievements.

THEMISTEUS: What presumption!

MAMERTINUS: Extreme presumption!

JULIAN: You can't bear seeing…! Oh, I know you better. I know all you old guard at this court. It's the gods whose glory you'd disparage. For isn't it to the glory of the gods they work great things by means of a man? But you hate them—these gods—whose temples you've destroyed, whose statues you've smashed to pieces and whose treasures you've plundered. You could hardly bear even the most beneficent of our gods. Or that the faithful still secretly cherished them in their hearts. And now you would destroy the temple of gratitude I've raised to them in my heart. You'd take from me that deep gratitude I owe the immortals for a new and ardently sought blessing— for isn't glory to be reckoned such?

URSULUS: The one true God of Heaven is my witness that—

JULIAN: The one true—there we have it! It's always the same with your lot! What intolerance! Take us as your model. Do we say our gods are the only ones? Don't we honor the gods of the Egyptians and the Jewish Jehova, who surely brought about great things for his people? But you, on the contrary— yes, even a man like you, Ursulus—! Are *you*, a Roman, born of Greek ancestors? The one true—what barbaric shamelessness!

URSULUS: You've promised you'll not hate anyone for his beliefs.

JULIAN: Yes, I've promised—but I won't tolerate your trampling on us. The envoys couldn't have come to—in other words you're saying the great god Dionysos, who has the marvelous power to make manifest to men what lies hidden—that he can no longer act as he did in former times? Am I to tolerate that? Is that not overweening impertinence? Aren't I compelled to call you to account?

URSULUS: Then all Christians will say it is their faith you're persecuting.

JULIAN: There'll be no one persecuted for his faith. But have I the right to cancel out whatever you are guilty of just because you're Christians? Are your misdeeds to shelter behind your errors? What haven't you misguided men already committed all these years, both here in court and elsewhere? You've flattered every vice and bowed to every folly. Yes, you yourself, Ursulus, what haven't you meddled in? I'm thinking of that shameless, decked-out barber, that perfumed poltroon, who just now filled me with disgust. How could you, the Chancellor go along with his impudent extravagance?

URSULUS: Is it a crime that I served my master?

JULIAN: I've no use for luxurious servants. I'll chase all such eunuchs out of the palace—and all the chefs and acrobats and dancers, too. A fittingly frugal style will now be established. *(To THEMISTEUS and MAMERTINUS.)* You, my friends, shall give me a hand in this. And you, Nevita, so that you'll enjoy the proper public regard, I now raise to the rank of commander-in-chief, appointing you to look into how the government departments have been run under my predecessor these last years. Appoint what men you think proper in judging these matters. *(To the older courtiers and councilors.)* I've no use for any of you. When my late lamented cousin on his deathbed made me his heir, he bequeathed also that justice his own long sickness hindered him from administering. Go home; and when you've given a good account of yourselves, take yourselves off to wherever you like.

URSULUS: The Lord God preserve and safeguard your Majesty. *(He bows and goes out the back with the older men. NEVITA, THEMISTEUS, and MAMERTINUS together with all the younger men gather round the EMPEROR.)*

NEVITA: My most exalted Emperor, how shall I render thanks sufficient for the sign of your favor you've just—

JULIAN: Don't thank me. These past few days I've learnt to value your loyalty and judgment. I'm giving you the responsibility of drafting the statement about the eastern envoys. Write in such a way that the benevolent gods won't find any ground for displeasure against any of us.

NEVITA: I shall perform my Emperor's will in all matters. *(He goes out to the right.)*

JULIAN: And now, faithful friends, let's praise the immortal powers who've shown us the right way.

THEMISTEUS: The immortals and their more than mortal favorite! What shouts of joy we'll hear throughout the empire when it's known you've got rid of those greedy and selfish men!

MAMERTINUS: With what excitement and eager expectation the choice of their replacements will be awaited!

THEMISTEUS: All Greeks will proclaim with one voice: "Plato himself has taken over the helm of state!"

MAMERTINUS: No, no, my worthy friend: All the Greeks will proclaim: "Plato's words have become reality: only a god can rule over men."

THEMISTEUS: My only wish is that those powers that bring luck to men may accompany Nevita. He's embarking on a great and difficult task; I don't know him all that well; we must all hope he shows himself to be the right man—

MAMERTINUS: Quite right. Though there could well be other men who—

THEMISTEUS: Not that by any means I imply your choice, incomparable Emperor—

MAMERTINUS: No, no, not in any way!

THEMISTEUS: But if it be a fault to wish fervently to serve a beloved master—

MAMERTINUS: Then in truth you've more than one erring friend—

THEMISTEUS: Even though you may not honor them as you honored the fortunate Nevita—

MAMERTINUS:—even though they may have to forgo any visible sign of your favor—

JULIAN: We won't allow any worthy man to be neglected or unrewarded. As far as you're concerned, Themisteus, I appoint you chief magistrate here in Constantinople; and you, Mamertinus, can get ready to go to Rome within the year to take over one of the vacant consulships.

THEMISTEUS: My gracious lord! Such an distinction makes me dizzy—!

MAMERTINUS: So high an honor! Consul! Was ever a consul so highly honored as I? Was Lucius, was Brutus, was Publius Vallerius? What are their honors to mine? They were chosen by the people—I by Julian!

A COURTIER: All praise to him whose very name strikes terror in the barbarians!

THEMISTEUS: Praise to all the gods above who with one accord cast their loving eyes on this one man so that it may be said of him alone when—may it be far hence—he causes us to grieve for the first time by leaving us, he has put Socrates, Marcus Aurelius, and Alexander in the shade!

JULIAN: You've got to the core of it, Themisteus! It's to the gods we lift our hands and our hearts. I say this not to instruct you, but to remind you of what has been neglected so long at this court. Far be it for me to compel anyone. But can I be blamed for wanting others to take part in the sweet rapture that streams through me when I feel myself cradled in the company of the immortals? All praise, all praise to you, vine-wreathed Dionysos! Because you, above all, bring about such great and mysterious things. Go now, all of you, each to your own affairs. For my part, I've promised a joyful procession through the city streets. This is no mere celebration for my courtiers, nor a party for private guests within four walls. The citizens are free to take part with me or to stay away; I will distinguish the pure from the impure, the pious from those deluding themselves—Oh, Sun-King, cast your light and beauty over this day. Oh Dionysos, flood your glory over our thoughts; fill our souls with your holy rapture, fill them until the bonds shall burst and joy, liberated, draws breath in dance and song! Life, life, life in beauty!

(He goes out to the right. The COURTIERS gather into whispering groups and eventually withdraw.)

(A narrow street in Constantinople. A great crowd of people—all are looking in the same direction down the street. Noise, singing, and music from flutes can be heard in the distance.)

A SHOEMAKER: *(In his doorway, shouting across the street.)* What's going on, neighbor?

A SHOPKEEPER: *(In the house, opposite.)* They say it's some Syrian dancers that have come to town.

A FRUIT SELLER: *(In the street.)* No, that's not it. It's an Egyptian group traveling with monkeys and camels.

EUNAPIUS: *(Shabbily dressed, trying vainly to slip through the crowd.)* Make way, you fools! How the devil can anyone jabber and clown around on such a disastrous day.

A WOMAN: *(At a little window.)* Pst, pst. Eunapius! You gorgeous fellow!

EUNAPIUS: Don't call to me in the open street, you old bawd!

THE WOMAN: Nip in the back way, sweetie!

EUNAPIUS: Shut up! You think I'm in the mood for that kind of game?

THE WOMAN: You'll soon be. Come, Eunapius my pet. I've just got in a fresh
supply of really juicy—

EUNAPIUS: Oh, you sinful world! *(Tries to pass.)* Out of the way, out of the
way, in the name of Satan, let me come through!

HECEBOLIUS: *(In traveling clothes and followed by a pair of slaves, enters from a
side street.)* Has the town lost its senses? They're all screaming at one another
and no one can tell me what's going on. Ah, there's Eunapius—my brother
in faith!

EUNAPIUS: Let me greet you, most worthy lord! So you've come back to the
city?

HECEBOLIUS: An instant ago. I've been spending the hot autumn months in
quiet devotion on my estate in Crete. But tell me everything that's going on
here.

EUNAPIUS: Misfortune and confusion. The new Emperor—

HECEBOLIUS: Yes, yes, I've been hearing incredible rumors—

EUNAPIUS: It's ten times worse than rumor can report. All the loyal servants
have been chased out of the palace—

HECEBOLIUS: You're telling the truth—?

EUNAPIUS: Believe me; I was the first to go—

HECEBOLIUS: Appalling! Then maybe I too—

EUNAPIUS: You can be sure of it. All the accounts are being investigated; all
gifts are to be given back; all discrepancies in the revenues—

HECEBOLIUS: *(Going pale.)* God help me!

EUNAPIUS: Lord be praised, I've a clear conscience!

HECEBOLIUS: Mine too, mine too; but all the same—ah, then is it true the
Emperor's sacrificed to Apollo and Fortuna?

EUNAPIUS: It's true, but why bother with such a trifle?

HECEBOLIUS: Trifle? Don't you see, my blind friend, it's our characters as
good Christians he's really after?

EUNAPIUS: What's that you say? By our Savior's Cross, can that be possible?

WOMEN: *(In the crowd.)* There they come!

A MAN: *(On a housetop.)* I can see him!

OTHER VOICES: Who's coming? Who? Who?

MAN ON THE ROOF: Emperor Julian. With vine leaves in his hair.

PEOPLE IN THE STREET: The Emperor!

EUNAPIUS: The Emperor!

HECEBOLIUS: Come, come, my pious brother.

EUNAPIUS: Let go of me! I'm not at all pious!

HECEBOLIUS: Not pious—?

EUNAPIUS: Who dares say that—? Do you want to ruin me? Pious? When was I ever pious? I did once belong to the Donatist sect; that was many years ago. The devil take the Donatists! Hey, Barbara, Barbara, open up, you old whore! *(Someone lets him in through the house door.)*

THE CROWD: Here he is! Here he comes!

HECEBOLIUS: All discrepancies in the revenues—! Investigators! Oh, what a dreadful blow! *(He creeps away with the two slaves.)*

(The Dionysian procession proceeds down the street. Flute players are in the lead; drunken men, some of them dressed as fauns and satyrs, dance to the rhythm. At the center of the procession is EMPEROR JULIAN, riding on a donkey which is covered with a panther-skin; he is dressed like the god Dionysos, with a panther skin over his shoulders, a crown of vine leaves on his brow, and in his hand a staff wound round with green leaves and tipped with a pine cone, like a thyrsus. Half-naked painted women and youths, dancers and acrobats, surround him; some are carrying wine jars and drinking bowls, others beat on tambourines, gesturing and leaping wildly forward.)

THE DANCERS: *(Singing.)*

Draughts of sweet fires from cups overflowing
Draughts of sweet fires!
Wine all-entrancing
Eyes ever glancing
Goatish legs dancing
We raise up our prayer, wine-god who inspires!

WOMEN: *(Singing.)*

Night, on our love games, your blessing bestowing.
Bacchantes preparing
Joys for the light of day, frenzied and glowing
Panther eyes flaring
Our glorious god's steed!
Your ecstasy sharing
Embrace us, bacchantes, our frenzy you feed.
Singing and playing
Dancing and swaying
Your ecstasy sharing.

JULIAN: Make room! Stand back all of you. Show respect, not for us but for him we honor!

A VOICE IN THE CROWD: The Emperor's in the company of tumblers and whores!

JULIAN: It's your shame I have to make do with no better. Don't you blush at finding more piety and zeal among them than among yourselves?

AN OLD MAN: May Christ enlighten you, my lord!

JULIAN: Ah! You're a Galilean! So you have to speak out! Didn't your own great master sit at the table with sinners? Didn't he regularly visit a house of dubious reputation? Come, answer me!

EUNAPIUS: *(Surrounded by girls from Madam Barbara's house.)* That's right, answer, answer if you can you idiot!

JULIAN: Well, isn't it the barber—?

EUNAPIUS: I'm a man made free, gracious Emperor! Make way, you bacchantes, make way for a brother! *(He and the girls dance into the Dionysian procession.)*

JULIAN: That's what I like to see. Follow this Greek if you possess a spark of the old spirit in you. And it's what we need, my people; because no god's been so misunderstood—so ridiculed, even—as this bringer of ecstasy, Dionysos, whom the Romans call Bacchus. Do you think he's a god of mere drunkards? Oh, you ignorant ones, I pity you if that's what you believe. Who else do the poets and seers look to for their miraculous gifts? Oh, I know some credit Apollo with this faculty, not entirely without justification; but that's to be understood in a different context—as I can prove from various writers. However, I'm not going to argue this in the open street. In any case, there's hardly time. Go on, laugh! Make the sign of the cross! I can see clearly. You'd like to mock me, throw stones at me if you dared. Oh, how ashamed I am of this city that's sunk far below barbarism and doesn't know any better than to cling to the crazy creed of an ignorant Jew! Move on! Stand aside and don't get in our way!

DANCERS:
Panther eyes flaring
Our glorious god's steed!

WOMEN:
Embrace us, bacchantes, our frenzy you feed
Your ecstasy sharing.
(The procession turns off into a side street; meanwhile the crowd stares in dumb amazement.)

(The EMPEROR'S library in the palace. An entrance-door to the left; a smaller door opening with a curtain before it, right. EUTHERIUS, the chamberlain, followed by two servants carrying carpets.

EUTHERIUS: *(Calling to the room on the right.)* Agilo, Agilo, warm rosewater! The Emperor wants a bath.

(JULIAN enters quickly from the left. He still carries the panther skin and the

crown of vine leaves. In his hand is the wreathed stave. He walks a while up and down, and then flings the stave into a corner.)

JULIAN: Was there beauty in any of that? Where were the elders with their white beards? Where the pure young virgins with bands on their brows and modest gestures, virtuous in the joy of dance? Ecchh! not you, you whores. *(He tears off the panther skin and throws it to one side.)* Where has Beauty fled? Can't the Emperor command her to return and reveal herself? Ecchh! these stinking obscenities! Those faces! Every debauchery screaming out of those twisted mouths. Infected in flesh and spirit. Ecchh, ecchh! A bath! Agilo! The stench is choking me.

AGILO: *(In the doorway, right.)* The bath is prepared, gracious lord!

JULIAN: The bath? Forget it. What's our body's filth compared to that other? *(AGILO goes out again. The EMPEROR stands awhile in thought.)* The seer of Nazareth sat at the table with publicans and sinners. Where lies the abyss between that and this?

(HECEBOLIUS enters from the left and stands anxiously by the door.)

JULIAN: What do you want, sir?

HECEBOLIUS: *(On his knees.)* My lord!

JULIAN: What's this? Hecebolius; is it really you?

HECEBOLIUS: The same, and yet another.

JULIAN: My old teacher? What is it you want? Stand up?

HECEBOLIUS: No, no, let me stay here beneath you. And don't be angry I make use of my former right to enter unannounced.

JULIAN: *(Coldly.)* I asked what you wanted.

HECEBOLIUS: "My old teacher," you said. Oh, could I but cast a veil of oblivion over those days!

JULIAN: *(As before.)* I see. You mean that—

HECEBOLIUS: Oh, that I might sink into the earth and bury my shame! See, see, here I kneel before you, a man whose hair's growing gray—who has studied, stooped over books, all of his days, and who now must confess he went astray—and led his beloved pupil astray.

JULIAN: What do you wish to tell me?

HECEBOLIUS: You called me your old teacher. See, here I kneel at your feet, looking up in wonder at you, and call you my new teacher.

JULIAN: Rise, Hecebolius!

HECEBOLIUS: *(Getting up.)* You shall hear everything, my lord, and then judge after your own righteousness. When you went away, I found it almost unbearable living with your illustrious predecessor. I don't know if you were informed I was promoted to the post of the Empress's tutor and distributor of alms? But ah, could posts even of honor compensate for the loss of my

Julian? I could hardly bear seeing men making a show of their virtuous deeds while taking all kinds of favors and bribes. I came to detest associating with those greedy opportunists whose services were for hire to anyone matching ringing words with ringing gold. Oh, my lord, you can't know the things that went on—

JULIAN: I know, oh, I know.

HECEBOLIUS: An austere life in solitude beckoned me. As often as I could, I fled to Crete, to my modest Tusculum—my little holding in the country— where all virtue did not seem to have departed this world. There I've been living all this summer, meditating on human affairs and on heavenly truths.

JULIAN: Fortunate Hecebolius!

HECEBOLIUS: Then there came to Crete rumors of your marvelous achievements—

JULIAN: Ah!

HECEBOLIUS: I asked myself: Is he more than mortal, this incomparable youth? Under whose protection does he stand? Is it this way the Christian God is wont to reveal his power—?

JULIAN: *(Tense.)* Well; well!

HECEBOLIUS: So I set myself the task of studying the ancient writers once more. The light of truth again and again flared up within me; oh, that I must confess this!

JULIAN: Tell me everything—I beseech you!

HECEBOLIUS: *(Dropping to his knees.)* Punish me, in your own righteousness, my lord; but turn from the religious errors of your youth! Yes, gracious lord, you're ensnared in error; and I—oh, how incomprehensible that shame does not end my life—I, I've been party to leading you astray—

JULIAN: *(With outstretched arms.)* Come, come I say, into my welcoming arms!

HECEBOLIUS: Oh no, I implore you, give your thanks to the immortal gods, whose favorite you are! And if you cannot, chastise me for doing so on your behalf—

JULIAN: Come, come into my arms, I say! *(He raises him, folds him in his arms, and kisses him.)* My Hecebolius! What a great and unexpected joy!

HECEBOLIUS: My lord, how am I to understand this?

JULIAN: Then you don't know that—? What time did you arrive in town?

HECEBOLIUS: I left the ship but an hour ago.

JULIAN: And hurried straight here?

HECEBOLIUS: On wings of fear and remorse, my lord.

JULIAN: Without speaking to anyone?

HECEBOLIUS: Yes, that's right. Without speaking to anyone, but—?

JULIAN: Oh, then you can't know—*(He embraces him again.)* My Hecebolius, now you shall learn! I, just like you, have cast off the yoke of error. The immortal Sun God, he to whom we mortals owe so much, I've restored to his ancient rights; Fortuna has accepted her sacrifice from my humble hands, and if at this moment you find me tired and a little listless, it is because I've just conducted a festival in honor of the divine Dionysos.

HECEBOLIUS: I hear, and I am struck with wonder!

JULIAN: Look...the wreath's still in my hair. All through the crowd's shouts of joy—ah yes, there were a good number of them—

HECEBOLIUS: And I'd no suspicion of such a great event!

JULIAN: Now we'll gather around us all lovers of truth and lovers of wisdom— all meritorious and honorable devotees of the gods—already there are some—though not all that many—

(CAESARIUS, accompanied by a number of officials and men of the former court, enter from the left.)

JULIAN: Ah, here's the good Caesarius, with a sizable suite and a face presaging something of importance.

CAESARIUS: Gracious majesty, will you permit your servant a question on behalf of himself and these troubled men?

JULIAN: Ask, my dear Caesarius! Aren't you brother to my beloved Gregory? Ask, ask!

CAESARIUS: Then tell me, my lord—*(He notices HECEBOLIUS.)* What's this! Hecebolius here?

JULIAN: Just this moment returned—

CAESARIUS: *(About to retire.)* Then I ask that I may wait—

JULIAN: No need to, my Caesarius; our friend can hear everything.

CAESARIUS: Friend, you say? Oh, my Emperor, then these incarcerations are not your doing?

JULIAN: What are you talking about?

CAESARIUS: You don't know, then? General Nevita—commander-in-chief, as he now styles himself—is setting about—under the pretext it's on your authority—starting proceedings against all your predecessor's most trusted servants.

JULIAN: Investigations, most necessary investigations, my Caesarius!

CAESARIUS: Oh, but then my lord, forbid him to use such violence. The accountant, Pentadius, is being hunted down by soldiers, and so is a certain Praetorian Prefect, whose name you've forbidden to be mentioned; you know who I mean, my lord—that unfortunate man who, with all his household, is hiding in fear from you.

JULIAN: You don't know the man. In Gaul, he came out with the most audacious proposals.

CAESARIUS: That may be; but now he's completely harmless. And he isn't the only one threatened with destruction; the Chancellor, Ursulus, is imprisoned, too.

JULIAN: Ah, Ursulus? That, too, was undoubtedly necessary.

CAESARIUS: Necessary! Was *that* necessary, my lord? Only think of Ursulus, that old man of unstained reputation, whose word was revered by high and low—

JULIAN: A man totally lacking in judgment, I tell you! Ursulus was too extravagant; he'd no qualms satisfying the greed of courtiers. And besides, he's useless in state affairs. I've found that out myself. I'd never dare trust him with receiving foreign ambassadors.

CAESARIUS: And yet we implore you, my lord, all who stand here before you; be magnanimous—both with Ursulus and with the others.

JULIAN: Who are the others:

CAESARIUS: All too many, I fear. I will but name Evagrius, the deputy chancellor; Saturninus, the former chamberlain; Chief Justice Kyrenus and—

JULIAN: Why do you stop?

CAESARIUS: *(Hesitantly.)* My lord, among the accused is also court theologian Hecebolius.

JULIAN: What?

HECEBOLIUS: I? Impossible!

CAESARIUS: Accused of taking bribes from unqualified seekers after office—

JULIAN: Hecebolius should be—a man like Hecebolius—?

HECEBOLIUS: What an outrageous slander! O Christ—that is, I mean—oh you heavenly gods!

CAESARIUS: Ah!

JULIAN: What do you mean?

CAESARIOS: *(Coldly.)* Nothing, my gracious Emperor!

JULIAN: Caesarius!

CAESARIUS: Yes, my noble lord?

JULIAN: Not lord, call me your friend.

CAESARIUS: Dare a Christian call you that?

JULIAN: I beg you, don't think like that, Caesarius! You mustn't believe that! Can I help it if all the accused are Christians? Doesn't it only show the Christians managed to get all the lucrative positions? Dare an emperor allow all the empire's most important offices to be abused? *(To the others.)* You can't think it's their religion has drawn my anger against these corrupt men. I call on all the gods to witness I'll not permit any proceedings against you Christians outside the law; and neither shall any man be allowed to do you injury. You, or at least a good many of you, are certainly devout, in that you also worship the Lord who is almighty and who rules over the whole visible world. Oh, my Caesarius, is it not he, also, whom I worship, though under other names.

CAESARIUS: Allow me, gracious lord!

JULIAN: Furthermore it's my intention to show clemency, wherever I rightfully can. As regards Hecebolius, his secret enemies ought not imagine they'll be allowed to harm him with accusations and other such spurious tactics.

HECEBOLIUS: My emperor! My shield and my safeguard.

JULIAN: Nor is it my desire that minor officials be unmercifully deprived of their means of support. I'm thinking in particular of that barber I sent away. I regret that. The man can stay. He seemed to me a man who knows his job. Such men should be honored. That's as far as I can go, Caesarius, no further. Ursulus must take the consequences. I must conduct myself so that the blind but perceptive Goddess of Justice finds no reason to frown on a mortal in whose hands she's placed so great a responsibility.

CAESARIUS: If that's so, I've no more to say on behalf of those unfortunate men. I only ask I be allowed to leave the Court and the city.

JULIAN: That's what you want?

CAESARIUS: Yes, most gracious lord.

JULIAN: You're stiff-necked, just like your brother.

CAESARIUS: The new events have given me a lot to think about.

JULIAN: I'd great plans for you, Caesarius! You'd be very dear to me if only you'd leave your path of error. Can't you do that?

CAESARIUS: God knows what I could have done a month ago; now I cannot.

JULIAN: A marriage into one of the most powerful families could be open to you. Won't you think about it?

CAESARIUS: No, most gracious lord!

JULIAN: A man such as you could quickly climb from one position to another. Caesarius, wouldn't it be possible for you to join me in advancing the new order?

CAESARIUS: No, most gracious lord!

JULIAN: I don't mean here; somewhere else. It's my intention to leave this place. Constantinople doesn't agree with me. You Galileans have ruined it for me in every way. I'm going to Antioch; I'll find it more congenial soil. You were to accompany me. Will you, Caesarius?

CAESARIUS: Most gracious lord, I too will be going eastward; but I'll be going alone.

JULIAN: What will you be doing there?

CAESARIUS: To visit my old father; to help Gregory strengthen him for the coming battle.

JULIAN: Go!

CAESARIUS: Farewell, my emperor!

JULIAN: A happy father, to have such unhappy sons! *(He gestures with his hand; CAESARIUS and his companions bow deeply and exit to the left.)*

HECEBOLIUS: What audacity! What unseemly impudence!

JULIAN: My heart is sorely wounded over this and much else. You, Hecebolius, shall accompany me. The earth burns beneath me in this poisoned, Galilean city! I'll write to the philosophers Chytron and Priscus, who've won such a great reputation in recent years. Maximus I'm expecting here any day. He shall go with us. I tell you, Hecebolius, joyful and victorious days lie ahead. In Antioch, my friend, we'll meet the incomparable Libanius—and there be closer to Helios, as he rises. Oh, this yearning for the Sun-King...!

HECEBOLIUS: Yes, yes, yes—!

JULIAN: *(Embracing him.)* Hecebolius! Wisdom, light, beauty!

END OF ACT ONE

ACT TWO

A huge entrance-hall in the Emperor's palace in Antioch. Open access at the back; on the wall, left, a door that leads to the inner rooms.

On a raised seat, downstage, right, JULIAN is sitting, surrounded by his court. Judges, Orators, Poets, and Teachers—among the latter HECEBOLIUS— are sitting on lower seats beneath him. Leaning up against a wall, near the exit, a MAN is standing, dressed as a Christian Priest; he hides his face in his hand and seems deep in prayer. A large group of citizens fill the hall. By the exit door at the back stand guards also at the door on the left.

JULIAN: *(Addressing the gathering.)* So great a success the gods have granted me. Hardly a single town I visited on my journey lacked its great gatherings of Galileans streaming out to greet me along the road, lamenting their errors, and placing themselves under the protection of the divine powers. What are the contemptible antics of our opponents compared with this? Aren't these blasphemers more like dogs howling futilely at the moon? Yet I won't deny being exasperated to learn how a few of this city's inhabitants felt free to cast scorn on the code of behavior I required of the priests of Cybele, that gracious goddess. Surely reverence for so sublime a deity should spare her servants becoming objects of derision? To these foolish fellows I say: Are you barbarians, seeing you don't know who Cybele is? Must I seriously remind you that when Roman rule itself was threatened by the Punic general— whose tomb I recently saw in Libyssa—the Sibyl counseled the statue of Cybele be taken from the temple at Pessinus to Rome? As far as the priests' way of life is concerned, some have worked themselves up over the fact they're forbidden to eat roots or anything that grows along the ground, yet can eat herbs and fruits that strain to grow high. Oh, you great blockheads, how I pity you for not grasping that! Can the human spirit nourish itself on what creeps along the ground? Doesn't the soul flourish on all that strives upward toward the heavens and the sun? I won't go at length into such things today. What's still to be said you'll learn from a tract I'm working on at nights which I expect to be heard in the classrooms and the marketplace. *(He rises.)* And with that, my friends, unless anyone has anything else to bring up—

A CITIZEN: *(Shoving forward.)* Oh, most gracious Emperor, don't let me go unheard!

JULIAN: *(Resuming his seat.)* Of course not, my friend! Who are you?

THE CITIZEN: Medon, a corn merchant. Oh my lord, if my love for you, most sublime and godlike—

JULIAN: Come to the point man!

MEDON: I have a neighbor, Alites, who for many years has damaged me in every imaginable way; he's also in the corn trade and does the most shameful things to harm my business—

JULIAN: Aha, my good Medon, you look as if your business is doing well.

MEDON: That's not really the issue, most gracious Emperor! Oh, most worthy gods, whom I've learned to love and venerate more highly every day, I could overlook the harm he does to my business; but what it's impossible for me to tolerate—

JULIAN: He disrespects the gods—?

MEDON: He does worse than that—well, at least something equally as reckless; he—oh, I don't know if my indignation will let me disclose it—he shows disrespect to you, gracious lord!

JULIAN: Indeed? What were the words he used?

MEDON: It's not words he's used at all. He's used something far worse.

JULIAN: And what is worse?

MEDON: A purple robe—

JULIAN: He wears one. Well, well, that does look bad.

MEDON: Yes. Oh great, wing-footed Mercury, when I think what wearing that robe would have cost him in your predecessor's time! And this arrogant garment is thrust in my face every day.

JULIAN: This garment, bought with cash that could have been yours—

MEDON: Oh, most gracious Emperor—punish this impertinent man; let him be chased out of the city; my love for our great and sublime ruler won't let me witness such shameless arrogance.

JULIAN: Tell me, good Medon, what kind of clothes does Alites wear apart from the purple robe?

MEDON: I don't exactly recollect, my lord; I think quite ordinary ones; all I could notice was the purple robe.

JULIAN: So, a purple robe and untanned sandals—

MEDON: Yes, my lord, it looks as outlandish as it's outrageous.

JULIAN: We must see to this situation, Medon!

MEDON: *(Delighted.)* Ah, most gracious lord—!

JULIAN: Early in the morning come here to the palace—

MEDON: *(More delighted.)* I'll come very early, most gracious majesty!

JULIAN: You will meet with my chamberlain—

MEDON: Yes, yes, my more than gracious majesty—

JULIAN: From him you'll receive a pair of purple shoes, embroidered with gold.

MEDON: Ah, my most generous lord and master!

JULIAN: These shoes you'll take to Alites, put them on him and tell him—from now on, he must wear them every time he takes it into his head to show himself outdoors in daylight in the purple robe—

MEDON: Oh!

JULIAN:—and when you've done that, tell him from me he's a fool if he thinks he's exalted by a purple robe without possessing the purple's power. Go; and come back for the shoes tomorrow!

(MEDON slinks out, crestfallen, amid the laughter of the citizens, the courtiers, orators, poets, and the rest applaud and cry their approval.)

ANOTHER CITIZEN: *(Steps from the crowd.)* All praise to the Emperor's justice! That spiteful corn miser got what was coming to him. Oh hear me and let your favor—

JULIAN: Aha! I think I know that face. Aren't you one of those cheering in front of my carriage when I drove into the city?

CITIZEN: One of the loudest, incomparable Emperor! I'm Malchus, a tax collector. Oh, give me your help. I'm pursuing a case against a wicked, stingy individual—

JULIAN: But why come to me? Aren't there judges here—?

MALCHUS: It's a complicated business, your Majesty. It all involves a field I leased out to the wretched man, and which I got hold of seven years ago when part of the land belonging to the Church of the Apostles was sold.

JULIAN: I see. Church property, then?

MALCHUS: Bought honestly, but now this fellow won't pay the rent nor give me the land back, under the pretext this field once belonged to the temple of Apollo and so, he says, illegally confiscated a long time ago.

JULIAN: Listen, Malchus, you must be one of the followers of the Galilean?

MALCHUS: Most gracious Emperor, it's an old tradition in our family to acknowledge Christ.

JULIAN: And it doesn't trouble you to say that?

MALCHUS: My opponent's more audacious than me, my lord! He goes in and out of his house as brazenly as before; he didn't flee the city when it was reported you were coming.

JULIAN: Didn't flee? Why should he do that, a man who stood for the rights of the gods?

MALCHUS: Most gracious Emperor, you've no doubt heard about the accountant, Thalassius?

JULIAN: What! The same Thalassius who ingratiated himself with my predecessor, when I was being slandered and my life menaced in Gaul—who got up in the marketplace and told the citizens to ask the Emperor to send them the head of Julian Caesar!

MALCHUS: My lord, it's this same mortal enemy of yours who now wrongs me.

JULIAN: Truly, Malchus, I've as much against that man as you

MALCHUS: Ten times more, my most gracious Emperor!

JULIAN: So what do you think? Shall we two join forces and sue him together?

MALCHUS: Oh, how exceedingly gracious! I'm fortunate ten times over!

JULIAN: You're ten times worse off! Thalassius goes in and out of his house just
as before, you say? He didn't flee the city when I arrived. Thalassius knew me
better than you. Go off, man! When I sue Thalassius for my head, you can
sue him for your field.

MALCHUS: *(Wringing his hands.)* Now I'm ten times unfortunate. *(He goes out
the back; the assembly applauds the EMPEROR'S judgment.)*

JULIAN: Very good, my friends, let's celebrate that I've succeeded, not
unworthily I hope, in inaugurating this day dedicated to the radiant Apollo.
Isn't it fitting a philosopher should overlook slights against himself while
firmly punishing wrongs committed against the immortal gods? I don't
recall if that supreme devotee of learning, Marcus Aurelius, was ever in a
similar situation; if he was, let's hope he conducted himself not entirely
unlike myself, who thinks it an honor to follow humbly in his footsteps.

Let this serve you as a guide to your conduct in the future. In the palace,
in the marketplace, yes, in the theatre—if it didn't disgust me entering
such a place of folly—it is suitable you greet me with praise and applause.
That kind of homage was, I know, well received by both the Macedonian
Alexander and by Julius Caesar—men favored by the Goddess Fortune to
shine above other mortals.

But if you see me enter the temple, that's another matter. It's my wish
you then keep silent or direct your praises to the gods, not to me, as you
watch me advance with downcast eyes and head bowed. Above all, do this
today when I sacrifice to a supreme and powerful god we know under the
name of the Sun-King, and who is all the greater in our eyes when we
reflect he is the same god many in the East call Mithra. And so—if no one
has anything more to say—

THE PRIEST AT THE DOOR: *(Straightening himself up.)* In the name of
the Lord God!

JULIAN: Who's that speaking?

THE PRIEST: A servant of God and the Emperor.

JULIAN: Come closer. What do you want?

THE PRIEST: To speak to your heart and your conscience.

JULIAN: *(Jumps up.)* That voice! What do I see? In spite of the beard and
cloak—! Gregory!

GREGORY: Yes, my noble lord!

JULIAN: Gregory! Gregory from Nazianzus!

GREGORY: Yes, gracious Emperor!

JULIAN: *(Has stepped down and grasped his hands, looking long at him.)* A bit older, browner, brawnier. No, that was the first glance, now you're just the same as before.

GREGORY: I wish it were so with you, my lord!

JULIAN: Athens. That night in the colonnade. No man's ever been closer to my heart than you.

GREGORY: Your heart? Ah, my Emperor, you've cast from your heart a better friend than I.

JULIAN: You mean Basil?

GREGORY: I mean a greater one than Basil.

JULIAN: *(Darkening.)* Ah, yes! That's what you've come to tell me. And in that outfit!

GREGORY: I haven't chosen this dress, my lord.

JULIAN: Not so? Who then?

GREGORY: He, who is greater than the Emperor.

JULIAN: I know this Galilean jargon. For the sake of our friendship, give it up.

GREGORY: Let me start by explaining why you see me here, dressed as a priest of the church you persecute.

JULIAN: *(With a sharp glance.)* Persecute! *(He climbs the dais again and sits.)* Now you can go on.

GREGORY: You knew what I believed about religious matters during our happy life together in Athens. But it was far from my thoughts, then, to renounce the joys of the world. Ambition, and the craving for wealth, I can claim, never tempted me. But I wouldn't be honest if I denied both my eyes and my soul clung in rapture to all the glory revealed to me in the ancient wisdom and arts of the Greeks. The squabbling and the small-minded bickering in our church, deeply pained me; but I took no part in any of that.; I served my countrymen in worldly things; nothing more—

Then news came from Constantinople. It said Constantius had died of fright over your achievements and had set you up as his heir. Hailed as someone superhuman, and with reports of your victories flying ahead, you, hero of Gaul and Germany, were able without a fight to ascend the throne of Constantinople. The world lay at your feet.

Then followed other news. The lord of the world was arming for war against the lord of Heaven.

JULIAN: Gregory, what are you daring to say—!

GREGORY: The lord of the flesh has armed against the lord of the soul. I stand here before you in bodily fear and trembling, but I daren't dissemble. Do you want to hear the truth or shall I keep silent?

JULIAN: Go on speaking, Gregory!

GREGORY: What haven't my fellow-believers had to suffer already in these few months? How many death sentences passed and carried out in the most cruel manner? Gaudenzios, the undersecretary; Artemius, the former Governor of Egypt; both tribunes, Romanus and Vinzentius—

JULIAN: You don't understand these things. I tell you the Goddess of Justice would have wept openly if those traitors escaped with their lives.

GREGORY: Well, let that pass my Emperor; but I tell you there's one sentence of death the God of Justice can never forgive you. Ursulos! That man who was your friend in your days of need. Ursulos, who put his own life in danger providing you with money in Gaul. Ursulos, whose whole offense was his Christian faith and his integrity—

JULIAN: Ah, you get this from your brother Caesarius!

GREGORY: Punish me, my lord; but spare my brother.

JULIAN: You know perfectly well you're in no danger, Gregory! What's more, I'll grant you Nevita has been much too harsh.

GREGORY: Yes, that barbarian whose Greek surface can't conceal his origins—!

JULIAN: Nevita's a fanatic on his job and I can't be aware of all he's up to. Over Ursulos, I'm genuinely sorry, and I deeply regret neither time nor circumstance allowed me to take up his case personally. I definitely would have spared him, Gregory! I've also considered returning to his heirs anything of his that was left.

GREGORY: Great Emperor, you don't owe me any account of your actions. I came only to tell you all this news struck like a bolt of lightning in Caesarea and Nazianzus and the other Cappadocian cities. How can I describe the effect it's had? Our internal squabbles were silenced by the danger we now shared. Many of the church's less sound members deserted; though in many of the fainter-hearted the light of the Lord burned with an unprecedented brightness. And now hard times have fallen upon our people. The heathens—yes, my Emperor, those *I* call heathens, begin to threaten us, to harm and persecute us—

JULIAN: Retribution—retribution, Gregory!

GREGORY: I'm far from defending all my fellow-believers may have done through misguided zeal for the church's cause. But you, who are so enlightened, the Emperor of us all, can't allow that the living shall be punished for the crimes of the dead. And that's what's happened in Cappadocia. The enemies of the Christians, though few in number, thirsting for plunder and burning to gain the favor of the new officials, have roused anxiety and alarm among the people in the cities and in the country. I'm not thinking mainly of the insults we must put up with nor of the violations we've been exposed to of our well-established property rights. What worries me and all my concerned brethren most, is the danger all this entails for men's souls. Many are infirm in their faith and lack the strength to turn away from earthly goods. The harsh treatment now endured by any who bear the name of Christian has led many to fall into apostasy. My lord, this is a rape of souls from God's Kingdom!

JULIAN: Oh, my clever Gregory, how can you speak that way? I'm astounded! Shouldn't you rather, as a good Galilean, rejoice for your community in being quit of these folk?

GREGORY: Most gracious Emperor, that's not how I think. I was once faint in the faith myself and I hold all such people to be invalids who can be cured so long as they keep in the bosom of the church. And that's the thinking of our little community in Nazianzus. Our deeply troubled brothers and sisters met to determine the best way to deal with the needs of the times. They were joined by delegates from Caesarea and the other towns. My father is sickly, and—as he sorrowfully concedes—doesn't possess that firmness of mind these troubling days require from one who sits on the bishop's throne. Therefore the congregation decided a younger man should be chosen who could hold the Lord's flock together. The choice fell on me.

JULIAN: Ah!

GREGORY: At the time I was away on a journey. But in my absence, and without consulting me, my father ordained me a priest and sent me the priestly vestments. The order came to me in Tiberia, on my estate, where I was spending some days with my brother and my old friend, Basil of Caesarea. My lord, if my doomsday had been pronounced, I could not have been more terrified than at that moment. I, a priest! I wanted it, and I didn't want it. I had to, yet I didn't dare. I wrestled with the Lord God, like the patriarch wrestled with him in the days of the Old Covenant. What went on inside me during the night that followed, I don't know. But this I know, that before the cock crowed, I spoke face-to-face with the Crucified One. Then I was his.

JULIAN: Delusion, delusion. I know all about these dreams.

GREGORY: On my journey home I traveled through Caesarea. Oh, what a distressing situation I found there! The city full of refugees from the countryside who'd abandoned house and home because the summer drought had shriveled the crops and destroyed all the vineyards and olive groves. To escape starvation they'd fled to the starving. There they languished—men, women and children—huddled in groups along the walls of houses; fever shook them, hunger ravaged their bellies. What did Caesarea have to offer them, this impoverished, unfortunate city only half recovered from the great earthquake of two years before? And in the midst of all this, under the burning heat and with continuing earth tremors, we had to witness ungodly sacrificial festivals by day and night. Demolished altars had been hastily rebuilt; blood of sacrifice ran in streams; acrobats and whores paraded through the city streets.

My lord—can you wonder how my sorely tried brethren see in the afflictions besetting them heaven's punishment for permitting unbelief and the signs of unbelief to flourish among them?

JULIAN: What signs do you mean?

GREGORY: The clamor, the screams of the fever-stricken people rose higher; they demanded the city authorities render for Christ a palpable example by razing to the ground whatever yet stood to remind them of paganism's former power in Caesarea.

JULIAN: You are not about to tell me—?

GREGORY: The city authorities called a council at which I also was present. You know, most gracious Emperor, all the temples are the city's property. The Citizens can dispose of them as they see fit.

JULIAN: Well, well. And if that's so?

GREGORY: In the dreadful earthquake that overwhelmed Caesarea two years ago, all temples were destroyed, save one.

JULIAN: Yes, yes. The temple of Fortuna.

GREGORY: At the meeting I'm speaking of the gathering resolved to resume God's chastising work as a testimony that they will hold firmly to Him alone and no longer tolerate any abomination in their midst.

JULIAN: *(Tensely.)* Gregory, you were my friend—do you value your life?

GREGORY: The gathering passed a resolution I could not support, yet it passed with almost everyone's consent. But as we feared the matter might come to your ears in a garbled version, and prompt you to react in rage against our city, it was decided someone should come here and tell you what was resolved and what is about to happen.

Most noble Majesty—no one could be found willing to take on this task. So I assumed the mission. That's why, my lord, I'm standing here humbly before you to tell you we Christians in Caesarea have decided the temple in which the heathens in their day worshipped a false god under the name of Fortuna, shall be demolished and razed to the ground.

JULIAN: *(Springing up.)* And I must hear this with my own ears! A single man dares tell me such unheard of things!

COURTIERS, ORATORS, AND POETS: Oh, pious Emperor, don't let this pass. Punish the blasphemer!

HECEBOLIUS: He's insane, my lord! Let him go. Look, look—that's madness glaring from his eyes!

JULIAN: Yes, you can well call it madness. But it's more than madness. To wish to pull down that splendid temple built for an equally splendid goddess! Isn't it this very goddess whose favors to me created the achievements now renowned in the remotest nations? What hope of triumph or of victory could I cherish if I let this violation stand? Gregory, I command you to return to Caesarea and let the people know I forbid this blasphemous act.

GREGORY: It's not possible, my lord! The matter's now gone so far that we're left with the choice of fear of man or obedience to God. We can't yield.

JULIAN: Then you'll feel how far the Emperor's arm can reach!

GREGORY: The Emperor's arm is mighty in earthly matters; and I, like others, tremble beneath it.

JULIAN: Then show it by your behavior! Ah, you Galileans, you count on my patience. Don't! Because truly—

(Noise at the entrance; the barber, EUNAPIUS runs in followed by a number of citizens.)

JULIAN: What's this? Eunapius, what's happened to you?

EUNAPIUS: Oh, that my eyes should witness such a sight!

JULIAN: What have you seen?

EUNAPIUS: See, most gracious Emperor, I come to you bloody and beaten and therefore happy to be the first to demand you punish—

JULIAN: Go on, man; who has beaten you?

EUNAPIUS: Allow me, lord, to lodge my complaint. This morning I left town to visit the little temple of Venus that you recently restored. When I arrived, I was met with the sound of songs and flute playing. Women gracefully danced in the forecourt, and inside I found the whole place filled with a joyous crowd, whilst priests in front of the altar performed the sacrifices you decreed.

JULIAN: Yes, yes. and then?

EUNAPIUS: Scarcely had I time to direct my thoughts to the delightful goddess I especially honor and worship than a great swarm of young men broke into the temple—

JULIAN: Surely not Galileans?

EUNAPIUS: Yes, my lord, Galileans.

JULIAN: Ah!

EUNAPIUS: Then what a riot followed! The dancing girls fled from the forecourt and to us inside, weeping from the abuse and blows of that violent mob. The Galileans fell upon us all, manhandled and insulted us in the most outrageous ways.

JULIAN: *(Stepping down from the throne.)* Wait, wait!

EUNAPIUS: Oh, had that outrage rained down on us alone! But the ruffians went further. Yes, most gracious Emperor, in *one* word: The altar is toppled, the statue of the goddess smashed in pieces, the entrails of the sacrifice cast to the ground for dogs—

JULIAN: *(Pacing up and down.)* Wait, wait, wait.

GREGORY: My lord, this man's word alone is not enough—

JULIAN: Quiet! *(To EUNAPIUS.)* Did you recognize any of these temple violators?

EUNAPIUS: I didn't, my lord; but these citizens knew many of them.

JULIAN: Take the guard with you. Arrest as many of the culprits as you can lay your hands on. Throw them into jail. The prisoners shall name the others; and when I have them all in my power—

GREGORY: What then, my lord?

JULIAN: The executioner will be able to tell you that. You and your fellow-citizens of Caesarea must learn what to expect if you continue in your Galilean obduracy.

(The EMPEROR goes out, left, in a violent rage. EUNAPIUS and his witnesses retire with the guards; the rest of the gathering disperses.)

(A marketplace in Antioch. In the foreground to the right a street leads from the market; to the left, in the background, a winding, narrow alley. A large crowd fills the marketplace. Street traders call out their wares. At various places townspeople have gathered in intensely debating groups.)

A MAN: By our heavenly God, what time did this disaster happen?

A SECOND MAN: In the morning, as I said; quite early this morning.

PHOCION: *(Who has come from the street on the right.)* My friend, do you think "disaster's" the right word? I'd call it a crime; what's more, a most insolent crime.

THE SECOND MAN: Yes, yes, you're probably right; it was an insolent thing to do.

PHOCION: Just consider—er, it *is* the attack on the temple of Venus you're talking about? Good. Well, just consider, I say, at a time when the Emperor himself is in town? And then to choose this of all days…a day…

A THIRD MAN: *(Joining the speakers.)* Excuse me—tell me, friends, what's actually…

PHOCION: I mean, a day like this when our great Emperor himself is officiating at the festival of Apollo.

THE THIRD MAN: Yes, of course, I know that. But why are they jailing these Christians?

PHOCION: What? Jailing them? Are they really onto their tracks? *(Loud shouts are heard.)* Hush! What's that? Yes, by the gods if they haven't bagged them. *(An OLD WOMAN, frantic and with disheveled hair, pushes her way through the crowd; she is surrounded by other women, who vainly try to hold her back.)*

OLD WOMAN: Let go of me! He's my only boy; the child of my old age! Let me go; let me go! Will no one tell me where to find the Emperor?

PHOCION: What do you want with the Emperor, old mother?

OLD WOMAN: I want my son back! Help me! My son! Hilarion! Imagine, they took him from me! They broke into our house, and then they took him!

A MAN: *(To PHOCION.)* Who's this woman?

PHOCION: What? You don't know the widow Publia—the psalm singer.

THE MAN: Ah, yes, yes, yes.

PUBLIA: Hilarion! My child! What will they do with him? Ah, Phocion, you're here? It's God's blessing I've found a Christian brother…

PHOCION: Hush, quiet, quiet; don't shout like that; the Emperor's on his way.

PUBLIA: Oh, this ungodly Emperor! The Lord of Wrath is punishing us for his sins; famine is stalking the land; the earth shakes beneath us!
(A squad of soldiers enters from the street, right.)

SQUAD-LEADER: Move aside; make way!

PUBLIA: Come, good Phocion, help me for the sake of friendship and fellowship…

PHOCION: Are you mad, woman: I don't know you.

PUBLIA: What? You don't know me? Aren't you Phocion the dyer? The son of…

PHOCION: I'm not the son of anyone. Get away from me, woman! You're crazy. I don't know you; I've never seen you. *(He dives into the crowd.)*

AN OFFICER: *(Enters right with soldiers.)* Clear a space, there!
(The soldiers push the crowd against the houses. PUBLIA collapses in the arms of the women, left. Everyone stares expectantly down the street.)

PHOCION: *(In a crowd behind the guards to the right.)* Yes, by the Sun-God, here he comes now, our blessed Emperor!

A SOLDIER: Stop shoving back there!

PHOCION: Do you see him? The man with the white band round his forehead, that's the Emperor!

A MAN: That man dressed all in white?

PHOCION: Yes, yes. That's him all right.

THE MAN: But why is he dressed all in white?

PHOCION: Very likely because of the heat; no, wait a moment, I think it's because, as a priest, he…

ANOTHER MAN: The Emperor himself's doing the sacrifice?

PHOCION: Yes, Emperor Julian does everything himself.

A THIRD MAN: He doesn't look as impressive as Emperor Constantius.

PHOCION: I think he does. He's not as tall as the previous Emperor, but his arm's longer. And then the way he looks…oh, my friends! It's not so easy to see just now; he's lowering his eyes modestly as he walks. Yes, he's a modest man, believe me. He doesn't notice women. I'd dare swear that since his wife died he's hardly ever…; he writes all through the night you know. That's why his fingers are often as black as a dyer's; yes, in fact, just like mine. You should realize I know the Emperor better than most. I was born in this city, but I lived some fifteen years in Constantinople, until quite recently…

A MAN: Is there anything to the rumor the Emperor's thinking of settling in this city?

PHOCION: I know the Emperor's barber and he says so. I just hope these shameful outrages don't rile him too much.

A MAN: Acch, that would be a nuisance.

THE SECOND MAN: If the Emperor settles here there'd be something for all of us.

PHOCION: That's what I had in mind; it's why I moved here. And now we must give of our best, my friends; when the Emperor passes by we'll send up a rousing cheer for him and for Apollo.

A MAN: (To another.) Who's this Apollo people have begun talking so much about?

THE SECOND MAN: Oh, he's a priest in Corinth—the one who watered what St. Paul planted.

THE FIRST MAN: Ah, yes. I think I remember that.

PHOCION: No, no no, it's not *that* Apollo; it's a completely different one; it's the Sun-King—the great Apollo who plays the lyre.

THE SECOND MAN: I see; *that* Apollo. Is *he* better?

PHOCION: Yes, I should think so. Look, look, there he comes. Oh, most blessed lord!

(JULIAN *dressed as a High Priest, enters surrounded by SACRIFICIAL PRIESTS and TEMPLE SERVANTS. COURTIERS and SCHOLARS, including HECEBOLIUS, have joined the procession, as well as townspeople. In front of the EMPEROR walk flute and harp players. SOLDIERS and STATE OFFICIALS with long batons clear the way in front and on either side.*)

THE CROWD IN THE MARKET: Hail to the Emperor! Long live Julian our hero and benefactor!

PHOCION: Welcome to Julian and the Sun-King! Long live Apollo!

CITIZENS: (In the foreground, to the right.) Emperor, emperor, stay long among us!
    (JULIAN *gives a signal and the procession stops.*)

JULIAN: Citizens of Antioch! I can't immediately call to mind anything that could warm my heart more than these, your cheers of encouragement. And my heart has sore need of this comfort. It was with drooping spirits that I set out on this procession, that should have been a joyful and uplifting occasion. Yes, I'll not hide the fact that this morning I wasn't far from losing that spiritual serenity a philosopher must preserve under all circumstances. But who has the heart to reproach me? I ask you to consider what blasphemies are being prepared elsewhere and here are already taking place.

PUBLIA: My lord, my lord!

PHOCION: O devout and righteous Emperor, punish these audacious people!

PUBLIA: Hear me. Give back my Hilarion!

PHOCION: All good citizens entreat your goodwill for this city.

JULIAN: Seek to win the goodwill of the gods, then you will certainly have mine. And isn't it only right that Antioch should take the lead? Isn't it as if the eye of the Sun-God rests with special delight on this city? Ask those among us who have traveled far, and you shall learn to your sorrow how in other places misguided ones have destroyed our holy places. What remains? A relic here or there; and nothing of the best. But here with us, citizens of Antioch! Oh, my eyes filled with tears of joy when I first saw that incomparable sanctuary, Apollo's own house, which one can scarcely believe was built with human hands. Doesn't the image of the glorious god stand there as before in the purest beauty? Not one corner of his altar has been hacked away or crumbled; not a crack to be seen in the straight, sturdy columns. And when I reflect on this…while I now feel the band round my brow…when I look down on these vestments that are more dear to me than the imperial purple, then, with a sacred thrill, I feel the presence of the god.

See, see, the light quivers about us in glory!

Feel, feel the air filled with the fresh scent of garlands!

Beautiful earth, home of life and light, home of joy and of beauty…what you once were you shall become again! Into the Sun-King's embrace! Mithra, Mithra!

Forward on our victory march!

(The procession starts up again accompanied by the cheers of the crowd, but those at the front halt at the opening of the narrow street through which another procession comes toward the marketplace.)

JULIAN: What's preventing us?

HECEBOLIUS: Most gracious emperor, something's going on ahead up there.

HYMN: *(In the distance.)*

Bliss is the torment, bliss our death greeting

Bliss through this valley of tears to arise.

PHOCION: These are Galileans, my lord! They've been caught!

PUBLIA: Hilarion!

PHOCION: They've got them! I can hear their chains!

JULIAN: Go on past them—!

EUNAPIOS: *(Pushing eagerly through the crowd.)* We've done better than we could have imagined, my lord.

JULIAN: Who are these shameless people?

EUNAPIOS: Some live in this city, but most are refugee country folk from Cappodocia.

JULIAN: I won't see them. Go on, as I said.

PRISONERS' HYMN:
Bliss, through our death, our saints to be meeting
Bliss to be sharing the martyrs' sweet prize.

JULIAN: What madmen! Don't let them come near! Guards! Guards!
(Both processions meanwhile have run against each other in the crowd. Apollo's procession is forced to halt while the procession of prisoners, men in chains surrounded by soldiers and accompanied by a large crowd, marches forward.)

PUBLIA: Hilarion, my child!

HILARION: *(Among the prisoners.)* Be happy, mother!

JULIAN: You unfortunate fools. When I hear such insanities from you I almost doubt I've the right to punish you.

ANOTHER VOICE: *(Among the prisoners.)* Stand aside; don't take the crown of thorns from us.

JULIAN: A voice from the night! Who is that?

CAPTAIN OF THE GUARD: My lord, this is the one who spoke out. *(He drags one of the prisoners, a young man, who is holding a half-grown youth by the hand.)*

JULIAN: *(With a cry.)* Agathon!
(The PRISONER regards him silently.)

JULIAN: Agathon, Agathon! Answer me; you *are* Agathon?

THE PRISONER: Yes.

JULIAN: You among these! Speak to me

AGATHON: I don't know you.

JULIAN: You don't know me. You don't know who I am?

AGATHON: I know you are the lord of the earth; therefore I don't acknowledge you.

JULIAN: And the child—? Is he your young brother? *(To the CAPTAIN OF THE GUARD.)* This man must be innocent.

EUNAPIOS: This one's the ringleader. He's admitted as much himself; he's even bragged about it.

JULIAN: So this is what hunger and sickness and misery can do a man's mind.

(To the prisoners.) Just one word to say you repent, and no harm shall
come to you.

PUBLIA: *(Screams.)* Don't say it, Hilarion!

AGATHON: Be brave, little brother!

PUBLIA: Go, go to whatever's waiting for you, my only one!

JULIAN: Listen, and think about it, you others —

AGATHON: *(To the prisoners.)* Choose between Christ and the Emperor!

PRISONERS: Glory to the Lord on high!

JULIAN: Terrible, the Galilean's power of perverting. It must be destroyed. Pass
by them, these abominations! They cast a shadow on our joy; they make the
day dark with their morbid longing for death. Flute players, men, women,
strike up! A song, a song of praise for life and light and joy!

PROCESSION OF APOLLO: *(Singing.)*
Blest is the cool caress of the rose;
Blest to regale where the golden sun glows!

PROCESSION OF PRISONERS:
Blissful to sink in the blood-drenched tomb!
Blissful to die for our heavenly home!

PROCESSION OF APOLLO:
Blest to breathe deeply the incense-flood

PROCESSION OF PRISONERS:
Blissful to choke on the upswelling blood

PROCESSION OF APOLLO:
Pleasures increasing, cups overflowing
Apollo provides, his riches bestowing.

PROCESSION OF PRISONERS:
The burning of flesh, the breaking of bone
He heals alone!

PROCESSION OF APOLLO:
Blest with the sunlight in joy to draw breath.

PROCESSION OF PRISONERS:
Blissful the pain of the martyr's sweet death.

*(The sacred grove round the temple of Apollo. The portico, supported by columns
and reached by broad steps leading up, can be seen between trees in the
background. A crowd of people are running in terror, crying out in distress. In the
far distance the music of the procession can be heard.)*

WOMEN: Help! The earth's shaking again!

A FLEEING MAN: How horrible! It's thundering beneath our feet—

A WOMAN: Is that what's happening? Was the earth shaking?

MANY VOICES: Hear it, hear it, hear it!

SOME: It's the chariot on the cobblestones

OTHERS: It's the drums. Listen to the music—the Emperor's arriving!

> *(The procession of Apollo can be seen coming through the grove from the right; it forms a semicircle in front of the temple, accompanied by the sound of flutes and harps.)*

JULIAN: *(Faces the temple and raises his hands.)* I accept the omen! I've never felt so close a kinship with the immortal gods. The divine Archer's among us. The earth drums under his heels just as it thundered when he stamped in anger on the Trojan shore. But it isn't against us he directs his angry brow. It's against those unfortunates who hate him and his sunlit realm. Yes, just as good fortune or misfortune's a measuring-stick we mortals may use to judge the favors of the gods—so clearly here the difference between them and us is shown.

> Where are the Galileans now? Some in the hands of the executioner, others fleeing through the narrow streets, faces ashen with terror, eyes flaring, screams forced through their lips and hair upraised in fright or torn out in despair.

> And where are we? Here, in Daphne's fresh grove with the breath of dryads cooling our foreheads—here, before the glorious god's glorious temple, laved by the waves of melodies from flute and lyre—here, in light, in gladness, in the god's revealed presence.

> Where is the Galileans' god? Where is the Jew, that crucified son of a carpenter? Let him reveal himself. He takes good care not to.

> Therefore it's fitting we fill this sanctuary; that with my own hands I perform the ceremony. I feel it so far from unbecoming and beneath me, I set it above all others. *(He heads the procession through the crowd toward the temple.)*

A VOICE: *(Shouting from the crowd.)* Stop, ungodly man!

JULIAN: A Galilean among us?

THE SAME VOICE: No further, you that deny God!

JULIAN: What man is speaking there?

OTHER VOICES IN THE CROWD: A Galilean priest. A blind old man. He's standing here.

STILL OTHER VOICES: Get rid of him. The shameless fellow!

> *(An OLD, BLIND MAN in priest's robes, supported by two younger men, also dressed as priests, is helped forward until he stands at the temple steps and before the EMPEROR.)*

JULIAN: Ah, what do I see! Tell me, old man, aren't you Bishop Maris of Chalcedon?

THE OLD MAN: Yes, I am that most unworthy servant of our church.

JULIAN: The most unworthy, you style yourself; and I think maybe you're not entirely wrong. Unless I'm mistaken, you've been one of those who's most fanatically fomented divisions among the Galileans.

BISHOP MARIS: I've done those things that crush me, deep in contrition. When you came to power, with the rumors of your sympathies, my heart was seized with unspeakable dread. Enfeebled by age and blind as I was, I could not think of going against earth's mightiest ruler. Yes, God forgive me—I forsook the flock it was my duty to guard, drew back like a coward from the dangers gathering round God's community, and sought safety here on my Syrian estate—

JULIAN: And so, amazing mystery! You, the man who betrayed your faith and once reckoned the emperor's favor so highly, step up to me as you've just now done, and fling your insults in my face.

BISHOP MARIS: I'm no longer afraid of you because now my heart is Christ's alone. In the Church's time of trouble her light and glory shone for me. All the blood you shed—all the violence and wrong you commit—cry out to heaven, re-echo in my deaf ears and show me in my night of blindness the way I have to go.

JULIAN: Go home, old man!

BISHOP MARIS: Not before you promise to abandon these, your satanic doings. What are you attempting? Shall the dust rise against the spirit? Will the lord of the world dethrone the lord of Heaven? Don't you see the day of wrath drawing upon us for your sins? Our wells are like eyes that have wept themselves dry. The clouds that should rain restoring manna upon us, pass over our heads in arid indifference. The earth that was cursed from the day of creation, heaves and trembles under the Emperor's bloodguilt.

JULIAN: What gain from your god do you look for from this fanaticism, foolish old man? Are you hoping your Galilean master, as in the old days, will perform a miracle and restore your vision?

BISHOP MARIS: I have the vision I wish for; and I thank the Lord he's taken my sight from me so I'm spared from seeing a man walking in a more ghastly night than mine.

JULIAN: Out of my way!

BISHOP MARIS: Where are you going?

JULIAN: To the house of the Sun-King

BISHOP MARIS: You shall not go. I forbid you in the name of the one God!

JULIAN: Insane old man! Take him away!

BISHOP MARIS: Yes, lay hands on me! But who so dares, his hand shall wither. The God of Wrath shall reveal himself in all his power—

JULIAN: Your god is no god of power. I shall show that the Emperor is stronger than he—

BISHOP MARIS: You are lost! Then I lay a curse on you, apostate son of the church!

HECEBOLIUS: *(Pale.)* Lord and Emperor, don't let this happen!

BISHOP MARIS: *(In a loud voice.)* Cursed be thou, Julianos Apostata! Cursed be thou, Emperor Julian! The Lord God has spat thee out of his mouth! Cursed be thine eyes and thy hands! Cursed be thy head and all thy deeds! Woe, woe, woe to the apostate. Woe, woe, woe—

(A hollow rumbling is heard. The temple's roof and pillars sway and are seen to collapse while the whole building is enveloped in a cloud of dust. The crowd gives out a cry of terror; many flee, others fall to the ground. For a moment there is a breathless silence. Gradually, the cloud of dust settles and Apollo's temple is seen in ruins.)

BISHOP MARIS: *(Whose two attendants have fled, stands alone and says in a hushed voice.)* God has spoken.

JULIAN: *(Pale, and with a hushed voice.)* Apollo has spoken. His temple is defiled; therefore he destroyed it.

BISHOP MARIS: And I tell you, it was the Lord who laid the temple of Jerusalem in ruins.

JULIAN: If that's so, then the churches of the Galilean shall be closed, and his priests shall be scourged until they've raised up that temple once more.

BISHOP MARIS: Try, you without power! Who is capable of raising up the temple of Jerusalem since the Prince of Golgotha destined its overthrow?

JULIAN: I have that power! The Emperor has that power! Your god shall be exposed as a liar. Stone by stone I'll rebuild that temple in Jerusalem in beauty and glory, as it was in the days of Solomon.

BISHOP MARIS: Not a stone shall be laid upon another, for it is cursed by heaven.

JULIAN: Wait, wait, you shall see—had you eyes to see—you who stand there abandoned and helpless, fumbling in the night, not knowing where to direct your feet.

BISHOP MARIS: For me, my path is lighted by the lightning that shall one day strike you and yours. *(He gropes his way out. JULIAN remains behind, surrounded by a small, pale, and terrified group.)*

END OF ACT TWO

ACT THREE

In Antioch. An open colonnade with statues and a fountain in the foreground. On the left, within the colonnade, a flight of stairs leads to the imperial palace.

A group of courtiers, teachers, poets, and orators, among them ORIBASES, the court physician, and the poet HERACLIUS, have gathered partly in the colonnade partly round the fountain. Most of them are dressed in shabby cloaks and their hair and beards are matted.

HERACLIUS: I can't take this life much longer. Up at sunrise, then a cold bath, running and fencing until you're ready to drop—

ORIBASES: At least it's very good for your health.

HERACLIUS: Is it good for you to eat seaweed and raw fish?

A COURTIER: Or good for you gobbling down great chunks of meat, all bloody and straight from the butcher?

HERACLIUS: I haven't seen much in the way of meat this last week. Most of it goes to the sacrifices. I think we'll soon be able to say the most venerable gods are the only carnivores left in Antioch.

ORIBASES: Still the malcontent, Heraclius?

HERACLIUS: What can you mean, my friend! I'm far from making fun of the Emperor's wise decrees. Blessings on Emperor Julian! Is he not following the immortals' footsteps? Because, tell me, doesn't it look like some economizing's also going on in the celestial household?

A COURTIER: Ha! ha! ha! You're not far off in that!

HERACLIUS: Only look at Cybele, the erstwhile so overflowing goddess, whose statue the Emperor resurrected from a rubbish dump—

A COURTIER: It was a dunghill—

HERACLIUS: Very likely; Cybele has dealings in fertilizers. But just look at this goddess, I'm telling you; for all her hundred breasts she's flowing with neither milk nor honey.

(An amused circle has gathered round him. As he speaks JULIAN enters from the top of the stairs in the colonnade without being seen by those below. He's wearing a ragged cloak fastened with a rope; his hair and beard are unkempt, his fingers stained with ink; in both hands, under his arms and stuck in his belt are piles of parchment-rolls and papers. He stands and listens to Heraclius and is visibly angry.)

HERACLIUS: *(Continuing.)* Yes, it really looks like our world-nurse has been sucked dry. One might almost think she's passed the age when women—

A COURTIER: *(Eyeing the EMPEROR.)* Tsch, tsch, Heraclius, shame on you! *(JULIAN signals to the courtier to keep quiet.)*

HERACLIUS: *(Continues.)* So much for her. But isn't it the same with Ceres? Doesn't she show a most miserable—I could almost say most imperial—miserliness these days? Yes, believe me, were we on nodding terms with the high Olympians these days, we'd hear all about it. I'll swear nectar and ambrosia are being rationed to the limit. Oh Zeus, how skinny thou must be! Oh Dionysos, how much now is left of thy plump loins? And thou, oh lusty, quick-blushing Venus—and thou, oh havoc to all husbands, Mars—

JULIAN: *(In fury.)* What a piece of impudence you are, Heraclius! What a vile, venom-spewing mouth—

HERACLIUS: Ah, my most gracious Emperor!

JULIAN: You insult everything sublime! And I had to encounter this—hearing your croaking tongue the instant I stepped out of my library into the fresh morning air. *(He approaches nearer.)* Do you know what I'm holding under my arm? No, you don't know. It's a polemic against you, Heraclius you silly, blasphemous fool.

HERACLIUS: Against me, my Emperor?

JULIAN: Yes, a polemic against you. A tract I wrote in fury this very night. Or should I not have been fired up in fury over your outrageous behavior yesterday. What was it you took it on yourself to say in the classroom in the hearing of myself and many serious men?

Didn't we have to put up for hours with those shocking fables of the gods you take such pleasure in? How dared you come out with such fabrications? Weren't they a pack of lies form beginning to end?

HERACLIUS: Ah, my Emperor, if you call *that* lying then both Ovid and Lucan have lied.

JULIAN: What else? Oh, I can't describe my indignation when I saw where your impious speech was leading. "Man, let nothing surprise you" I was tempted to say with the comic playwright when I heard you carrying on like some scruffy mongrel—not words of gratitude but just a lot of absurd nursery tales—which, moreover, were most miserably written. Because your verses are awful, Heraclius—as I've demonstrated here in this essay. I wanted to get up from my seat and walk out when I saw you, as if in a theatre, playing both Dionysos and the immortal one you're named after. And why I restrained myself and sat where I was, I assure you, was less out of regard for the author than for the actors—if I could call them such. But mostly it was out of regard for myself, being afraid it might seem I was fleeing like a frightened dove. So I made out to be unconcerned but repeated to myself in silence that verse of Homer;

Bear it awhile, my heart; heavier things hast thou endured
Be patient, as before, when a mad dog mocks the eternal gods.[1]

Yes, we must put up with this and more. The times are no better than they are. Where's the happy man who's managed to keep eyes and ears unpolluted in this age of iron!

ORIBASES: I implore you, my noble lord, don't excite yourself. Let it be a comfort that we listened most unwillingly to this man's foolishness.

JULIAN: That isn't true in the least! I noted most of your faces and they appeared not at all unwilling to laugh every time this brazen joker rattled off his indecencies and then looked round the gathering with an oily smile just as if he'd done something to be proud of.

HERACLIUS: Oh, my emperor, I am most unhappy—

JULIAN: Yes, you certainly ought to be, because in truth this is no trifling matter. Or is there in these stories of the gods perhaps no deeper meaning, no serious purpose? Weren't these stories conceived with the aim of leading the human spirit along an enjoyable and easy path up to those mysterious dwellings where the supreme god rules—and by this means preparing men's souls for union with him? What else can be the reason? Wasn't it with this in mind the ancient poets invented such stories and isn't that why Plato and others repeated them, even adding more to their number? I tell you, without this purpose, the stories are suitable only for children and barbarians— indeed, hardly for them. But were they children or barbarians you had before you yesterday? Where did you find the gall to speak to me as though I were a child? Do you imagine you're a seer and have a seer's license to say what you like because you've put on a ragged cloak and carry a beggar's staff?

A COURTIER: Ah, how true, my emperor! No, no, much, much more is needed.

JULIAN: Is there really? And what then? Maybe it's to let your hair grow and never clean your nails. Oh you hypocrite, Cleon! But I know you, all of you. Here, in my writings I've given you a name which—now you'll get to hear it—*(He rummages through the bundles of papers. At this moment, LIBANIUS enters from the right, splendidly dressed and with a haughty expression.)*

ORIBASES: *(In a lowered voice.)* Ah, what a relief you've come, my highly esteemed Libanius.

JULIAN: *(Searching his papers.)* Where is it?

LIBANIUS: *(To ORIBASES.)* Why is it a relief?

ORIBASES: The Emperor's in a rage. Your arrival might calm him down.

JULIAN: Ah, here it is—*(Vexed.)* What does that man want?

ORIBASES: My lord, it is—

JULIAN: Good, good, good. Now you'll hear whether I know you or not. Among the miserable Galileans are a number of fanatics who call themselves penitents. They reject all earthly goods but still demand sumptuous gifts from all the foolish folk who pay homage to them as if they were holy men worthy to be venerated. See, you are like these people, except I give you nothing. Because I'm not foolish like them. Yes, yes, if I weren't firm on that matter you'd soon overrun the court with your insolence. Or don't you already? Aren't there may among you who would come back here, even if I drove you away? Oh, my dear friends, what will this lead to? Are you lovers of wisdom? Are you followers of Diogenes, whose clothes and ways you've taken on? In truth, you're seen less often in the classroom than with my treasurer. How pitiful and wretched philosophy has become in your hands. You hypocrites and most ignorant orators! You—but what does that fat fellow want over there?

ORIBASES: My lord, it's the chief magistrate—

JULIAN: The chief magistrate can wait. What we're dealing with here is more important. Or isn't it? The man seems very impatient. Is it so urgent?

LIBANIUS: By no means, my lord. I can come back another day. *(He makes to go.)*

ORIBASES: My lord, you don't recognize this distinguished man? It's Libanius, the teacher of rhetoric.

JULIAN: What, Libanius? Impossible. Libanius, the incomparable Libanius—is here? I can't believe it!

LIBANIUS: I presumed the Emperor knew the citizens of Antioch elected me chief magistrate.

JULIAN: Certainly I knew that. But when I made my entry into the city, and the magistrates met me with a speech of welcome, I looked in vain for Libanius. Libanius was not among them.

LIBANIUS: The Emperor hadn't indicated any desire of hearing Libanius speak on that occasion.

JULIAN: Libanius ought to know what the Emperor would wish in that respect.

LIBANIUS: Libanius had no idea what time and separation might have done. Libanius therefore found it more appropriate to place himself in the crowd. He stood in a clearly not inconspicuous position; but it did not suit the Emperor to let his eye fall upon him.

JULIAN: I believe you received my letter the day after—?

LIBANIUS: Priscus, your new friend, brought it me.

JULIAN: And all the same—or perhaps because of that—you kept away—?

LIBANIUS: A headache, and important business—

JULIAN: Ah, Libanius, previously you were not so unavailable.

LIBANIUS: I come when I'm invited. Ought I be a petitioner? Should I block the path of the Emperor's highly honored favorite, Maximus?

JULIAN: Maximus never shows up at court.

LIBANIUS: Understandably. Maximus holds his own court. The Emperor's installed him in an entire palace.

JULIAN: Oh, my Libanius, haven't I installed you in my heart? How can you envy Maximus his palace?

LIBANIUS: I envy no one. I don't envy my colleagues Themisteus and Mamertinus, although you've given them great proofs of your favor. Neither do I envy Hecebolius whose wealth you've augmented with such lavish gifts. Yes, I'm even glad I'm the only one to whom you've given nothing. Because I grasp the reason for this exception. You intend the cities of your empire should have abundance of everything and especially of rhetoric, well knowing this to be the quality that distinguishes us from the barbarians. You were concerned that I—like certain others—might become lukewarm in my art, if you showered me with wealth. The Emperor therefore chose to let the teacher of his youth remain poor, so he would be more firmly dedicated to his calling. This is how I interpret a behavior which has astonished some whom I shall not name. It is for the health and well-being of the city you've given me nothing. You want to scant me in wealth to grant me abundance in eloquence.

JULIAN: And I, my dear Libanius, have also grasped the reason why the teacher of my youth allowed me to spend several months here in Antioch without once calling on me. Libanius naturally felt the services his former pupil has rendered to the gods, to the state, and to learning were not great enough to merit the praise of the man who is named the king of eloquence. Libanius undoubtedly believed meaner talents best suited such mediocre matters. Quite reasonably, Libaniuis's reticence might proceed from concern for my spiritual harmony. Yes, you doubtlessly feared seeing the Emperor drunk with arrogance, raving like one who, from thirst, has drunk too copiously from some leaf-fringed wine bowl, if you'd lavished on him some of that art for which all Greeks admire you, and by doing that, raised him to the level of the gods through so precious a sacrifice.

LIBANIUS: Ah, my Emperor, if only I could believe my words possessed such power—

JULIAN: And that is what you can't believe, my incomparable friend? Leave me. I'm angry with you, Libanius! But it's a lover's anger toward the one he loves.

LIBANIUS: Is that really so? Oh, my kingly brother, then let me tell you that since your arrival, not a day has passed but I haven't cursed the mulishness that stopped me making the first move. My friends suggested—not without a vestige of reason—that you'd undertaken this long journey mostly to see me and hear me speak. But from Julian himself came no such sign. What was I to do? Flatter the Emperor, when I loved the man?

JULIAN: *(Embracing and kissing him.)* My Libanius!

LIBANIUS: *(Returning the kiss.)* My friend and brother!

ORIBASES: How this honors them both!

COURTIERS AND TEACHERS: *(Applauding.)* How beautiful! How sublime!

JULIAN: Oh, Libanius, you rascal—how could you set your heart against granting me this happiness for so long? In the weeks and months waiting for this moment, my face wore a dark shroud of melancholy.

LIBANIUS: Ah, you were better off than I; you had an audience you could speak to about your absent friend.

JULIAN: Don't say that. All I had was the forsaken lover's consolation: in grief reiterating your name aloud: Libanius, Libanius!

LIBANIUS: But while you called out to the empty air, my only audience was my little room's four walls. Most of my day I spent in my bed imagining who just then might be with you—now this man, now another—. "It was different before," I told myself, "when it was I who had Julian's ear."

JULIAN: And in the meantime you let me pine with longing. Look at me. Aren't I a hundred years older?

LIBANIUS: Ah, but then haven't I undergone a similar change? You didn't even recognize me!

JULIAN: This meeting, for us both, has been a bath from which we emerge restored to health. *(He embraces and kisses him once more.)* And now, my dearest friend, you must tell me what brought you here today; for I've no doubt you've come on an important errand.

LIBANIUS: Setting aside my longing—that is so. If only someone else had been sent! But the place of honor the citizens have given me makes it my duty to convey the pleasant and the unpleasant.

JULIAN: Speak, my Libanius and tell me how I can serve you.

LIBANIUS: Then let me begin by saying the inhabitants of this city are plunged in sorrow since you've withdrawn your favor from them.

JULIAN: Hm—!

LIBANIUS: And this sorrow's joined with anxiety and disquiet since your new governor, Alexander, took up office.

JULIAN: Aha, I see!

LIBANIUS: The promotion of such a man was truly unexpected. Alexander up to now has held only minor posts, and those in a manner not likely to gain the citizen's respect or love.

JULIAN: That I know quite well, Libanius.

LIBANIUS: Alexander is violent in all he does, and justice doesn't count for much in his eyes—

JULIAN: I know that. I know all about it. Alexander's a brute of a man, lacking all education and culture. There's no way Alexander's merited such a promotion. But you can tell the citizens of Antioch they've deserved Alexander. Oh yes, it's possible they deserved a worse ruler, those greedy, unteachable people.

LIBANIUS: Then it's what we feared; it's a punishment—

JULIAN: Listen to me Libanius! Why did I come here? With trust in the people of this city. Antioch, which the Sun-King chose especially for his seat, was to help me make good again all the wrongs and ingratitude that so long have been offered to the immortals. But how was I greeted? Some were against me, others lukewarm. What don't I have to endure here? That Cappadocian, Gregory from Nazianzus—doesn't he range the city inciting the witless Galileans with his seditious speeches? Isn't there even some poet they've produced—some Apollonaris—who works them into a frenzy with his wild songs?

And what don't I have to hear from elsewhere? In Caesarea, haven't they done what they threatened? Destroyed the temple of Fortuna! What shame and disgrace! And where were the goddess's votaries, meanwhile? Did they try to prevent it? No, they just let it all happen, Libanius, when they ought to have laid down their lives to protect the sanctuary. But wait, wait! The Galileans in Caesarea shall pay with their blood and the whole city shall go up in flames as soon as I've time at my disposal.

LIBANIUS: My lord and friend—if you will allow me—

JULIAN: First allow me. Tell me yourself if I ought tolerate this? Whether someone as devoted as I can put up with such contempt toward the divinities that watch over and protect me? But what should I decide? Haven't I written long nights through against these unhealthy heresies, writing, Libanius, till my eyes became red and my fingers black with ink? And what do you think is the result? Ridicule's all I've received for thanks, not just from the fanatics themselves but even from those who profess to share my opinions. Yes, and crowning all of these indignities, I must live to see you here as spokesman for some citizens raising a fuss about Alexander—of whom it must be said he's doing his best to keep the Galileans in control.

LIBANIUS: Oh, my noble friend, what he's doing is precisely our ground of complaint.

JULIAN: What am I hearing from you!

LIBANIUS: It's not my choice I'm here on the city's business. At the assembly I told the people that for such a mission they should choose the most distinguished man in the city, thus giving them to understand I didn't want the job. In spite of that, the choice still fell on me who am definitely not—

JULIAN: Well, well, well. But that I should hear from your own mouth, oh Libanius—

LIBANIUS: I beg my royal brother to remember I'm speaking on the city's behalf. As for myself, I revere the immortal gods as highly as anyone. What would the art of rhetoric be without the tales handed onto to us by the poets of the past? Aren't these tales like a rich mine from which a practiced orator can fashion both weapons and ornaments if he knows how to work the metal expertly. Indeed, wouldn't the lessons of philosophy seem flat and indigestible if expressed without images and allegories taken from the world above? But tell me, my friend, can you expect to find this way of thinking among the masses, especially in an age like our own? I assure you, in Antioch at any rate, it's not so promising. The citizens here—both Galileans and the better informed—have lived next to each other these past few years without bothering about such things. There was hardly a household in the city where quite different beliefs didn't co-exist about religious matters. And, until recently, this never hurt the general harmony. Now it's all changed. People are starting to set doctrine against doctrine. Families are being split apart. In fact, recently a citizen I shan't identify disinherited his son because the young man left the ranks of the Galileans. Business and trade are suffering under all this, doubly painful now, with prices so high and famine at the gates.

JULIAN: Enough, enough—more than enough, Libanius! You complain of high prices. But tell me, has luxury ever flourished more than at present? Is the amphitheatre empty any day it's rumored there's a new lion from Africa? Last week, when there was talk of helping the economy by getting rid of all drifters and idlers, didn't the citizens cry out there should be an exemption for gladiators and dancers because they couldn't do without them!

Ah, well may the gods stretch their hands in anger over your depravities. There are teachers of wisdom enough in this city; but where is wisdom? Why do so few tread in my footsteps? Why should one stop at Socrates? Why not go a small step further and follow Diogenes or—if I might say—me, since we lead you to happiness? For isn't happiness the goal of all philosophy? And what is happiness other than being in harmony with oneself? Does the eagle crave gold feathers? Or the lion claws of silver? Does the pomegranate tree aspire to bear fruit of sparkling stones? I tell you, no man has the right to pleasure until he's shown himself strong enough to do without it. Yes, he should not dare so much as touch pleasure with his fingertips before he is prepared to tread it under foot.

And, in truth, that's a distant prospect. But I'll devote all my strength to this. For the sake of these things I'll give up other, also important, matters. The King of Persia, alarmed at my approach, has made me an offer of peace. I'm thinking of taking that up, to free my hands to enlighten and improve you, you unwilling pupils. As far as the other matter stands, things shall stay the same. You're to accept Alexander. See you get along with him. You, my Libanius, I won't have it said I let you go away unrewarded—

LIBANIUS: Ah, my Emperor—

JULIAN: You spoke with some bitterness on how I'd rewarded Themisteus and Mamertinus so handsomely. But didn't I take something from them, too? Didn't I take from them my daily company? I intend giving you somewhat more than them.

LIBANIUS: Ah, what are you saying, my noble brother!

JULIAN: I don't intend rewarding you with gold or silver. I was only that stupid in the early days, until I saw how people thronged around me, like thirsty harvesters round a spring, all pushing and shoving each other, all holding out their cupped hands to get them filled first—and filled to the brim. I've got wiser since. Especially, I think it might be said the Goddess of Wisdom hasn't withdrawn her support from me in the policies I've pursued for the good of this city.

LIBANIUS: How true, how true!

JULIAN: So I'm commissioning you, my dear Libanius, to compose a eulogy on me.

LIBANIUS: Ah, what an honor—!

JULIAN: You shall write it putting particular emphasis on the benefits for which the people of Antioch owe me their gratitude. I hope you will compose something worthy of both the orator and the subject. This task, my dear Libanius, shall be my gift to you. I can't think of a better reward for a man like you.

LIBANIUS: Oh, my royal friend, what an overwhelming privilege!

JULIAN: And now we will go to the fencing hall. After, my friends, we'll stroll through the streets to give these arrogant natives a wholesome example of modest dress and decent behavior.

ORIBASES: Through the streets, my lord? Ouf, in this midday heat—

A COURTIER: Oh, my lord, please excuse me, I'm feeling extremely unwell—

HERACLIUS: Me too, gracious lord! The whole morning I've been struggling with a nauseous stomach—

JULIAN: Then take an emetic, and see you bring up your ignorance at the same time. Oh, Diogenes, what disciples you have! They're ashamed of wearing your cloak in the open street. *(He departs in anger through the colonnade.)*

(A dilapidated street in a suburb of the city. In a row of houses to the left is a small church. A large crowd of Christians, wailing. The hymn-writer, APOLLINARIS and CYRILLUS, a teacher among them. Women with children in their arms shrieking in anguish. GREGORY from Nazianzus is walking through the street.)

WOMEN: *(Running and clinging fast to his cloak.)* Oh, Gregory, Gregory, speak to us. Comfort us in our distress.

GREGORY: Only *one* can comfort you. Hold fast to him. Cling to your Lord and Shepherd.

A WOMAN: Do you know, oh man of God, the Emperor's ordered all our holy scriptures burnt!

GREGORY: So I've heard, but I can't believe such folly.

APOLLONARIS: It's the truth. Alexander, the new governor ordered the soldiers to search our brothers' houses. Even women and children are whipped till they bleed if they're suspected of having books hidden away.

CYRILLUS: The Emperor's order doesn't just involve Antioch or even just Syria; it extends to the empire and the whole world. The minutest reference to Christ is to be wiped out of existence and from the memory of believers.

APOLLONARIS: Oh mothers, grieve for yourselves and your children! The time will come when you shall quarrel with those you now carry in your arms over what really was written in the lost word of God. The time will come when your children's children will ridicule you and not know who and what Christ was. That time will come when there shall be erased from all hearts that the Savior once suffered and died. The last believer shall go blindly to his grave and from that moment Golgotha shall be swept away from the earth just like the place where the garden of Eden once lay. Woe, woe for the new Pilate! He is not content, like Pilate, to kill the Savior's body. He murders the word and the teaching.

WOMEN: *(Tearing their hair and rending their clothes.)* Ah, ah, ah!

GREGORY: And I say to you, be of good comfort! God does not die. It's not from Julian the danger comes. The danger's been there, long before him, in the weakness and discord of our hearts.

CYRILLUS: Oh, Gregory, how can you ask that we stand steadfast beneath all these terrors? Brothers and sisters, do you know what has happened in Arethusa? The unbelievers have assaulted Marcos, the old bishop, dragged him by the hair through the streets, thrown him into a sewer, pulled him out filthy and bloody, smeared him with honey and hoisted him up into a tree and set there to be stung by wasps and poisonous flies.

GREGORY: And hasn't God's strength gloriously revealed itself in Marcos! What was Marcos, formerly? A man of doubtful faith. When the disturbances broke out in Arethusa he even fled the city. But see, no sooner had he realized, in his hiding place, that those violent men were avenging the bishop's flight on innocent brothers, than he willingly went back. And how did he bear the tortures that so appalled even his tormentors, that to come out of the situation with some shred of respect, they offered to set him free for a paltry sum? Did he not answer: No, and no, and again no? The Lord God was with him. He neither died nor gave in. His face showed neither terror nor impatience. In the tree where he hung he gave praise for his good fortune in that he was raised closer to heaven while others, he said, crawled upon the earth.

CYRILLUS: A miracle must have taken place with that steadfast old man. If you'd heard, as I did, the screams from the prison that day this summer when Hilarion and the others were tortured—! The screams were indescribable; helpless cries mingled with hissing sounds every time the iron, white-hot, seared into the torn flesh.

APOLLINARIS: But Cyrillus, have you forgotten how songs were born from the screams? Didn't Hilarion sing as he died? Didn't the brave Cappadocian boy sing under the torturer's hands until he gave up the ghost? And Agathon, that boy's brother, didn't he sing until unconsciousness overcame him, and he woke up out of his mind? In truth I tell you, so long as song rises from our suffering, so long shall Satan never conquer!

GREGORY: Be comforted. Love one another and suffer for each other, just as Serapion in Doristora lately suffered for his brothers when, for their sake, he let himself be scourged and cast into the furnace. See, see, has not the vengeful hand of the Lord already struck down the ungodly? Or haven't you heard the reports from Heliopolis in Lebanon?

APOLLONARIS: I know. During the obscene festival of Aphrodite heathens broke into the house of our holy sisters, raped them, murdered them with tortures too horrible to describe—

WOMEN: Ah, ah!

APOLLONARIS: —yes, some of the monsters opened up the body of one of the martyred, ripped out the entrails and ate the liver raw!

WOMEN: Ah, ah, ah!

GREGORY: The God of Wrath seasoned that meal. And how did it agree with them? Go to Heliopolis and you will see those men with putrefying poison in their veins, with eyes and teeth falling out, all speech and understanding gone from them. Terror has seized the city. Many heathens have been converted since that night. Therefore I do not fear this ravaging beast that raises itself against the Church; I do not fear Hell's crowned hireling who thinks to fulfill the arch-fiend's work. Let him fall upon us with fire, with sword, with the wild beasts of the arena! Yes, should his insanity drive him further than what he has done so far, what of it? Against all of this there is a cure and a path to victory!

WOMEN: Christ, Christ.

OTHER VOICES: There he is! There he comes!

SOME: Who?

OTHERS: The Emperor! The murderer! The enemy of God!

GREGORY: Quiet! Let him go by in silence.

(A detachment of the Imperial Guard comes along the street. Behind, follows JULIAN, accompanied by courtiers and philosophers, all escorted by guards. Another detachment of the Palace Guard, led by the Captain, FROMENTINUS, concludes the procession.)

A WOMAN: *(Quietly to the others.)* Look, look, he's dressed himself in rags like a beggar.

ANOTHER WOMAN: He must be out of his mind.

A THIRD WOMAN: God's already stricken him.

A FOURTH WOMAN: Hide your children against your breasts. Don't let their eyes see the horror.

JULIAN: Well, well, here's a whole pack of Galileans! What are you doing in the sunshine, in the open street, you spawn of darkness?

GREGORY: You've closed our churches; therefore we stand outside and praise the Lord our God.

JULIAN: Ah, so it's you, Gregory! Yes, you're still active around here. But be warned; I won't put up with it much longer.

GREGORY: I'm not looking for martyrdom; I don't wish it in the least; but if it happens to me, I'll count it an honor to die for Christ.

JULIAN: Your kind of talk tires me. I don't want to see you here. Why don't you stay in your stinking lairs? Go home, I tell you.

A WOMAN: Oh Emperor, where are our homes?

ANOTHER WOMAN: Where are our houses? The pagans have plundered them and driven us out.

OTHER VOICES: Oh Emperor, Emperor, why have you taken our possessions from us?

JULIAN: You ask that? Then I'll tell you, you ignorant folk! If we've taken your possessions from you, it was done for the good of your souls. Hasn't the Galilean said you should possess neither silver nor gold? Hasn't your Master promised you'll one day ascend to Heaven? Then shouldn't you thank me for making your journey as light as possible?

THE PHILOSOPHERS: Oh, incomparably put!

APOLLONARIS: My lord, you've taken from us more than silver and gold. You've taken God's own word. You've taken from us our holy scriptures.

JULIAN: I know you well enough, you hollow-eyed hymn-singer! You're Apollonaris, right? And if I took your ridiculous books from you, I expect you're the type of man who'll soon enough set about writing something equally as ridiculous. But let me tell you you're a pathetic scribbler and versifier. By Apollo, no self-respecting Greek would have your verses in his mouth. That stuff you recently sent me which you had the gall to call "The Truth" I can assure you I've read, understood, and condemned.

APOLLONARIS: You might have read it but you've not understood it; had you understood, you'd not have condemned it.

JULIAN: Ha! ha! The refutation I'm working on will show I've understood. But as for those books whose loss you're howling and wailing over, let me tell you the time is soon coming when you'll think more poorly of them—when you'll be shown your Jesus of Nazareth's a liar.

WOMEN: Ah! Alas for us!

CYRILLUS: *(Stepping from the crowd.)* Emperor, what did you just say?

JULIAN: Didn't the crucified Jew prophesy the temple of Jerusalem shall lie in ruins until the end of time?

CYRILLUS: So it shall be!

JULIAN: Oh, you fools! At this moment my general, Jovian, with two thousand workers, is in Jerusalem rebuilding the temple in all its magnificence. Wait, wait, you stiff-necked unbelievers—you shall discover who is mightier, the Emperor or the Galilean.

CYRILLUS: My lord, your will discover that to your confusion. I kept silent until you blasphemed the Holy One and called him a liar; but now I must tell you you've not the slightest power against the Crucified God.

JULIAN: *(Restraining himself.)* Who are you? What is your name?

CYRILLUS: *(Approaching.)* You shall hear. First and foremost I am a Christian and that is the most glorious name; for it shall never be wiped from the earth. Next, I bear the name Cyrillus and under that name I'm known to my brothers and sisters. But if I preserve the first name untainted, then I'll be rewarded with eternal life.

JULIAN: You're mistaken, Cyrillus. You're aware I know something of the mysteries of your doctrine. Believe me, him you're pinning your hopes on is not what you think he is. He died, thoroughly died at the time when Pontius Pilate was Governor in Judea.

CYRILLUS: I'm not mistaken. It's you, Emperor, who are mistaken in this. It was you who renounced Christ the moment he granted you dominion over the world. Therefore, I declare in his name that he soon will take from you both dominion and your life, and you shall come to learn, too late, how powerful he is whom you so blindly despise. Yea, just as you have forgotten his beneficence, so shall he not allow his love to flow for you, when he rises to punish you. You have cast down his altars, he shall cast you from your throne. You have found joy in trampling his law under foot—that same law you yourself once proclaimed to believers. In the same manner the Lord will tread you under his heel. Your body shall be swept away in the wild winds, and your soul shall journey where there are greater torments than you can think up for me and mine!

(The women flock around CYRILLUS, weeping and lamenting.)

JULIAN: I'd gladly spare you, Cyrillus! The gods are my witness that I do not hate you for your faith. But you have insulted my imperial power and authority, and that I must punish. *(To the CAPTAIN OF THE GUARD.)* Fromentinus, take this man to jail and let the executioner, Typhon, give him as many lashes as are necessary for him to proclaim that it is the Emperor, not the Galilean, who hold power on earth.

GREGORY: Be strong, brother Cyrillus!

CYRILLUS: *(With upraised hands.)* How blest am I to suffer for the glory of the Lord! *(The soldiers grab him and drag him away.)*

THE WOMEN: *(Weeping and lamenting.)* Ah, alas for us; alas for him who denies God.

JULIAN: Drive them away from here, these lunatics. Chase them like rebels out of the city. I'll no longer put up with their defiance and depravity.

(The Guards drive the clamorous crowd into the side streets. Only the EMPEROR and his followers remain. A man, until now hidden, is revealed lying in front of the church door; his cloths are in shreds and he has strewn ashes on his head.)

A SOLDIER: *(Prodding him with the shaft of his lance.)* Up, get up; beat it!

THE MAN: *(Looking up.)* Tread beneath your feet this worthless salt, thrown away by the hand of the Lord!

JULIAN: You eternal gods—Hecebolius—

THE COURTIERS: Why it's true—it's Hecebolius!

HECEBOLIUS: That's no longer my name. I have no name. I've betrayed the baptism that named me.

JULIAN: Rise, my friend! Your mind is sick—

HECEBOLIUS: Judas's brother is plague-ridden. Keep away from me—

JULIAN: Oh, you inconstant man—

HECEBOLIUS: Away from me, tempter! Take back your thirty pieces of silver! Is it not written: "You shall give up wife and children for the sake of the

Lord"? And I——? For the sake of wife and children I have betrayed the Lord my God! Ah, alas, alas! *(He throws himself once more to the ground.)*

JULIAN: It's madness like this such writings spread like wildfire on earth. Ought I not burn them? Wait! Within a year the temple of the Jews shall rise up again on mount Zion—it's golden roof shining over the lands to be witness: liar, liar, liar. *(He leaves quickly, followed by the philosophers.)*

(A road outside the city. To the left, at the edge of the road, stands the statue of Cybele among mere stumps of trees. A little farther away, left, is a fountain with a stone basin. It is approaching sunset.

On a step at the base of the goddess's statue sits an old priest with a covered basket in his lap. A group of men and women surround the stone basin, drawing water. People are seen passing back and fourth along the road. From the left PHOCION enters, shabbily dressed with a large bundle on his head. He meets the barber, EUNAPIUS, arriving from the city.)

PHOCION: What do I see—my friend Eunapius in full court dress.

EUNAPIUS: How can you make fun of a poor fellow?

PHOCION: You call that making fun? I meant it as a high compliment.

EUNAPIUS: That could be. These days it's become the fashion to go around in rags, all the more if they've been lying a good while in the gutter.

PHOCION: How do you imagine all this will end?

EUNAPIUS: I try not to think about it. I know how it's ended for me and that's enough.

PHOCION: You're not longer in the Emperor's service?

EUNAPIUS: What would the Emperor want with a barber? Does he get a haircut? Or get his beard trimmed, do you imagine? He doesn't even comb it once. But how are things with you? You're not looking too cheerful, yourself.

PHOCION: Ah, Eunapius, the days of the purple-dyers are over.

EUNAPIUS: You're right there. It's only the backs of Christians that are getting any purple now. But what's that you're dragging about?

PHOCION: A bunch of willow-bark. I've got to dye fools' cloaks for philosophers.
(A detachment of soldiers enter from the right and takes up position by the statue of Cybele.)

PHOCION: *(To one of the men by the stone basin.)* What's going on?

THE MAN: The statue's to be fed again.

PHOCION: Is the Emperor sacrificing here this evening?

ANOTHER MAN: Doesn't he sacrifice morning and evening—now here, now there?

A WOMAN: It's a misfortune for poor folk that the new Emperor's so fond of the gods.

ANOTHER WOMAN: Oh, Dione, don't say that. Shouldn't we all be fond of the gods?

THE FIRST WOMAN: Maybe so—it's a misfortune, just the same—

ONE OF THE MEN: *(Pointing to the right.)* Look there—here he comes.

(JULIAN enters, dressed as a priest and carrying a sacrificial knife. Several philosophers, priests of the temple, teachers, and guards accompany him. Behind them follows a crowd of people, some jeering, others indignant.)

ONE OF THE ARRIVALS: Over there's the goddess. Now watch some fun.

AN OLDER MAN: You call that fun? How many hungry mouths could be filled with what's wasted here?

JULIAN: *(Goes up to the statue.)* Oh, this sight! It fills my heart with rapture and my eyes with tears of sadness. Yes, indeed I must weep when I think that this statue of the awe-inspiring goddess—overthrown by blaspheming and insolent hands—has lain so long as if in oblivious sleep, and, what's more, in a place it disgusts me to describe. *(Suppressed laughter among the curious onlookers.)*

JULIAN: *(Angrily turning.)* Yet my rapture is no less when I reflect it was I who was privileged to liberate the divine mother from so unseemly a situation. And shouldn't I rejoice at that thought? It's said I won some battles against the barbarians and I'm praised for it. I tell you, I set a far higher value on what I've accomplished for the well-being of the gods; to them we owe all our powers and all our knowledge. *(To those around the stone basin.)* Anyway, I am moved that there are still some in this pig-headed city who don't show themselves indifferent to my appeals but participate as a decent piety requires, and I don't doubt that you've brought suitable sacrificial gifts with you. *(Goes over to the old priest.)* What do I see here! Only one old man! Where are your temple brothers?

THE OLD PRIEST: None are still living apart from myself.

JULIAN: All dead. The road encroaching without any reverence. The sacred grove cut down. Old man, where are the sacrificial gifts?

THE OLD PRIEST: *(Pointing to the basket.)* Here, my lord!

JULIAN: Good, good. And the rest?

THE OLD PRIEST: This is all. *(He opens the basket.)*

JULIAN: A goose! This goose is all?

THE OLD PRIEST: Yes, my lord!

JULIAN: And who was the pious man who remembered to present so generous a gift?

THE OLD PRIEST: I brought it myself. Oh, my lord, don't be angry. This one's all I had.

SUBDUED VOICES: It's plenty. One goose is more than enough.

JULIAN: Oh, Antioch, you put my patience to a hard test!

A MAN IN THE CROWD: Bread first, offerings after.

PHOCION: *(Nudging him.)* Well said, well said!

ANOTHER MAN: Give the people something to eat; let the gods look after themselves.

A THIRD MAN: We were better off under Chi and Kappa!

JULIAN: You insolent whiners, with your Chi and Kappa! Maybe you imagine I don't know what you mean with your Chi and Kappa? Oh, I know well enough. They've become catchwords among you. You mean Christ and Constantius. But their rule's over, and I'll yet find a way to break the defiance and ingratitude you show both to the gods and to me. You resent the fact I make due sacrifices to the gods. You sneer because I go about in humble dress and let my beard grow untrimmed. Oh yes, that beard's a real thorn in your flesh! You call it, impertinently, a goat's beard. You fools, I tell you it's a wise man's beard. Yes, I'm not ashamed you should know this beard's a host to vermin, as a clump of willows is a host to wildlife—yet I bear this despised beard of mine with greater honor than you your clean-shaven chins.

EUNAPIUS: *(Muttering.)* A ridiculous thing to say; quite absurd!

JULIAN: But do you imagine I'll let these insults go unanswered? No, no, you'll find otherwise. Only wait, you'll be hearing from me sooner than you think. Just now I'm working on a piece called "The Beard-Hater." It's directed against you, people of Antioch—that's right, against you whom I call "ignorant dogs." There you'll find my reasons for doing things that now seem to you so strange.

FROMENTINUS: *(Entering from the right.)* Great Emperor, I bring you a joyful message. Cyrillus has already come to his senses—

JULIAN: Ah, just as I thought.

FROMENTINUS: Typhon's done a first-class job, too. The prisoner was bound by the wrists and hoisted, naked, roofwards so that the tips of his toes just touched the ground; then Typhon flogged his back with a whip of ox-sinews so that the strokes reached round to his chest.

JULIAN: Oh, these degenerates, forcing us to use such methods!

FROMENTINUS: To prevent him dying we finally had to untie the obstinate man. He was quite still for a while, and seemed to be thinking; but suddenly he asked to be brought before the Emperor.

JULIAN: That pleases me. So you're bringing him here?

FROMENTINUS: Yes, my lord—here they are with him.

(A group of soldiers lead in CYRILLUS.)

JULIAN: Ah, my good Cyrillus, you're not so cocky as before, I see.

CYRILLUS: Maybe you've searched the entrails of some beast or bird to find out what I've got to say to you?

JULIAN: No, I hardly imagine I need omens to assume you've come to see reason and have got rid of your illusions about the power of the Galilean. You recognize both the Emperor and our gods to be greater than he?

CYRILLUS: Don't imagine anything of the sort. Your gods are powerless; and if you cling to these stone images which can neither see or hear, then you'll soon be as impotent as they are.

JULIAN: Cyrillus—is this what you have to tell me?

CYRILLUS: No, I come to thank you. Until now I trembled at you and your tortures. But in the hour of agony I won the victory of the spirit over that which perishes. Yes, my Emperor, when your henchmen imagined I hung in anguish from the prison roof, I lay, peaceful as a child, in my Savior's arms; and when my tormentors believed they tore strips from my body, the Lord stroked his healing hands over my wounds, taking away the crown of thorns and setting upon me the crown of life. Therefore I thank you; no other man has shown me such mercy as you. And so you'll never think I'll fear you again, watch this—*(He pulls open his cloak, tears at his wound and throws pieces of flesh at the Emperor's feet.)*—see, see, glut on the blood of mine you thirst for! But know I quench my thirst on the blood of Christ! *(Shrieks of horror amongst the crowd.)*

MANY VOICES: This brings disaster on us all!

JULIAN: *(Who has drawn back.)* Grab the madman lest he harm us!

(The soldiers surround CYRILLUS and drag him to the fountain; at the same time women are heard singing off to the right.)

JULIAN: Look over there, Fromentinus, what's that strange procession—

FROMENTINUS: Gracious Emperor, they're psalm-singers—

JULIAN: Ah, that band of crazy women—

FROMENTINUS: Governor Alexander has confiscated some scriptures they consider sacred. Now they wander the city to lament on the graves of Christians.

JULIAN: *(With clenched hands.)* Rebellion, rebellion—from both women and men!

(OLD PUBLIA and a large group of women come down the road.)

PUBLIA: *(Singing.)*

Their gods are marble and silver and gold,
They'll crumble to mold.

CHORUS OF WOMEN:

To mold, to mold.

PUBLIA:

They murder our brothers; the sons that we love.

Rise, doves of song, pray for vengeance above.

CHORUS OF WOMEN:

For vengeance above.

PUBLIA: *(Seeing the EMPEROR.)* There he is! Woe to the godless man who has burnt the word of God. Do you think you can burn away the word of God? I'll tell you where the word burns. *(She snatches a knife from a priest, cuts open her breast and twists the knife in the wound.)* Here's where the word burns. Burn our books. The word will burn in men's hearts until the final day! *(Throws the knife from her.)*

WOMEN: *(Singing with rising frenzy.)*

Let scriptures be banned; let bodies be slain

The word shall remain

The word shall remain.

(Taking PUBLIA with them, they go on their way into the country.)

PEOPLE AT THE FOUNTAIN: Alas, the Galilean's word is the strongest!

OTHER VOICES: What power have all our gods against this one alone!

YET OTHERS: No sacrifice! No worship! It will arouse the terrible one against us.

JULIAN: Oh, you fools! You fear to arouse one long since dead—a false prophet—yes, you shall see for yourselves. He is a liar, I tell you. Be patient a little longer. Every day, every hour, I expect a message from Jerusalem—

JOVIAN: *(Clothes covered in dust, enters hastily from the right with a few followers.)* Most gracious Emperor, forgive your servant for seeking you here.

JULIAN: *(With a cry of joy.)* Jovian! Oh, joyful news—!

JOVIAN: I came here direct from Judea. The palace told me you were here—

JULIAN: Oh, you bountiful gods—then the sun will not set on the lie! How much is done? Speak, my Jovian!

JOVIAN: *(With a glance at the crowd.)* My lord, shall I tell all?

JULIAN: All, all—from first to last!

JOVIAN: I got to Jerusalem with the masons and soldiers and two thousand workers. We immediately began clearing the site. Great ruins of temple walls were still standing. They quickly fell before our pickaxes and levers—as if an invisible power helped us dislodge them—

JULIAN: You see; you see!

JOVIAN: While this went on, immense piles of mortar were being carried to the new building work. Then, without any warning, a whirlwind arose that scattered the mortar like a cloud over the whole area.

JULIAN: Go on, go on!

JOVIAN: The same night the earth shook many, many times.

VOICES IN THE CROWD: You hear? The earth shook.

JULIAN: Go on, I tell you!

JOVIAN: We didn't allow our courage to be daunted by this strange occurrence. But when we dug deeper in the ground and made an opening to the vaults and the stone breakers went into them to work by torchlight—

JULIAN: Jovian, what happened?

JOVIAN: My lord, a huge and terrifying torrent of fire shot out of the caverns. A thunderous noise shook the whole city. The vaults burst apart and hundreds of workers died in the depths. The few who survived fled with terrible injuries.

VOICES WHISPERING: The God of the Galileans!

JULIAN: Can I believe all this? Did you see it?

JOVIAN: I was there myself. We started again. My lord, in the sight of many thousands—fearful, kneeling, jubilant, praying—the same miracle was repeated twice.

JULIAN: *(Pale and shaking.)* And then—In one word, what has the Emperor accomplished in Jerusalem?

JOVIAN: The Emperor has fulfilled the Galilean's prophecy.

JULIAN: Fulfilled—

JOVIAN: Through you the word has become truth: Not one stone shall be left upon another.

MEN AND WOMEN: The Galilean is victorious over the Emperor. The Galilean is greater than Julian!

JULIAN: *(To the priest of Cybele.)* You may go home, old man! And take your goose with you. We'll not make a sacrifice this evening. *(Turns to the crowd.)* I've heard many of you here say the Galilean is victorious. It may seem so; but I tell you, it's a delusion, you ignorant blockheads—believe me: It shall not be long before the tables are turned! I shall—I shall! Yes, only wait! I'm preparing a piece against the Galilean. It shall be in seven chapters; and when his followers have *that* to read—and the Beard-Hater, too— Give me your arm, Fromentinus! This conflict's tired me out. *(To the guards as he goes past the fountain.)* Let Cyrillus go! *(He leaves with his following for the city.)*

THE CROWD BY THE FOUNTAIN: *(Shouting after him in scornful laughter.)* There he goes, the sacrificial butcher! There goes the scraggy bear! There goes the long-armed monkey!

(Moonlight. Among the ruins of Apollo's temple. JULIAN and MAXIMUS both in long robes, enter between the overturned columns in the background.)

MAXIMUS: Where are you going, my brother?

JULIAN: Where there's most solitude.

MAXIMUS: But here—in this horrible place? Among these heaps of ruins?

JULIAN: Isn't the whole world a heap of ruins?

MAXIMUS: You've surely shown that what has fallen can be restored.

JULIAN: Cynic! In Athens I saw a cobbler who set up a work stall in the temple of Theseus. In Rome, I heard a corner of the Julia basilica was doing service as an ox-stall. Do you call that a restoration?

MAXIMUS: Why not? Don't all things happen piece by piece? What is the whole but the total sum of the pieces?

JULIAN: Feeble wisdom! *(Pointing to the overturned statue of Apollo.)* Look at this head without a nose. Look at this shattered elbow, these splintered loins. Do all this ugly fragments add up to a totality of former beauty?

MAXIMUS: How do you know the former beauty was beautiful in itself— except in the imagination of the beholder?

JULIAN: Ah, Maximus, that's precisely the point. What *is* anything in and for itself? I can name nothing after today. *(He kicks the head of Apollo.)* At any time, have you been mightier than yourself? Strange, Maximus, that such power can lie in an illusion. Look at the Galileans. And look at me, earlier, when I believed it possible to resurrect the fallen world of beauty.

MAXIMUS: Friend, if illusion is necessary to you, go back to the Galileans. They will take you back with open arms.

JULIAN: You know too well that's unthinkable. Emperor or Galilean! How to reconcile those opposites? Yes, this Jesus Christ is the greatest rebel who ever lived. What was Brutus, what was Cassius compared with *him?* They murdered just the one Julius Caesar; but *he* murders every Caesar and every Augustus alike. Is it even thinkable there could be a reconciliation between the Galilean and the Emperor? Is there room for the two in the entire world? And he lives on earth, Maximus, the Galilean lives, I tell you, however much the Jews and the Romans imagined they finally killed him; he lives in men's stubborn minds; he lives in their defiance and contempt of all visible power.

"Give to the Emperor what is the Emperor's,—and to God what is God's!" The mouth of man never uttered more cunning words than these. What's behind them? What and how much belongs to the Emperor? These words are like a club to strike the crown from the Emperor's head.

MAXIMUS: Yet the great Constantine knew how to come to terms with the Galilean—and your predecessor likewise.

JULIAN: Yes, if one could be as satisfied as they were. But do you call that ruling the world? Constantine enlarged his empire's boundaries. But didn't he shrink the boundaries of his spirit and his will? You rate the man too highly whom you call "the great." My predecessor I won't even consider; he was more a slave than an Emperor; and I can't be content with just the name. No, no, one can't think of compromise in these things. And yet, to have to give up! Oh, Maximus, after these defeats I can't go on being Emperor—but neither can I decide not to go on. Maximus, you who can interpret omens whose meanings are hidden from other men, who can read the eternal book of the stars, can you tell me the outcome of this contest?

MAXIMUS: Yes, my brother, I can tell you the outcome.

JULIAN: You can? Then say what it is! Who shall conquer, the Emperor or the Galilean?

MAXIMUS: Both the Emperor and the Galilean will disappear.

JULIAN: Disappear—? Both—?

MAXIMUS: Both. In our time or in centuries to come, I don't know. But it will happen when the right one appears.

JULIAN: And who is this right one?

MAXIMUS: He that combines both the Emperor and the Galilean.

JULIAN: You answer the riddle with a darker riddle.

MAXIMUS: Listen to me, brother and friend of truth. I tell you, they will both disappear—but not be destroyed. Doesn't the child disappear in the youth, and the youth in the man? But neither the child nor the youth is destroyed. And you, my most beloved pupil, have you forgotten our talk in Ephesus about the three empires?

JULIAN: Ah, Maximus, so many years lie between. Speak on!

MAXIMUS: You know I've never approved what you've done as Emperor. You wanted to turn the youth back into a child again. The empire of the flesh has been absorbed into the empire of the spirit. But the empire of the spirit is no more the ultimate state, than that of the youth is. You tried to stunt the youth's maturing—preventing him becoming a man. Oh, you fool, who drew your sword against the future—against the third empire where the twin-natured one shall rule!

JULIAN: And this—?

MAXIMUS: The Jews have a name for him. They call him the Messiah, and they wait for him.

JULIAN: *(Slowly and thoughtfully.)* The Messiah? Neither Emperor nor Redeemer?

MAXIMUS: Both in one and one in both.

JULIAN: Emperor-God and God-Emperor. Emperor of the realm of the Spirit and God of the realm of the Flesh.

MAXIMUS: *That* is the third empire, Julian!

JULIAN: Yes, Maximus, *that* is the third empire.

MAXIMUS: In *that* empire the transient call to rebellion shall become reality.

JULIAN: "Give to the Emperor what is the Emperor's, and to God what is God's." Yes, yes, that is the Emperor in God and God in the Emperor. Ah, dreams, dreams—who shall break the Galilean's power?

MAXIMUS: Where does the power of the Galilean lie?

JULIAN: I've searched into that in vain.

MAXIMUS: It is written somewhere: "Thou shalt have no other gods before me."

JULIAN: Yes, yes, yes!

MAXIMUS: The seer of Nazareth did not proclaim this god or that; he said "God is me; I am God."

JULIAN: Yes, this is beyond me—! And so the Emperor is powerless. The third empire? The Messiah? Not of the Jews but Messiah of the empires of the spirit and the world?

MAXIMUS: The God-Emperor.

JULIAN: The Emperor-God.

MAXIMUS: Logos in Pan—Pan in Logos.

JULIAN: Maximus, how will he manifest himself?

MAXIMUS: He will be manifested in the one who wills himself.

JULIAN: My beloved teacher, I must leave you.

MAXIMUS: Where are you going

JULIAN: To the city. The Persian King has offered terms of peace which I too hastily accepted. My envoys are on their way. They must be overtaken and recalled.

MAXIMUS: You're going to re-open the war with King Sapor?

JULIAN: I'll do what Cyrus dreamt of and Alexander attempted—

MAXIMUS: Julian!

JULIAN: I'll possess the world. Good night, my Maximus! *(He waves farewell and quickly leaves. MAXIMUS looks thoughtfully after him.)*

CHORUS OF PSALM-SINGERS:
Gods men have made of silver and gold
Shall crumble to mold.

END OF ACT THREE

PAGE 135

1 The second line is not in Homer. Julian (or Ibsen) seems to have misattributed a scholiast's annotation.

ACT FOUR

*On the empire's eastern borders. Wild mountain landscape. A deep valley
divides the high foreground from the background mountains. JULIAN, in
military dress, stands at the edge of a knoll and looks down into the valley. A little
apart from him NEVITA stands, with the Persian Prince HORMISDAS, the
General JOVIAN, and other commanding officers. To the right, by a hastily
constructed stone altar, the soothsayer NUMA and two other Etruscan soothsayers
are kneeling, searching the entrails of offerings for omens. Further forward,
MAXIMUS is sitting on a stone surrounded by the philosophers PRISCUS
and CHYTRON among others. Now and then small detachments of lightly
armed troops cross the mountain from right to left.*

JULIAN: *(Pointing downward.)* See there, the legions winding like an armored
    snake through the ravine.

NEVITA: Those right under us, in the sheepskin tunics, are the Scythians.

JULIAN: Such piercing howls—

NEVITA: It's the Scythians customary song, my lord!

JULIAN: More of a howl than a song.

NEVITA: Here come the Armenians. Arsaces is leading them.

JULIAN: The Roman legions must be out on the plains already. All the tribes in
    the area are hurrying to surrender. *(He turns to the commanders.)* On the
    Euphrates we've gathered twelve hundred ships with all our supplies and
    needs. I know for sure the fleet can navigate the old canal and sail right up
    to the Tigris. The entire army's to cross in the ships. Then we'll advance
    along the east bank as fast as the fleet can follow us upstream. Tell me,
    Hormisdas, what you think of these arrangements.

HORMISDAS: Invincible commander, I know that under your victorious
    protection, I'll be privileged again to set foot in my fatherland.

JULIAN: How good it feels getting away from that narrow-minded lot in the
    city. The terror in their eyes as they surrounded my chariot when I left them!
    "Come back soon, and be gentler to us than now," they shouted. I'll never
    go back to Antioch. I'll not look on the ungrateful city again. After I've won,
    I'll take my route home through Tarsus. *(Goes over to the soothsayers.)*
    Numa, what do you read in the omens for our action this morning?

NUMA: The omen says this year you shouldn't cross the empire's frontiers.

JULIAN: Hm! What do you make of the omen, Maximus?

MAXIMUS: This is how I see it: The omen's advising you to subjugate all the
    land you pass through. That way you'll not be crossing the empire's frontiers.

JULIAN: That's it. We need to look cannily at these obscure signs; so often a
    double meaning lies in them. At times it seems the mysterious powers like to

lead humans astray, especially in their major enterprises. Weren't there some who saw a sign of ill luck for us when the portico in Hierapolis collapsed and buried some fifty soldiers, just as we were passing through the city? But I claim it indicates a double blessing. First, it predicts the Persian kingdom will collapse; next it prophesies the fall of the unfortunate Galileans. Because those soldiers who were killed—who were they? Galilean prisoners, most reluctantly recruited into the war and so by destiny ordained for a sudden and dismal end.

JOVIAN: Most gracious Majesty, here comes a captain from the vanguard.

AMMIAN: *(Entering from the right.)* My lord, you've ordered me to report anything unusual occurring during our advance.

JULIAN: Well? Has something occurred this morning?

AMMIAN: Yes, my lord, a double omen.

JULIAN: So, Ammian—say what it is!

AMMIAN: First, my lord, when we'd marched some way past the village of Zaita, a huge lion broke out of the thickets and made straight for our soldiers, who then killed it with a shower of arrows.

JULIAN: Ah!

THE PHILOSOPHERS: What a happy omen!

HORMISDAS: King Sapor is called the Lion of the Lands.

NUMA: Turn back; turn back, Emperor Julian!

MAXIMUS: Go boldly forward, Victory's chosen one!

JULIAN: Turn back after this? Like that lion at Zaita, so the Lion of the Lands will fall before our arrows. Aren't there previous examples to back me up when I interpret this in our favor? Need I remind such learned men when Emperor Maximinian conquered the Persian king, Narses, there was a similar lion—and also a huge wild boar—who were slain in front of the Roman columns? *(To AMMIAN.)* But the other—? You mentioned two signs, I think.

AMMIAN: The other one's more doubtful, my lord. Your horse, Babylonius, as you instructed, was fully saddled and led out to wait for your coming down the other side of the mountain. But just then a company of Galilean prisoners was marched past. As they were heavily burdened they were less than willing, so we had to use the lash on them. In spite of this they raised their arms as if in joy, and burst into a song of praise for their god. This sudden noise made Babylonius shy, rear up in alarm and fall over backwards, and while he rolled on the ground the gold trappings were spattered and soiled with mud from the path.

NUMA: *(At the altar.)* Emperor Julian, turn back, turn back!

JULIAN: The Galileans did that out of malice but in fact, against their will, they've created an omen I welcome with joy. For, just as Babylonius fell, so Babylon likewise shall fall, stripped of its glories and magnificence.

PRISCUS: Wisely interpreted!

CHYTRON: By the gods, so it is!

THE OTHER PHILOSOPHERS: There's no other answer!

JULIAN: *(To NEVITA.)* Let the army continue its advance. Then this evening, to make absolutely sure, I'll make sacrifices and see what the omens determine. But as for you, you Etruscan clowns whom I brought here at such great cost, know I'll no longer tolerate you in the camp; you only serve to hurt the soldiers' morale. I tell you, you know nothing of the difficult skill you profess. What audacity! What overweening gall! Take them away! I don't want to see them again. *(Some of the guards drive the soothsayers out, left.)*

JULIAN: Babylonius fell. The lion struck down by my soldiers! Yet still we don't know what unseen help we can count on. There are times when the gods, whose nature we've not searched into enough, seem—dare I say?—either to be sleeping or to take very little part in human affairs. We seem to be living in such a sad time, my friends. We've even witnessed how certain gods have failed to support well-meant efforts to further their own interests and honor. We shouldn't judge further in this. It might be, the immortals who steer and sustain the world, choose certain times to transfer their powers to human hands—which in no way degrades the gods, since it's through them the especially favored man—if he's to be found—can advance in the world.

PRISCUS: Aren't your own actions, peerless Emperor, sufficient witness to that?

JULIAN: I don't know, Priscus, if I ought rate my own actions so highly. I won't go into the fact the Galileans consider the Jew, Jesus of Nazareth, just such a chosen one; since these people are mistaken—as I'll conclusively prove in my tract against them. But I will name Prometheus from ancient times, who heroically granted humans greater gifts than the immortals thought we merited—for which he suffered both great agony and contempt, until he was admitted at last into the company of the gods—where he truly belonged all the time.

And can't the same be said of Heracles and of Achilles and finally of the Macedonian Alexander, with whose exploits some have likened mine, while I was in Gaul and more especially regarding my aims in this campaign?

NEVITA: Your Majesty, The rearguard is below us now, maybe it's time to—

JULIAN: At once, Nevita! But first I want to tell you about a strange dream I had last night.

I dreamt I saw a child pursued by a rich man who owned numberless cattle, but disdained to serve the gods.

This evil man wiped out the child's whole family. But over the child himself Zeus held his pitying hand.

Then I saw this child grow into a youth under the protection of Minerva and Apollo.

I dreamt further that the youth fell asleep on a stone under the open sky.

Then Hermes descended to earth in the shape of a young man saying; "Come, I will show you the way that leads to the dwelling of the highest god!" Then he led the youth to the foot of a fearfully steep mountain. There he left him.

The youth then burst into tears and wailed and cried out to Zeus in a loud voice. And lo, Minerva and the Sun King who rules over the earth, came down to him, lifted him up to the mountain's summit, and revealed to him all his family's inheritance.

But this inheritance was the entire globe, from ocean to ocean and beyond.

They told the youth all this would belong to him. But they laid down three conditions: He should not sleep, as his kinsmen had done; he should not listen to the advice of hypocrites; and he should honor as gods those who resemble the gods. "Do not forget," they said before they left him, "you have an immortal soul, and this soul is of divine origin. And if you follow our advice you shall see our father and become a god like us."

PRISCUS: What sign and omens can compare to this?

CHYTRON: It's not too much to say the divine fates will think twice if their counsels don't match yours.

JULIAN: We can't confidently build on such an exception. But I really find this dream remarkable although my brother Maximus, from his silence— contrary to what one might expect—seems neither to like the dream nor the interpretation I put on it. Well, we must bear with that for the moment. *(He pulls out a scroll of paper.)* See this, Jovian? Early this morning in bed I set down what I dreamt. Take this, get a large number of copies made, and have it read to different regiments. I believe it's important that in a hazardous campaign like ours, with all its dangers and hardships, the soldiers should confidently place their fates in the hands of their leader, holding him infallible in things that affect the outcome of the war.

JOVIAN: I beg you, your Majesty, to excuse me from this.

JULIAN: What's this you're saying?

JOVIAN: That I daren't lend my hand to something contrary to the truth. Oh, listen to me, my noble lord and Emperor! Is there a single soldier who doubts he is safe in your hands? On the frontiers of Gaul, against horrendous numbers and disadvantages of every kind, didn't you win greater victories than any other leader of our time can boast of?

JULIAN: So—is this news?

JOVIAN: Everyone knows that up until now fortune has favored you in the most wonderful way. In learning you've no rivals among the living and in the fine art of eloquence you bear the prize among the best.

JULIAN: And so—in spite of all this—

JOVIAN: In spite of all this, my emperor, you are yet a man. But if you proclaim this dream to the army you're declaring you're a god—and in this I can't make myself your accomplice.

JULIAN: What do you say, friends, to this speech?

CHYTRON: It's impertinent enough to suggest ignorance.

JULIAN: It seems as if in your zeal for truth, Jovian you forget that the Emperor Antoninus, named the "Pious," was worshipped in a special temple in Rome as an immortal god. And not him alone, but also his wife, Faustina, and other emperors, both before and after that time.

JOVIAN: I know that, my lord—but our forefathers were not privileged to walk in the light of the truth.

JULIAN: *(With a long look at him.)* Ah, Jovian! Tell me, yesterday evening when I was reading the omens for the night, you approached and brought a message while I was ritually rinsing the blood from my hands.

JOVIAN: Yes, your Majesty!

JULIAN: In my haste I happened to splash some drops of water on your cloak. You drew back sharply and shook off the water as though your cloak had been polluted.

JOVIAN: My Emperor—that didn't escape you?

JULIAN: Did you intend it to escape me?

JOVIAN: Yes, my lord, that was a matter between me and the one true God.

JULIAN: Galilean!

JOVIAN: My lord, it was you who sent me to Jerusalem and I was a witness to everything that happened there. I've been thinking a lot since then; I've read the Christians' writings, have spoken with many of them, and I've concluded that in this teaching lies the divine truth.

JULIAN: Is it possible! Is this really possible? That's how this infectious insanity spreads itself. My closest companions—my own generals, are falling away from me.

JOVIAN: Place me foremost in front of your enemies, my lord, and you'll find I'll gladly give the Emperor that which is the Emperor's.

JULIAN: How much—?

JOVIAN: My life, my blood.

JULIAN: Life and blood are not enough. The one who shall rule, must rule over the wills and the minds of men. And here Jesus of Nazareth stands against me and wages war on my power. Don't imagine I will punish you, Jovian! The kind you belong to yearn for that happiness. And they call you martyrs afterwards. Right? Isn't that how they exalt those I've been forced to chastise for their obstinacy? Go to the front ranks! I don't need to see you again. Oh, this fraud you practice on me cloaked under talk of a double loyalty and a double empire! This shall be changed. Other kings as well as the Persian shall feel my foot on their neck. To the front ranks, Jovian!

JOVIAN: I will do my duty, my lord! *(He goes out to the right.)*

JULIAN: We'll not let this morning, so big with so many happy omens, become overcast. We'll take this, and much more, with a tranquil mind. My dream *shall* be announced to the army. You, Chytron, and you, my Priscus, and you other friends, shall see this is done in a worthy manner.

THE PHILOSOPHERS: With joy, with unutterable joy, my lord! *(They take the scroll and exit to the right.)*

JULIAN: I beg you, Hormisdas, not to doubt my power, though it might seem some headstrong spirits speak out here. Go, and you as well, Nevita, and all the rest of you, each to his duty; I'll follow when the army's assembled on the plain.

(All exit, right, except the EMPEROR and MAXIMUS.)

MAXIMUS: *(After a moment, he rises from the stone where he was sitting, and goes over to the EMPEROR.)* My sick brother!

JULIAN: More wounded than sick. When a deer's struck by a hunter's arrow it seeks out the thicket where the others can't see it. I could no longer bear to show myself in the streets of Antioch—and now I feel I can't show myself before the army.

MAXIMUS: No one sees you, friend, because they fumble in their blindness. You must become the doctor for their eyes; then they'll see you in your glory.

JULIAN: *(Staring down into the ravine.)* How deep it is beneath us! How distant and tiny they are, winding their way forward through the thorns and thickets by the stony river bed.

When we stood at the entrance to that narrow pass everyone to a man rushed into the gap. It cut the marching time by an hour, a fragment of effort saved—on the journey to death.

And the others eagerly flocked after. No thought of taking the path over the top; no longing for the fresh air up here expanding the chest and letting you breath freely. There they trudge, and trudge and trudge, and can't see how they've shrunk the heavens over them and don't know there are heights where its vaster. Maximus, isn't it as if men live only so that they die? The

Galilean's ghost's in this. If it's true, as it's said, his father created the world, then the son despises his father's work. And precisely for this blasphemous insanity he's praised so highly! Think what Socrates was compared to him! Didn't Socrates love pleasure, and joy and beauty? Yet he renounced them. But what a fathomless gulf between on the one side not desiring, and on the other desiring yet renouncing. It was this lost treasure of wisdom I wanted to give back to mankind. Like Dionysos before, I came to them full of joy and youth, with vine leaves on my brow and with grapes full and ripe in my arms. But they rejected my gifts and I am mocked and hated and reviled by friends and enemies.

MAXIMUS: Why? I'll tell you why. Close to a town where I once lived was a vineyard famous far and wide for its grapes; and when the townspeople wanted sweet fruit on their tables, they sent their servants out to that vineyard to fetch the grapes. Many years later I returned to that same town; but there was no one who any longer knew of those once so highly prized grapes. So I went to find the owner of the vineyard and asked him "Tell me, my friend, have your vines died since no one knows of them anymore." "No," he replied, "but, as you know, young vines give good grapes, but poor wine; old vines give poor grapes but good wine. "Therefore, Stranger," he answered, "I continue to gladden the hearts of my countrymen with this vineyard's abundance, but in another form—as wine, not as grapes."

JULIAN: *(Thoughtfully.)* Yes, yes, yes!

MAXIMUS: That's something you didn't consider. The world's vine has grown old but you believe that, as of old, you can go on offering grapes to those who now thirst after the new wine.

JULIAN: Ah, my Maximus, who is it who thirsts? Give one name, beyond our band of brothers, who yearns with spiritual needs. My misfortune's to be born in this age of iron.

MAXIMUS: Don't condemn the age. If the age had been greater, you would have been less. The world-soul is like a rich man who has countless sons. If he shares his riches equally among all the sons, all will be comfortable but none will be rich. If, instead, he disinherits all except one to whom he gives all, that one will be rich in a circle of poor men.

JULIAN: No parable applies less than this to me. Is that my situation? Don't many already share precisely what the ruler of the world should possess more richly than all the others; yes, I'd claim, what he alone should possess? See how power is divided! Doesn't Libanius possess the power of eloquence so richly he's called the king of orators? Don't you, Maximus, have the power of occult wisdom. Even the deranged Apollinaris of Antioch has the power of song and ecstasy to such a degree I envy him! And take the Cappadocian

Gregory! Doesn't he possess a raw power to such excess that many give him a name no mere subject should be given—the great! What's even more strange, the same name's applied to Gregory's friend, Basil, the gentle-hearted one with the girlish eyes. And he's not even active in the world, he lives *here*, this Basil, in this remote region, got up in hermit's dress, in the sole company of his disciples, with his sister, Macrina, and other women named pious and holy. And what don't they achieve, both he and his sister, through the letters that often issue from them! Everything, even self-denial and seclusion becomes a power against my power. But worst of all is the crucified Jew.

MAXIMUS: Then put an end to these spreading divisions of power! But don't think you can crush the rebels by attacking them like a commander-in-chief sent by a ruler they don't know. You must come in your own name, Julian! Did Jesus of Nazareth appear as if sent by another? Didn't he claim *he* was the one who sent him? In truth, the fulfillment of time is in you and you don't see it. Don't all signs and omens point like an infallible finger to you? Must I remind you of your mother's dream—?

JULIAN: She dreamt she gave birth to Achilles.

MAXIMUS: Must I remind you that fortune has borne you, as if on powerful wings, through a stormy and dangerous life? Who are you, lord? Aren't you the resurgent Alexander, earlier unready, but now equipped for the full task?

JULIAN: Maximus!

MAXIMUS: There is *one* who re-emerges at certain intervals in the life of the human race. He's like a rider entering the arena to tame a wild horse. Each time the horse throws him. In a moment the rider's in the saddle again, always more assured, always more skillful than before; but *down* he had to fall in his various shapes until the present day. He had to fall as the god-begotten man in the garden of Eden; he had to fall as founder of the world-empire; he had to fall as the Prince of God's Kingdom. Who knows how many times he's wandered among us without anyone recognizing him? Can you know, Julian, you weren't once in him you now persecute?

JULIAN: *(Gazes in the distance.)* Oh, unfathomable riddle!

MAXIMUS: Shall I remind you of that ancient prophecy which once again is circulating? It predicts that for as many years as the year has days—just so many years shall the Galilean's kingdom remain in power. In two years it will be three-hundred-and-sixty-five years since that man was born in Bethlehem.

JULIAN: You believe in this prophecy?

MAXIMUS: I believe in the one who is to come.

JULIAN: Always riddles!

MAXIMUS: I believe in the freedom of necessity.

JULIAN: Even more enigmatic.

MAXIMUS: Look, Julian, when Chaos seethed in the empty, horrible waste, and Jehovah was alone—that day when, according to the ancient Jewish writings, he stretched out his hand and parted light from darkness, sea from land—that day the great God of creation stood at the peak of his power. But with humankind other wills emerged on earth. And men and beasts and trees and plants shaped their kind after their own laws; and according to such eternal laws all the stars proceed in the firmament. Did Jehovah repent? The legends of all peoples speak of a repentant Creator. But he implanted the law of self-preservation in his Creation. Too late to repent! The created *wills* to preserve itself: and so it is preserved. But the two one-sided empires wage war on each other. Where is he, where is he, the King of Peace, the twin-natured one, who shall reconcile them?

JULIAN: *(To himself.)* Two years? All the gods inactive. No capricious power lurking, plotting to cross my plans. Two years? In two years I can subject the earth to my rule.

MAXIMUS: You spoke, my Julian—what did you say?

JULIAN: I'm young and strong and healthy. Maximus, it's my intention to live long. *(He goes out to the right. MAXIMUS follows him.)*

(A hilly forested area with a stream running between the trees. Upon the heights a small estate. It is almost sunset.

Detachments of troops march past from the left to the right at the base of the hill. BASIL OF CAESAREA and his sister, MACRINA, both in hermit dress, stand below by the wayside and hand out water and fruit to the weary soldiers.)

MACRINA: Look, Basil, each one paler, each more wearied than the previous one.

BASIL: And such a multitude of Christian brothers among them! A curse on Emperor Julian! This is more fiendishly conceived than all the agonies of the torture chamber. Who is he leading his armies against? Much less against the King of Persia than against Christ.

MACRINA: You think it's as appalling as that?

BASIL: Yes, Macrina, I see more and more it's against *us* the fight's directed. All the setbacks he suffered in Antioch, all the opposition he met with, all the humiliation and disappointment he had to endure for his ungodly actions, he now wishes to bury in oblivion by a victorious campaign. And he'll succeed. All men are like that. They see success conferring right; and most will submit to power.

MACRINA: *(Pointing to the left.)* New battalions. Countless. Endless—

(A detachment of troops pass by; a young man in the ranks falls down on the wayside, exhausted.)

AN OFFICER: *(Striking him with his baton.)* Get up there, you lazy dog!

MACRINA: *(Rushing forward.)* Oh, don't hit him!

THE SOLDIER: Let them hit me—I'll suffer gladly.

AMMIAN: *(Arriving.)* Still more delay! Ah, it's him. Can he really go no further?

OFFICER: I hardly know what to say, sir; he falls down every other minute.

MACRINA: Ah, be patient! Who is this poor man? Here, suck the juice from this fruit. Who is he, sir?

AMMIAN: A Cappadocian, one of those madmen who defiled the temple of Venus in Antioch.

MACRINA: Oh, one of those martyrs—!

AMMIAN: Try to get up, Agathon! I have to pity the fellow. They punished him more than he could take. He's not been in his right mind ever since.

AGATHON: *(Gets up.)* I can take it well enough. And I'm completely in my right mind, sir! Beat me, beat me—I'll suffer it gladly.

AMMIAN: *(To the OFFICER.)* Move forward, we can't waste time here.

OFFICER: *(To the soldiers.)* Forward, forward.

AGATHON: Babylonius fell; soon shall the Babylonian fall. The lion of Zaita was brought down—the crowned lion of the world shall be brought down. *(The soldiers are driven out, right.)*

AMMIAN: *(To BASIL and MACRINA.)* You're strange people. Wrong-headed yet you do good. Thanks for comforting my weary men; I only wish the Emperor's cause let me treat your brethren as leniently as I'd like. *(He exits right.)*

BASIL: God go with you, noble pagan!

MACRINA: Who could that man be!

BASIL: I don't know him. *(Pointing to the left.)* Look, look, there he is himself!

MACRINA: The Emperor? Is it the Emperor?

BASIL: Yes, it's him.

(JULIAN, with several generals, enters left accompanied by a detachment of the IMPERIAL BODYGUARD commanded by ANATOLUS.)

JULIAN: *(To his companions.)* What's this—you're tired? Because a horse falls, I should stand still? Rather, isn't it more fitting to go on foot than to ride a poor animal? Tired! My ancestor declared an emperor should die standing. I say an emperor ought show an example of endurance as long as he lives and not only at the hour of his death. But, by the great light of heaven, do my eyes look upon Basil of Cesarea?

BASIL: *(Bowing low.)* Your humble servant, oh mighty Emperor!

JULIAN: Yes, I should believe that! A fine way you serve me, in truth, Basil!

(Approaches.) So this is the house that's become famous for the letters issuing out of it! Throughout all the land this house is more talked about than are the classrooms, though I've spared neither effort nor pains to get *them* on their feet again. And I take it this woman must be your sister, Macrina.

BASIL: That's so, my lord!

JULIAN: You're a beautiful woman, and still young. And yet I'm told you've renounced life.

MACRINA: My lord, I've renounced life to live in truth.

JULIAN: Ah, I know all about these delusions of yours. You sigh for what lies in the beyond, of which you can know nothing certain; you mortify the flesh; you shrink from all human desires. And yet, I tell you, this can be a form of vanity as much as any other.

BASIL: Don't imagine, my lord, I'm blind to the danger that lies in renouncing. I know very well my friend Gregory's right when he writes that he's convinced he can be a hermit in his heart without being one in the flesh. And I know, too, this rough garment won't profit my soul if I reckoned wearing it a virtue. But I don't feel it that way. This life of seclusion fills me with inexpressible joy; that's all. The violent convulsions the world is going through in our time, in all their hideousness, don't disturb me here. Here I find my body lifted up in prayer, and my soul purified by this simple way of life.

JULIAN: Oh, my self-effacing Basil, I feel you're after more than that. If what they say is true, your sister here has assembled a circle of young women to be molded in her own image. And you yourself, just like your Galilean master, have selected twelve disciples. What do you intend doing with them?

BASIL: To send them out into the world to strengthen our brothers in the struggle.

JULIAN: Just so! And, equipped with all the weapons of eloquence, this army's to be sent against me. And all that eloquence, that beautiful art of Greece, where did you get it from? From our classrooms. And what right do you have to it? You've sneaked like a spy into our camp to find out where we're most vulnerable. And now you're using this knowledge to inflict the greatest damage. You must know, Basil, I'm no longer disposed to take this abuse any longer. I'll strike your weapons from your hands. Stick to Matthew and Luke and similar uncouth scribblers. From now on you won't be allowed to interpret our ancient poets nor our ancient philosophers; because I hold it unreasonable for you to draw knowledge and benefit from sources whose truth you don't believe in. For the same reason Galilean students will be banned from our classrooms. For why are they there? To steal our skills and use them against us.

BASIL: My lord, I'd already heard of this curious injunction. And I'm with Gregory when he writes you've no exclusive claim to Greek learning nor Greek eloquence. I must side with him when he says *you* use an alphabet invented by the Egyptians, and wear the purple first put to use by the people of Tyre. But more than this, my lord. You overrun lands and exercise rule over races whose languages you cannot understand, and whose customs you don't know. It's your right to do that. But that same right you have in the visible world, he whom you call the Galilean has in the invisible—

JULIAN: Enough of that! I'll no longer listen to such talk. You speak as if there were two rulers of the world, and with this construction, oppose me at every turn. You are ridiculous! You set the dead against the living. But you'll soon know the true situation. The treatise I've been writing against you for a long time now—don't think I've set it aside on account of the war. Maybe you imagine I spend my nights in sleep? You're sadly mistaken! The "Beard-Hater" earned me some mockery—even from many who might have benefited by taking its truths to heart. But that won't discourage me. Any more than a man with a stick in his hand can decently give way before a pack of barking dogs. Why do you smile, woman? What was it you laughed at?

MACRINA: My lord, why do your rage so furiously against one you call dead?

JULIAN: Ah, I understand! You want to say he still lives.

MACRINA: What I say, oh mighty lord, is that your heart feels he is still alive.

JULIAN: I? I should feel—?

MACRINA: What is it you hate and yet persecute? Not him, but your belief in him. Just as he lives in your hatred and persecution, so he lives in our love.

JULIAN: I know your riddling way of speaking. You Galileans say one thing but mean another. And this you call the art of rhetoric! Oh, you mediocrities! What idiocy! I feel the crucified Jew lives, you say? To what level has an age sunk that can be satisfied with that stuff! But people today are no better than that. Madness is reckoned wisdom. How many countless nights haven't I spent sleepless and searching for the true foundation of things? But where are those who will follow me? Many praise my words; but few or none let themselves be won over. However, it's not yet the end. Something's about to amaze you. You shall grasp how all that is scattered is striving to unite as one. You shall discover all you now despise possesses glory within it—that the cross you hang your hopes on I shall hammer into a ladder for him you do not know.

MACRINA: And I say to you, Emperor, you are no more than a scourge in God's hand—a scourge appointed to punish us for our sins. To our shame this has to be so. To our shame our divisions and loss of love have led us to stray from the true path! There was no longer any king in Israel. Therefore the Lord struck you with madness that you might chastise us. What a spirit has he not clouded so that it should rage against us. What a blossoming tree has he not stripped to make rods for our sin-laden shoulders? There were omens to warn you but you would not heed them. Voices called you but you would not hear them. Hands wrote their messages of fire on the wall for you, but you erased the writing you refused to decipher.

JULIAN: Basil, I wish I'd known this woman before today.

BASIL: Come, Macrina!

MACRINA: Alas, that I had to look into those shining eyes! Angel and serpent united in one; the apostate's yearning and the tempter's cunning. How have our brothers and sisters kept high their hopes of victory in the presence of such a Messenger? In him is someone greater. Don't you see, Basil, in him the Lord God will strike us so we die.

JULIAN: You have said it!

MACRINA: Not I!

JULIAN: The first soul is won!

MACRINA: Go away from me!

BASIL: Come—come!

JULIAN: Stay here! Anatalus, they're under guard! It's my will you shall go with the army—both you and your disciples, the young and the women.

BASIL: My lord, you cannot want this!

JULIAN: It's not wise to leave fortresses in the rear. See, I wave my hand and wipe out the shower of burning arrows you've launched from that little house.

BASIL: No, no, my lord—this violence—

MACRINA: Ah, Basil, here or elsewhere—all is finished!

JULIAN: Isn't it written you shall give to Emperor that which is the Emperor's? I need all the hands I can muster for this campaign. You can look after my sick and wounded. That will be serving the Galilean at the same time; and if you still consider that a duty make good use of your time. He hasn't many days left.

(Some soldiers surround BASIL and MACRINA; others march off quickly through the thicket toward the house.)

MACRINA: The sun is setting over our home, with it is sinking hope and the light of the world! Oh, Basil, that we should live to see the night.

BASIL: The light remains.

JULIAN: The light's yet to come. Turn your backs on the sunset, Galileans. Look to the east, to the east, where Helios dreams. For truly I say to you, you shall behold the Sun King claim this earth. *(He goes out to the right; all follow him.)*

(Beyond the Euphrates and the Tigris. A broad plain with the imperial camp. Bushes to the left in the background hide the windings of the Tigris. Masts of ships rise above the bushes and extend into the far distance. It is a cloudy evening.

SOLDIERS and MILITARY PERSONNEL of all kinds are preparing the camp. All kinds of stores are being brought from the ships. In the far distance watch fires can be seen. NEVITA, JOVIAN, and several commanders arrive from the fleet.)

NEVITA: Now you can see how right the Emperor's choice was. Here we stand on enemy soil without having struck a blow; no one opposed us as we crossed the river; not so much as a single Persian horseman in sight.

JOVIAN: No, my lord, the enemy didn't expect us to take this route.

NEVITA: You say that as if you still thought it an unwise route to take.

JOVIAN: Yes, my lord, it's still my belief we should have set out on a more northerly path. Then we'd have had our left flank covered by Armenia, which is friendly to us; and we'd have got all the provisions we needed from that fertile countryside. Whereas here? Our progress is hampered by the heavy supply ships. Surrounding us a barren plain—almost a desert—ah, here is the Emperor. I'll leave; he's not much pleased with me these days.

(He exits to the right. At the same moment JULIAN arrives from the ships with some of his attendants. ORIBASES, PRISCUS, and CHYTRON together with some others, appear between the tents to the right and go to greet the EMPEROR.)

JULIAN: And so we see the empire increase. Each step I take eastwards expands the empire's frontier. *(Stamps on the ground.)* This earth is mine! I'm still within the empire, not outside it. Well, Priscus—?

PRISCUS: Incomparable Emperor, your orders have been carried out. What you so miraculously dreamt we've had read out to the whole army.

JULIAN: Good, good. And what effect did the dream have on the soldiers?

CHYTRON: Some raised their voices in joyful praise, proclaiming you divine; others, however—

PRISCUS: These others were the Galileans, Chytron!

CHYTRON: Yes, yes, most of the others were Galileans; and they beat their breasts and sent up a howl of anguish.

JULIAN: I shan't stop there. The busts of myself I've had prepared to be set up in the cities I shall conquer, are to be placed by every paymaster's table in the camp. Lamps shall be lit either side of the busts, braziers of sweet-smelling incense shall burn before each, and every soldier, as he steps forward to receive his pay, shall throw some grains of incense on the fire.

ORIBASES: Most gracious Emperor, forgive me, but is that advisable?

JULIAN: Why not advisable? I'm astonished at you, my dear Oribases!

PRISCUS: Ah, my lord, you might well be astonished! Not advisable to—!

CHYTRON: Shouldn't a Julian dare what men less divine have dared?

JULIAN: My conviction is it would be far more risky to impose censorship on the advice of the mysterious powers. If we've come so far that the divine beings are placing their powers in earthly hands—as so many signs encourage us to infer—then truly it would be the height of ingratitude to conceal the fact. In such a dangerous situation as ours, it's hardly immaterial whether the soldiers should direct their worship to the wrong object when they could invoke a totally different one. I must tell you, Oribases and you others, if anyone else here would set such limits to the imperial power—that, precisely, would be the real impiety I'd be compelled to confront. Hasn't Plato already announced the truth that only a god can rule over men? What did he mean by that? Answer me—what did he mean? I'm far from insisting that Plato—that matchless philosopher—was prophesying with any particular person in mind, not even the most exalted. But I think we all can bear witness to the chaos that arises when the supreme power is broken up and shared by several hands. Enough of that. I've already ordered that the imperial busts be set up throughout the camp. But what brings you here, Eutherius, in such a state?

(EUTHERIUS the chamberlain enters from the ships accompanied by a man with his cloak hitched up.)

EUTHERIUS: Most High Emperor, this man from Antioch has been sent by Governor Alexander, with a letter he claims is important.

JULIAN: Ah, let's see! Light here! *(A torch is brought. The EMPEROR opens the letter and reads.)*

JULIAN: Can this be possible! More light! Yes, there it is—and here—what now? This truly goes beyond anything I could have imagined!

NEVITA: Bad news from the west, my lord?

JULIAN: Nevita, tell me how much time's needed to get from here to Ctesiphon?

NEVITA: It can't possibly be done in less than thirty days.

JULIAN: It's *got* to be done in less time! Thirty days! A whole month! And while we're creeping along here, should I let those madmen—

NEVITA: You know your self, my lord, we must follow all the windings of the river because of the ships. The current's strong and therefore shallow and stony. I don't think it's possible to go faster.

JULIAN: Thirty days! And after, there's the taking of the city; the Persian army to be put to flight—and then peace concluded. How much time will all that need? Yet some among you advised me to go via a longer detour. Ha! They're plotting my ruin.

NEVITA: My lord, be easy; the march will go forward with full vigor.

JULIAN: It certainly will need to. Can you imagine what Alexander reports? The Galileans' madness has broken all bounds since my departure. And the abomination gets worse every day. They realize my victory in Persia will bring about their destruction; and with the insolent Gregory as their leader they're like an enemy army active behind the lines. In Phrygia many secret plots are being hatched which no one can track down.

NEVITA: What does it mean, my lord? What are they up to?

JULIAN: What are they up to? Praying, preaching, singing, prophesying the end of the world. If only that were all—but they're dragging our followers down with them, luring them into their seditious company. In Cesarea the congregation's elected Eusebius as bishop—Eusebius the unbaptized—and the confused creature's accepted the call contrary even to their own church law. However, that's far from being the worst. Worse, worse, ten times worse, is that Athanasius has returned to Alexandria.

NEVITA: Athanasius?

PRISCUS: That enigmatic bishop who disappeared into the desert six years ago?

JULIAN: A church council expelled him for his unorthodox zeal. The Galileans were docile under my predecessor. Well, just think about it—now this raving visionary's returned to Alexandria. His entry was like a monarch's; the roadway strewn with carpets and green palm branches. And what happened after? What do you imagine? That same night revolt broke out among the Galileans. George, their lawful bishop, that moderate and accommodating man, whom they accused of being lukewarm in the faith, was murdered, torn to pieces in the city streets.

NEVITA: But my lord, how could things get so far out of hand? Where was the governor, Artemesius?

JULIAN: You may well ask where Artemesius was. I'll tell you. He's gone over to the Galileans! Artemesius himself, armed, broke his way into the Serapeum, the world's most superb temple, smashed the statues, plundered the altars, and destroyed the irreplaceable treasures of the library which our misguided and ignorant age has such desperate need of; and for which I could weep as for a friend snatched away by death, except I'm too angry for tears.

CHYTRON: Truly, this passes all understanding!

JULIAN: And not to be able to catch the culprits and punish them! To have to be a witness as such outrages take hold more and more! Thirty days, you say! Why do we hang back? Why are we setting up camp? Why are we sleeping? Don't my generals know what's at stake? We must hold a council. When I think of what the Macedonian Alexander could achieve in thirty days—

(JOVIAN, accompanied by an unarmed man in Persian dress, enters from the camp.)

JOVIAN: Don't be angry, my lord, for appearing before you; but this stranger—

JULIAN: A Persian warrior!

PERSIAN: *(Throwing himself on the ground.)* No warrior, most mighty one!

JOVIAN: He came unarmed, urging his horse across the plains, and reported to the outposts—

JULIAN: So your countrymen are close by?

PERSIAN: No, no!

JULIAN: Then where have you come from?

PERSIAN: *(Pulling aside his clothes.)* See these arms, lord of the world, bloody from rusted chains. Feel this flayed back, wound after wound! I come from the torture chamber, my lord.

JULIAN: Ah, you are fleeing from King Sapor?

PERSIAN: Yes, mighty one who knows all things. I stood high in King Sapor's esteem until, driven by fear at your approach, I ventured to predict this war would cause his downfall. Would you know, my lord, how he rewarded me? He gave my wife as a prize to the archers from the mountains; he had my children sold as slaves; all my possessions he gave to his servants to share among themselves. He had me tortured for nine days. Then he ordered me to ride out into the wilderness and die like an animal.

JULIAN: And what do you want with me?

PERSIAN: After such treatment? I want to help you destroy my persecutor.

JULIAN: Ah, unhappy man—how can you help?

PERSIAN: I can fasten wings to the feet of your soldiers.

JULIAN: What are you telling me? Stand up and say what you mean.

PERSIAN: *(Getting up.)* No one in Ctesiphon imagined you would choose this route—

JULIAN: That I know.

PERSIAN: It's no longer a secret.

JULIAN: You're lying man! You Persians know nothing of my plans.

PERSIAN: My lord, whose wisdom comes from the fire and the sun, know that my countrymen know of your plans. You've crossed the river in your ships; these ships, more than a thousand in all, and loaded with everything your army needs, are to be towed up the Tigris with your army advancing beside them.

JULIAN: Incredible—!

PERSIAN: When the fleet approaches Ctesiphon as closely as possible—which means two day's journey from the city—you will march on it at once, surround it, and force King Sapor to surrender.

JULIAN: *(Looking around.)* Who has betrayed us?

PERSIAN: This plan can no longer be carried out. My countrymen have hastily built stone dams across the river on which your ships will be stranded.

JULIAN: Do you realize, fellow, what this will cost you if you're not telling the truth?

PERSIAN: My body's in your power, mighty lord. If I'm not speaking the truth you're free to have me burned alive.

JULIAN: *(To NEVITA.)* The river blocked! It will take weeks to make it navigable again.

NEVITA: If it *can* be done, my lord. The equipment we'll need—

JULIAN: And this has to happen now, now that we urgently need a victory—

PERSIAN: Master of the world, I told you I could give your army wings.

JULIAN: Speak! You know a shorter route?

PERSIAN: If you promise me, after your victory, to restore my possessions and get me a new bride of noble birth—

JULIAN: I promise you all you want; just speak, speak!

PERSIAN: If you take the route straight across the plains you can stand before the walls of Ctesiphon in four days.

JULIAN: Aren't you forgetting the mountain range beyond the plains?

PERSIAN: My lord, have you not hard tell of a secret pass through the mountains?

JULIAN: Yes, a ravine. Ahriman's Way, they call it. Is it true such a thing exists?

PERSIAN: I rode through Ahriman's Way two days ago.

JULIAN: Nevita!

NEVITA: Indeed, my lord, if this *is* true—!

JULIAN: Miraculous help when we need it!

PERSIAN: But if you intend taking this route there's no time to lose. The Persian army's been recalled from the northern provinces to close the mountain passes.

JULIAN: Do you know this for sure?

PERSIAN: Delay, and you'll discover it.

JULIAN: How many days will your countryman take to get there?

PERSIAN: Four days my lord.

JULIAN: Nevita, we must get to the other side of that pass in three days!

NEVITA: *(To the PERSIAN.)* Is it feasible to cross the pass in three days?

PERSIAN: Yes, great warrior, it's feasible if you start tonight.

JULIAN: We must strike camp! No sleep, no rest tonight. In four days—five at the most—I must stand in front of Ctesiphon. What are you thinking about? Ah, I know.

NEVITA: The fleet, my lord!

JULIAN: Yes, yes, yes, the fleet.

NEVITA: If the Persian army arrives at the pass a day later than we, then—even if they can't inflict any other damage—they'll turn against your ships.

JULIAN:—And seize a huge booty with which to continue the war—

NEVITA: If we could leave twenty thousand men with the ships they'd be protected—

JULIAN: What are you thinking of? Twenty thousand? Almost a third of all fighting men. Where would be the forces I'd need to win with? Split, scattered, divided. I can't spare a single man for such a purpose. No, no, Nevita, there must be a third way—

NEVITA: *(Recoiling.)* My great Emperor—!

JULIAN: The fleet must neither fall into Persian hands nor use up our manpower. I say there's a third choice. Why do you hang back? Why not say what you think?

NEVITA: *(To the Persian.)* Do you know if Ctesiphon is stocked with corn and oil?

PERSIAN: Ctesiphon has abundant stocks of all kinds.

JULIAN: And once we get into the city, the whole rich land lies open before us.

PERSIAN: The people will open their gates for you, my lord! I'm not the only one who hates King Sapor. They'll rise up against him and fall at your feet if you appear swiftly and terribly with all your gathered strength.

JULIAN: That's right; that's right!

PERSIAN: Burn the ships, my lord!

NEVITA: Ah!

JULIAN: His hatred can see, while your loyalty's blinkered, Nevita!

NEVITA: My loyalty saw, my lord, but didn't like what it saw.

JULIAN: Aren't these ships like fetters on our progress. We've provisions for four whole days in camp. It's best the soldiers not be loaded down. And what use are the ships anyway? We've no more rivers to cross.

NEVITA: My lord, if that's really your will—

JULIAN: My will, my will? Oh, on an evening like this—wild and tempestuous— why can't lightning strike and—

MAXIMUS: *(Excitedly entering from the left.)* Child favored by the Sun, hear me!

JULIAN: Not just now, my Maximus!

MAXIMUS: No time more than now. You must hear me!

JULIAN: In the name of fortune and wisdom, then speak, my brother!

MAXIMUS: *(Draws him aside and says quietly.)* You know I've searched and studied in books and omens, to find out the fate of this campaign.

JULIAN: I know you've been unable to foretell anything.

MAXIMUS: The omens spoke and the books agreed; but the answers that kept coming were so strange I had to believe I was mistaken.

JULIAN: But now—?

MAXIMUS: When we left Antioch I wrote to Rome to consult the Sybilline books—

JULIAN: Yes, yes—!

MAXIMUS: The answer's just now arrived; a messenger from Antioch's Governor has brought it—

JULIAN: Ah, Maximus, and it says—?

MAXIMUS: It says what all the omens and books told me; and now I can interpret. Be happy, my brother, you're invincible in this battle.

JULIAN: The prophecy, the prophecy?

MAXIMUS: The Sybilline books say, "Julian must beware of Phrygia."

JULIAN: *(Recoiling.)* Of Phrygia—? Ah, Maximus!

MAXIMUS: Why so pale, my brother?

JULIAN: Tell me, beloved teacher—how do you read this answer?

MAXIMUS: Is more than one meaning thinkable? Phrygia? What's Phrygia to you? In Phrygia, a land lying out of the way and far behind you, where you've no need to set foot? No danger threatens you, lucky man—that's the meaning.

JULIAN: This oracle's ambiguous. No danger threatens me in battle—but from that distant place—Nevita! Nevita!

NEVITA: My lord—?

JULIAN: In Phrygia, then? Alexander writes of clandestine plots hatching in Phrygia. Once it was foretold the Galilean would return—burn the ships, Nevita!

NEVITA: My lord, is that your firm, unalterable decision—?

JULIAN: Burn them! Don't hold back. Secret perils threaten us from behind. *(To one of the captains.)* Pay close attention to this foreigner. He'll act as a guide. Give him food and drink and see he gets a good rest.

JOVIAN: My Emperor, I beg you, don't build your confidence on the words of such a deserter.

JULIAN: Aha! You seem dismayed, my Galilean counselor. Things aren't going the way you like. Maybe you know more than you care to say. Go, Nevita, and burn the ships!

(NEVITA bows and goes out left. The CAPTAIN leads the PERSIAN away between the tents.)

JULIAN: Traitors in my own camp! Wait, wait—I'll get to the bottom of all their craftiness. The camp shall strike! Go, Jovian, and see that the advance troops move out within the hour. The Persian knows the way. Go!

JOVIAN: As you command, noble Emperor! *(He goes out to the right.)*

MAXIMUS: You're burning the fleet? You must have something big in mind.

JULIAN: I wonder if the Macedonian Alexander would have dared this?

MAXIMUS: Did Alexander know from where the danger threatened?

JULIAN: True, true! *I* know it. All the powers that bring victory are in league with me. Omens and signs reveal their secret knowledge to fulfill my empire. Wasn't it said of the Galilean that spirits came and served him? Whom do the spirits serve now? What would the Galilean say were he invisibly among us?

MAXIMUS: He would say, "The third empire is at hand."

JULIAN: The third empire has come, Maximus! I sense that the world's Messiah lives in me. Spirit is made flesh, and flesh spirit. All creation lies within my will and my power. Look, look, there the first sparks are flaring. Flames are licking the rigging and the forest of masts. *(Cries out to the fire.)* Burn, burn!

MAXIMUS: The wind responds to your will. It rises to serve you.

JULIAN: *(Commanding, with clenched fist.)* Storm gather! Westerly! Obey my will!

FROMENTINUS: *(Entering from the right.)* Gracious lord, allow me to warn you. There's dangerous disturbance in the camp.

JULIAN: I'll not suffer any more trouble. The army will advance.

FROMENTINUS: Yes, my emperor—but the insolent Galileans—

JULIAN: The Galileans. What of them?

FROMENTINUS: The paymasters prepared to distribute pay to the soldiers and set up your noble bust before the tables—

JULIAN: That's to be the practice from now on.

FROMENTINUS: Each man was told, as he stepped forward, to cast some incense in the burners—

JULIAN: Well then—?

FROMENTINUS: Many Galilean soldiers did so without thinking about it further; but others refused—

JULIAN: What's that! They refused?

FROMENTINUS: At first, my lord; but when the paymasters explained it was an old custom with nothing to do with religion—

JULIAN: Aha, what then?

FROMENTINUS: Then they fell into line and did what they were told.

JULIAN: As you see; they fell into line!

FROMENTINUS: But later, my lord, our own men smiled and sneered at them and thoughtlessly told them it would be best they got rid of the signs of the cross and the fish which they tattoo on their arms; seeing they'd just worshipped the divine Emperor.

JULIAN: Yes, yes. And the Galileans?

FROMENTINUS: They broke out into loud wailing—listen, listen to them, my lord. It's impossible to speak reason to them. *(Wild cries are heard coming from the tents.)*

JULIAN: Madmen! Rebellious to the end. Don't they know their master's power is broken?

(Christian soldiers rush onto the plain. Some beat their breasts; others tear their clothes, all the time weeping and crying out.)

A SOLDIER: Christ died for me, and I betrayed him!

ANOTHER SOLDIER: God in Heaven who punishes, strike me; I've served false gods!

AGATHON: The devil on the imperial throne has destroyed my soul! Oh! oh! oh!

OTHER SOLDIERS: *(Ripping off the discs they wear round their necks.)* We will not serve idols!

STILL OTHERS: This God-forsaken one's not our ruler. We want to go home! Home!

JULIAN: Fromentius, seize these madmen. Cut them down!

(FROMENTINUS and many others move to attack the Christian soldiers. At that moment a huge fire flares; flames rise up from the ships.)

OFFICERS AND MEN: The fleet's on fire!

JULIAN: Yes, the fleet is burning. And more than the fleet is burning. On that red, flaring bonfire the crucified Galilean is burning to ashes; and the earthly Emperor is burning with the Galilean. But up from the ashes will rise—like that miraculous bird—the God of the Earth and the Emperor of the Spirit in *one,* in *one,* in *one!*

MANY VOICES: Madness has struck him!

NEVITA: *(Entering from the left.)* It is fulfilled.

JOVIAN: *(Rushing from the camp.)* Stop! Stop! Stop!

JULIAN: Burn, burn!

AMMIAN: *(From the camp.)* My lord, you're betrayed! The Persian deserter—he deceived you—

JULIAN: You're lying, man! Where is he?

AMMIAN: Fled!

JOVIAN: Those who escorted him said he seemed to be snatched from their hands.

AMMIAN: His horse has gone from its stall. He must have escaped over the plains.

JULIAN: Put out the fire, Nevita!

NEVITA: Impossible, my Emperor!

JULIAN: Put it out, put it out! It *shall* be possible!

NEVITA: Nothing's more impossible. All the moorings have been cut; all the ships are drifting toward the burning wrecks.

HORMISDAS: *(Entering from the tents.)* A curse on my countrymen! Oh, my lord, that you could listen to that crafty individual.

SHOUTS FROM THE CAMP: The fleet's burning. Cut off from home! Death in front of us!

AGATHON: Idolater, idolater, now bid the flames to die!

JOVIAN: The storm's increasing. The fire's like a raging sea—

MAXIMUS: *(Whispering.)* Guard yourself against Phrygia.

JULIAN: *(Calling out to the army.)* Let the fleet burn! In seven days you shall burn Ctesiphon.

END OF ACT FOUR

ACT FIVE

A barren stony plain without trees or grass. To the right is the EMPEROR's tent. Afternoon. Exhausted soldiers lie in groups on the ground. Now and then detachments of the army pass from left to right. Outside the tent PRISCUS and CHYTRON with several others of the Emperor's suite are waiting tensely ad anxiously. The Captain of the Bodyguard, ANATALUS, with other soldiers, stands before the entrance to the tent.

CHYTRON: It's unbelievable how long this war council's taking!

PRISCUS: Yes, you'd think they'd only one choice: Go forward or turn back.

CHYTRON: There's no sense in it. Tell me, Anatalus, why in the name of the gods don't we go forward?

PRISCUS: Yes, why alarm us like this, halting here in the middle of the desert?

ANATALUS: See that haze quivering on the horizon, north, east and south?

CHYTRON: Of course, of course; it's the heat—

ANATALUS: The plain's on fire.

PRISCUS: What's that? The plain's burning?

CHYTRON: Don't make such grim jokes, Anatalus. Tell us what it is.

ANATALUS: I'm telling you the plain's on fire. Out there, where the desert ends, the Persians have set fire to the grass. We can't go anywhere until the ground's cooled down.

CHYTRON: Oh, how appalling. There's barbarians for you! Resorting to such tactics.

PRISCUS: But that means there's no choice. No food, no water. Why don't we go back?

ANATALUS: Over the Tigris and Euphrates?

CHYTRON: And the fleet's burnt! Is that the way to fight this war? Really, the Emperor should be thinking more of his friends! How am I to get home again?

ANATALUS: You, like the rest of us, my friend!

CHYTRON: Like the rest? Like the rest? Oh, brilliantly put! It's different for you. You're soldiers. It's your calling to put up with inconveniences. I'm just not used to them. I didn't follow my Emperor to get into such a pickle. I'm being pestered by midges and poisonous flies—just look at my hands!

PRISCUS: We definitely didn't come here for this. We agreed to follow the army to compose panegyrics on the victories the Emperor's supposed to win. What's become of these victories? What's been accomplished in the six tedious weeks since the fleet went up in flames? The destruction of a few deserted towns not fit to describe. The display in the camp of a few prisoners the vanguard's reputed to have taken. I've not the slightest notion what battles this took place in. And those prisoners had the suspicious appearance of being hastily snatched up shepherds and farmers…

CHYTRON: And then they had to burn the fleet. Didn't I say at the time that would be a source of misfortune?

ANATALUS: It's not what I heard.

CHYTRON: What? I didn't say that? You heard me, Priscus; didn't I say that?

PRISCUS: I'm not exactly sure, my friend; but I know I protested in vain against that foolhardy decision. Yes, I can say I've been against the whole campaign at this time of the year. What impatience! What could the Emperor have had in mind? Is this the same hero who fought with such masterful success on the Rhine? It could make you think he's been struck with blindness or become sick in his mind.

ANATALUS: Sshh, sshh. What kind of talk is that?

CHYTRON: Yes, our Priscus certainly put it a little indelicately. But I'm bound to confess I detect a woeful lack of wisdom in a number of the imperial philosopher's latest actions. How rash to set up his bust in the camp and let himself be worshipped as a god! How foolish to so openly insult the strange teacher from Nazareth, who, it must be said, commands remarkable powers that could have brought us all some good under these dangerous circumstances. Ah, here comes Nevita himself. Now we'll get to hear—

(NEVITA enters from the tent. In the entrance, he turns and directs a sign inside. Immediately after, ORIBASES comes out.)

NEVITA: *(Drawing the physician aside.)* Tell me frankly, Oribases—is anything wrong with the Emperor's mind?

ORIBASES: Why do you ask that, sir?

NEVITA: How else should I explain his behavior?

ORIBASES: Oh, my beloved Emperor—!

NEVITA: Oribases, you mustn't hide anything from me.

CHYTRON: *(Approaching.)* Valiant commander, if it's not being intrusive—

NEVITA: Later, later!

ORIBASES: *(To NEVITA.)* Rest easy, sir! No harm will come. Eutherius and I have promised each other to keep an eye on him.

NEVITA: Ah, you're not telling me that—

ORIBASES: Last night he came close to ending his life. Fortunately, Eutherius arrived in time—oh but don't say anything to anyone!

NEVITA: Don't let him out of your sight.

PRISCUS: *(Approaching.)* It would put us much at ease to learn what the council—

NEVITA: Excuse me; I've important things to see to.

(He goes out behind the tent. At the same moment JOVIAN emerges from it.)

JOVIAN: *(Into the tent.)* It shall be done, most gracious Emperor!

CHYTRON: Ah, most worthy Jovian! Well? Has the retreat been decided on?

JOVIAN: I wouldn't advise anyone to call it a retreat. *(He goes out behind the tent.)*

CHYTRON: These military men! A philosopher's peace of mind means nothing to them. Ah!

(JULIAN comes out of the tent; he is pale and haggard. With him are EUTHERIUS and several generals. The latter at once go out right, across the plain.)

JULIAN:*(To the philosophers.)* Be joyful, my friends! Soon everything will be well.

CHYTRON: Ah, most blessed lord, have you found a way out?

JULIAN: We've several ways out, Chytron. All we need is to choose the best. We're now going to change the army's line of advance.

PRISCUS: Praise be to your wisdom!

JULIAN: This march eastward—it's getting us nowhere.

CHYTRON: No, no, that's for certain!

JULIAN: So we're going north, Chytron!

CHYTRON: What's that, my lord—north?

PRISCUS: Not westward, then?

JULIAN: Not westward. Far from westward. That would prove difficult because of the rivers. And we must leave Ctesiphon for later. Without ships we can't think of taking the city. The Galileans were the cause of their burning; I've been watching. Who dares call it a retreat if I go northwards? What do you know of my plans? The Persian army is based somewhere in the north; we're now pretty sure of that. Once I've defeated Sapor—it will need only one battle—we'll find plentiful supplies in the Persian camp. When I lead the Persian King prisoner through Antioch and the other cities, then we'll see if those people don't fall at my feet.

CHRISTIAN SOLDIERS: *(March across the plain, singing.)*
The ax strikes at the root of the tree
The world's great cedar falls.
From Golgotha, Christ's blood births free
The palm that never palls.*(They go out, right.)*

JULIAN: *(Following them with his eyes.)* The Galileans are always singing. Songs of death and wounds and pain. Those women I brought along as nurses— they've done more harm than they're worth. They've taught the soldiers strange songs which I've never heard before. Still, I won't punish any of them for that. It only leads to even greater idiocies. Do you know, Priscus, what happened with those rebels who just recently refused to show proper respect for the imperial busts?

PRISCUS: Just recently?

JULIAN: When, in order to instill a proper sense of fear in any who might be like-minded, I'd have had some of them executed, the oldest man stepped forward and begged, amid loud cries of joy, to be allowed to die first. So you see, Priscus, when I heard about it yesterday—

PRISCUS: Yesterday? My lord, you're mistaken. That all happened forty days ago.

JULIAN: So long? Yes, yes, yes. The Hebrews had to wander forty years in the desert. All the old ones had to die. A new generation was needed; but *that one*—mark this—*that one* entered the land promised them all.

EUTHERIUS: It's late in the day, my lord; won't you consider eating?

JULIAN: Not just now, my Eutherius! Some denial of the body's good for all of us. Yes, I tell you we must win our way to becoming a new generation. I can do nothing with you as you are now. If you want to escape the desert, you must pursue a pure life. Look at the Galileans. We can learn certain things from those people. No one's destitute or helpless among them. They live as brothers and sisters together—and most of all now when their obstinacy's forced me to chastise them. These Galileans, you should know, have in their hearts something I earnestly wish you would strive for. You style yourselves disciples of Socrates, of Plato, of Diogenes. Is there even one among you who'd go gladly to his death for Plato's sake? Would our Priscus sacrifice his left hand for Socrates? Would Chytron, for Diogenes' sake, suffer his ear to be cut off? You most certainly wouldn't! I know you, you whited sepulchers! Be gone from my sight—I've no use for you!

(The philosophers retire, humbled. The others move away also, anxiously whispering. Only ORIBASES and EUTHERIUS stay with the EMPEROR. ANATALUS remains with his soldiers outside the tent.)

JULIAN: How strange! Isn't it, at the deepest level, unfathomable? Oribases—can you explain this riddle to me?

ORIBASES: My lord, what riddle do you mean?

JULIAN: With twelve humble men, fishers, ignorant people, he founded all this.

ORIBASES: Oh my lord, these thoughts tax your strength.

JULIAN: And who are those who've held it together to this day? Women and simple folk for the most part—

ORIBASES: Yes, yes, my lord; but soon there'll be a favorable shift of fortune in this campaign—

JULIAN: Very true, Oribases; and as soon as fortune's changed, all will be well.

The kingdom of the carpenter's son is about to fall; that we know. As many years as the year has days, so long shall he rule; and now it is—

EUTHERIUS: My beloved lord, wouldn't a bath be good for you?

JULIAN: You think so? You may leave, Eutherius! Go, go! I've something to say to Oribases.

(EUTHERIUS goes out behind the tent. The EMPEROR draws ORIBASES over to the other side.)

JULIAN: Did Eutherius say anything to you this morning?

ORIBASES: No, my lord!

JULIAN: He's not said anything about last night?

ORIBASES: No, your Majesty, absolutely nothing. Eutherius is most discreet.

JULIAN: If he should tell you anything, don't believe it. It didn't happen the way he said it did. It's he himself who seeks my life.

ORIBASES: He—your old and faithful servant!

JULIAN: I'm keeping my eye on him.

ORIBASES: I will, too.

JULIAN: We'll both keep our eyes on him.

ORIBASES: My lord, I think you slept very poorly last night.

JULIAN: Yes.

(ORIBASES is about to speak but reconsiders.)

JULIAN: Do you know the reason I couldn't sleep?

ORIBASES: No, my emperor!

JULIAN: The victor of the Milvian Bridge was with me.

ORIBASES: The great Constantine?

JULIAN: Yes. These last nights I've had no peace from that ghost. He appears a little after midnight and doesn't leave until just before morning.

ORIBASES: My lord, it is full moon; that's always strangely influenced your mind.

JULIAN: According to the ancients signs like these usually—where has Maximus got to? But their opinions aren't sure enough to build on. We've seen how they've gone astray so often and so badly. Even what they say about the gods can't be taken completely on trust. Nor about the shades and the powers that work for men's well-being. What do we know about these powers? Nothing, Oribases, apart from their unpredictability and fickleness; for which we've ample proof. I wish Maximus would come—! *(To himself.)* Here? But it's not here the storm's predicted to break. It's supposed to be Phrygia—

ORIBASES: What place, my lord, and what storm?

JULIAN: Oh, nothing. Nothing.

NEVITA: *(Entering from the right.)* My lord, the army's now on the march—

JULIAN: Northwards?

NEVITA: *(Starts.)* Of course, my lord!

JULIAN: We really should have waited until Maximus—

NEVITA: What are you saying, my lord? There's nothing to wait for here. We're out of provisions; scattered enemy riders already have been sighted both to the east and the south—

JULIAN: Yes, yes, we must advance—northwards. Maximus will be here soon. I've sent for the Etruscan soothsayers from the rearguard; they shall try again to—I've also got hold of some Magi and they say they're well versed in the Chaldean mysteries. Our own priests are examining omens in nine different places—

NEVITA: My lord, whatever the outcome of the omens, we have to march forward. The soldiers are no longer to be relied on; they see clearly our only salvation lies in reaching the Armenian mountains.

JULIAN: It's what we'll do, Nevita—however the omens turn out. But it boosts confidence to know one's acting in accord with those unfathomable forces who, when they're inclined, can so profoundly shape a man's destiny.

NEVITA: *(Leaves him and says curtly.)* Anatalus, strike the Emperor's tent! *(He whispers some words to him and then goes out, right.)*

JULIAN: All the omens these forty days have been unpromising, which only shows one can rely on them, because all this time we've made only the most meager progress. But you must know, my good Oribases, I've now a new plan in mind—ah, Maximus!

MAXIMUS: *(Entering from the plain.)* The army's on the march, my lord. Get on your horse!

JULIAN: The omens—the omens?

MAXIMUS: Ah, yes—the omens! Don't ask about the omens.

JULIAN: Speak! I must know how they answer!

MAXIMUS: All the omens are silent.

JULIAN: Silent?

MAXIMUS: I went to the priests; the entrails of the sacrifices gave no sign. I went to the Etruscan frauds; the flights and cries of birds told them nothing. I visited the Magi, also; their writings had no answer to give. And I myself—

JULIAN: You yourself, my Maximus?

MAXIMUS: I can tell you now. Last night I studied the position of the stars. They told me nothing, Julian!

JULIAN: Nothing. Silence—silence, as if the sun were preparing an eclipse. Alone! No longer a bridge between me and the spirits. Where are you now, white, gleaming fleet of sails that came and went in the bright day, bearing messages between earth and heaven? The fleet is burnt. And this fleet, too, is burnt. Oh, all my gleaming ships! Maximus, what can you say about this?

MAXIMUS: I believe in you.

JULIAN: Yes, yes—do that!

MAXIMUS: The world-will has placed its power in your hand; therefore, it's silent.

JULIAN: And that's how we'll interpret it. And act accordingly—though we'd rather… This silence! To stand so utterly alone. But then, so do others, who can be said to stand almost alone. The Galileans. They've only one god, and *one* god is virtually no god. So how is it we see these people every day—?

ANATALUS: *(Who meanwhile has had the tents taken down.)* My Emperor, now you must mount your horse; I daren't let you stay here any longer.

JULIAN: Yes, now I'll mount my horse. Where is my good Babylonius? So now, sword in hand—Come, my dear friends! *(All go out to the right.)*

(Marshy wooded area. A dark still-standing lake between the trees. Watchfires in the distance. A moonlit night with drifting clouds. Some soldiers stand on guard in the foreground.)

MACRINA AND WOMEN: *(Singing offstage to the left.)*

In pain we cry
For man's bitter plight
Who suffers wrath's might.
We see we shall die.

ONE OF THE SOLDIERS: *(Listening.)* Hush. Do you hear? Over there—the Galilean women singing?

ANOTHER SOLDIER: They sing like owls and night-ravens.

A THIRD SOLDIER: I'd rather be among them just the same. It's safer with the Galileans than with us. The Galilean's god is stronger than ours.

FIRST SOLDIER: The Emperor's angered the gods, that's certain. What could he be thinking of, setting himself up as a god?

THIRD SOLDIER: What's worse, he's angered the god of the Galileans. Didn't you hear, they swear it's a fact that a few nights ago he and his magicians slit open the belly of a pregnant woman searching for omens in her entrails.

FIRST SOLDIER: Well, I don't believe that. In any case it wasn't a Greek woman; it must have been a barbarian.

THIRD SOLDIER: They say the Galilean's god looks after barbarians, too. If that's right, it doesn't look good for us.

SECOND SOLDIER: Oh, come on now—the Emperor's a great soldier.

FIRST SOLDIER: So is King Sapor a great soldier.

SECOND SOLDIER: Do you think we face the entire Persian army?

FIRST SOLDIER: Some say it's just the vanguard. No one knows for sure.

THIRD SOLDIER: I still wish we were over there, with the Galileans.

FIRST SOLDIER: *You're* thinking of going over to them?

THIRD SOLDIER: So many have gone over. In the last few days—

FIRST SOLDIER: *(Calling into the darkness.)* Halt—halt! Who goes there?

A VOICE: Friends from the outposts.

(Some soldiers appear between the trees with the Cappadocian, AGATHON among them.)

SECOND SOLIDER: Aha! Someone trying to run away.

ONE OF THE ARRIVALS: No, he's out of his senses.

AGATHON: Not out of my senses. Oh, in the name of the merciful God, let me go!

A SOLDIER FROM THE OUTPOSTS: He says he will kill a beast with seven heads.

AGATHON: Yes, yes, that's what I'll do. Oh, let me go free. Do you see this spear? Do you know what kind of spear it is? With this spear I'm going to kill the beast with seven heads and then I'll get back my soul. Christ promised that to me. He was with me last night.

FIRST SOLDIER: Hunger and thirst have done this to him.

ONE OF THE ARRIVALS: Take him to camp. He can sleep it off there.

AGATHON: Let me go! Oh, if only you knew what kind of spear this is!

(The soldiers lead him off downstage right.)

THE THIRD SOLDIER: What was all that about the beast?

FIRST SOLDIER: That's Galilean secret talk. They've a lot like that.

(EUTHERIUS and ORIBASES enter hurriedly from the right anxiously searching.)

EUTHERIUS: You can't see him?

ORIBASES: No. Ah, soldiers! Tell me, good friends, did anyone go by here?

FIRST SOLDIER: Yes, a squad of spearmen.

ORIBASES: Good, good! And no one else? No one of high rank? None of the generals?

SOLDIER: No, no one.

ORIBASES: Not here, either! Oh, Eutherius, how could you have—

EUTHERIUS: What could I have done? What could I? My old eyes haven't closed for three nights—

ORIBASES: *(To the soldiers.)* You must help us find him. I demand it in the supreme commander's name. Spread out among the trees; if you find any of our leaders, report to the watchfire over there.

SOLDIERS: I will, my lord.

(All go out in different directions, left. Shortly after, JULIAN appears behind a tree to the right. He listens, looks about him, and beckons behind him.)

JULIAN: Hush! Come out, Maximus! They didn't see us.

MAXIMUS: *(From the same side.)* Oribases was among them.

JULIAN: Yes, yes. Both he and Eutherius are keeping their eyes on me. They imagine I might... Have either of them said anything to you?

MAXIMUS: No, my Julian. But why did you waken me? And what do you want, here in the middle of the night?

JULIAN: To be alone with you for the last time, my beloved teacher!

MAXIMUS: Not for the last time, Julian!

JULIAN: Look at that dark lake. Do you think—if I vanished without a trace from this earth, and my body was never found and no one knew what had become of me—do you think it would get about that Hermes had come to me and carried me off, and I'd been taken into the company of the gods?

MAXIMUS: The time approaches when men won't need to die to live as gods on earth.

JULIAN: I am homesick, Maximus—homesick for the light and the sun and the stars.

MAXIMUS: Oh, I implore you—don't brood on sorrowful things. The Persian army faces you. Tomorrow will be your battle. You will conquer—

JULIAN: I—conquer? You don't know who was with me one hour ago.

MAXIMUS: Who was with you?

JULIAN: I'd fallen asleep on my bed in the tent. Then I was awakened by a strong reddish light that seemed to pierce through my closed eyelids. I looked up and saw a figure standing in the tent. Over its head was draped a long cloth which fell down at both sides, leaving the face free.

MAXIMUS: Did you recognize the figure?

JULIAN: It was the same face I saw in the light many years ago in Ephesus—that night we held a symposium with the two others.

MAXIMUS: The Spirit of the Empire.

JULIAN: It's since visited me once before in Gaul—on an occasion I don't like to think about.

MAXIMUS: Did it speak?

JULIAN: No. It seemed about to speak, but didn't. It stood motionless, gazing on me. Its face was pale and haggard. Suddenly it pulled the cloth together over its head, hid its face, and went out straight through the wall of the tent.

MAXIMUS: The moment of decision's at hand.

JULIAN: Yes, it's indeed at hand.

MAXIMUS: Don't give up, Julian. He who wills, wins.

JULIAN: And what does the victor win? Would it be worth the winning? What did the Macedonian Alexander, what did Julius Caesar win? Greeks and Romans speak of their fame with cold admiration—but that other, the Galilean, the carpenter's son, reigns as the King of Love in the warm hearts of the faithful. Where is he now? Is he active somewhere else since that time he endured Golgotha? I dreamt about him recently—dreamt I had subjected the whole earth. I commanded the memory of the Galilean to be wiped from the earth; and it was wiped away. Then the spirits came and served me and bound wings to my shoulders and I soared out into endless space until I set my foot upon another world. It was a different world from mine. Its circumference was greater, its sunlight more golden and several moons circled it. Then I looked down at my own world, the Emperor's world that I had rendered Galilean-free—and I found all I had done was exceeding good. But note, Maximus, there came past me a procession on this strange world where I stood. There were soldiers and judges and executioners at its head, and weeping women followed the procession. And behold, at the center of this slow, solemn procession walked the Galilean, in the clear day, carrying a cross on his back. I then called to him, saying: "Where to, then, Galilean?" And he turned his face toward me, smiled and nodded slowly, saying: "To the place of the skull." Where is he now? Was all that happened at Golgotha near Jerusalem a mere village episode done, as it were in passing, in an idle hour? Does he go on and on, suffering and dying and conquering yet again from one world to the next? Ah, if I could only lay waste to the world! Maximus, is there no poison, no consuming fire that could shatter creation to what it was when the solitary spirit brooded over the watery abyss?

MAXIMUS: I hear an alarm from the watchposts. Come, Julian—

JULIAN: To think that century after century will follow and in all of them men will live knowing it was I who gave in and he who conquered. I won't give in! I am young; I am invulnerable; the third empire is at hand—*(With a loud cry.)* There he stands!

MAXIMUS: Who? Where?

JULIAN: Do you see him? There, between the trees—in a crown and purple robe—

MAXIMUS: It's the moonlight playing on the water. Come—come, my Julian!

JULIAN: *(Goes truculently toward the vision.)* Away from me! You are dead. Your empire is finished. Off with that wizard's robe, carpenter's son! What are you up to there? What is it you're making?—Ah!

EUTHERIUS: *(From the left.)* The gods be praised! Oribases—here, here!

JULIAN: Where has he gone?

ORIBASES: *(From the left.)* Is he there?

EUTHERIUS: Yes. Oh, my dearly beloved Emperor!

JULIAN: Who was it just said: "I'm building the Emperor's coffin?"

ORIBASES: What do you mean, my lord?

JULIAN: Who spoke, I'm asking! Who was it said: "I'm building the Emperor's coffin?"

ORIBASES: Come with me to the tent, I beg you! *(Noises and cries are heard in the distance.)*

MAXIMUS: Battle cries! The Persians are upon us—

EUTHERIUS: The outposts are under attack!

ORIBASES: The enemy's in the camp. Ah, my lord, you are unarmed—

JULIAN: I'll sacrifice to the gods.

MAXIMUS: What gods, you fool? Where are they—and what are they?

JULIAN: I will sacrifice to one or another. I will sacrifice to many. One among them must hear me. I will call upon some power outside me and above me—

ORIBASES: There's not a moment to waste—

JULIAN: Ah, did you see that burning torch behind the cloud? It flared and died out in the same instant. A message from the spirits! A gleaming ship linking heaven and earth! My shield, my sword!
(He races out right. ORIBASES and EUTHERIUS follow him.)

MAXIMUS: *(Calling.)* Emperor, Emperor—don't do battle tonight! *(Exits right.)*

(Open plain with a village nearby. Daybreak. Misty. Sounds of battle. Cries and sounds of weapons out on the plain. In the foreground, ROMAN SPEARMEN led by AMMIAN engaged with PERSIAN BOWMEN. The latter are driven back toward the left.)

AMMIAN: That's right. Go at them! Cut them down. Don't give them time to shoot.

NEVITA: *(With more troops, from the right.)* Well fought, Ammian!

AMMIAN: Oh, my lord, why don't the cavalry come and help?

NEVITA: It's impossible. The Persians are using elephants in their front line. Just the smell fills the horses with fear. Slash, slash! That's right, thrust under their breastplates.

CHYTRON: *(In nightclothes, burdened with books and rolls of paper, enters from the right.)* To think I should get caught up in all these horrors!

NEVITA: Have you seen the Emperor, friend?

CHYTRON: Yes, but he ignores me. I beg you, most humbly, for a few sturdy fellows to protect me.

NEVITA: *(To his soldiers.)* They're falling back. Shield-bearers now advance!

CHYTRON: You're not listening to me! It's most essential I come to no harm. My work on "Fortitude in Adversity" is not completed—

NEVITA: *(As before.)* The Persians have reinforced their right flank. They're advancing again.

CHYTRON: Advancing again? Such appalling blood-lust! An arrow! It almost struck me! How indiscriminately they shoot: no respect for life and limb! *(Runs out, stage left.)*

NEVITA: The battle's even. It's not going either way. *(To FROMENTINUS.)* Hey there, Captain—have you seen the Emperor?

FROMENTINUS: Yes, my lord. He's fighting at the head of the white cavalry.

NEVITA: Not wounded?

FROMENTINUS: He appears invulnerable. Arrows and spears swerve away wherever he shows himself.

AMMIAN: *(Shouting from the center of the fighting.)* Bring help; we can't hold out much longer!

NEVITA: Keep going, my valiant Fromentinus.

FROMENTINUS: *(To the soldiers.)* Close your ranks, Greeks, and go at them! *(He rushes to AMMIAN's aid; the battle line retreats a little.)*

ANATALUS: *(With some men, right.)* The Emperor's not here?

NEVITA: The Emperor? Don't you answer for the Emperor's safety?

ANATALUS: His horse was shot from under him—then a crowd surrounded him; it was impossible to get to him—

NEVITA: Ah, do you think he's come to any harm?

ANATALUS: No, I don't think he has. There was a shout that he was unhurt, but—

MANY OF NEVITA'S FOLLOWERS: There he is! There he is!
(JULIAN without helmet or armor, with only his sword and shield, and leading men of the Imperial Guard, enters, right.)

JULIAN: I'm glad I've found you, Nevita!

NEVITA: Ah, my lord—without armor—how unwise—!

JULIAN: In these parts weapons are powerless against me. But go, Nevita; take supreme command; the horse was shot under me but—

NEVITA: My emperor, then you have been hurt?

JULIAN: No, only a blow to the head, a little dazed. Go, go—what's *that?* There's so many strange figures crowding around us.

NEVITA: *(Softly.)* Anatalus, you're responsible for the Emperor.

ANATALUS: Keep calm, my lord.
(NEVITA goes out to the right with his group. JULIAN, ANATALUS, and some of the Imperial troops remain behind. The battle on the plain recedes more and more into the distance.)

JULIAN: How many of our men have we lost, Anatalus?

ANATALUS: Certainly no small number, my lord; but I'm sure there's greater loss among the Persians.

JULIAN: Yes, yes. But still many fallen, both Greeks and Romans, don't you think?

ANATALUS: My Emperor, you're not well. Your face is quite pale—

JULIAN: You see those men lying there, some on their back, some face downward with outstretched arms? They're most certainly dead?

ANATALUS: Yes, my lord—no doubt of that.

JULIAN: They're dead, yes! So they know nothing, either of my setback in Jerusalem or of the other reversals. Do you think, Anatalus, many more Greeks will die in this battle?

ANATALUS: My lord, we must hope the bloodiest work is over.

JULIAN: Many more will die, I tell you! To no avail. What use if *many* die? Those that follow will still find out—. Tell me, Anatalus, what do you think the Emperor Caligula had in mind with that sword?

ANATALUS: What sword is that, my lord?

JULIAN: You remember, he wanted a sword which, with only one stroke, he could—

ANATALUS: Hear that shout from the army, my lord! Now I'm sure the Persians are retreating.

JULIAN: *(Listening.)* What's that singing in the air?

ANATALUS: My lord, allow me to fetch Oribases—or, even better—come, come, you are sick!

JULIAN: There's singing in the air—a song. Can't you hear it?

ANATALUS: If that's so, it will be the Galileans—

JULIAN: Yes, for sure, it's the Galileans. Ha-ha-ha, they're fighting in our ranks and don't see who's standing on the other side. Oh, you pack of fools! Where's Nevita? Why's he attacking the Persians? Can't he see the Persians are not the danger? You're all betraying me.

ANATALUS: *(Quietly to one of the soldiers.)* Run to the camp; fetch the Emperor's doctor! *(The soldier goes out to the right.)*

JULIAN: What legions of them! Do you think they've caught sight of us, Anatalus?

ANATALUS: Who, my lord? Where?

JULIAN: Can't you see them—look!—high above us, and far away! You're lying—you can see them clearly.

ANATALUS: By the immortal gods, those are only the morning clouds; it's the day breaking.

JULIAN: They're the Galilean hordes, I tell you! Look—look, those in robes edged in crimson; they're the ones who were martyred. Women, singing, surround them, twisting bowstrings from the long hair they've torn from their heads. Children follow, plaiting slings from their drawn-out entrails.

Burning torches! What multitudes—countless waves! They're heading this way! They all gaze on me, coming straight for me!

ANATALUS: They are Persians, my lord. Our ranks are breaking—

JULIAN: They *shall* not break. You *shall* not! Stand fast, you Greeks! Stand, stand, Romans! Today we will liberate the world.

(The battle meanwhile has moved back across the plain. JULIAN rushes with raised sword into the thickest of the battle. General confusion.)

ANATALUS: *(Shouting to the right.)* Help! The Emperor's in the greatest danger!

JULIAN: *(In the middle of the fighting.)* I see him! I see him! A longer sword! Who can lend me a longer sword?

SOLDIERS: *(Storming forward from the right.)* With Christ for the Emperor!

AGATHON: *(Among them.)* With Christ for Christ! *(He hurls his spear; it grazes the Emperor's arm and enters his side.)*

JULIAN: Ah! *(He grips the spear head to draw it out, but it slices his hand. He gives out a cry and falls.)*

AGATHON: *(Shouting in the confusion.)* The Roman spear from Golgotha! *(Unarmed, he throws himself against the Persians; he is seen to be cut down.)*

CONFUSED CRIES: The Emperor! Is the Emperor wounded?

JULIAN: *(Attempts to rise, but falls back, calling out.)* Your victory, Galilean!

MANY VOICES: The Emperor's fallen!

ANATALUS: The Emperor's wounded! Shield him, shield him, in the name of the gods! *(He rushes desperately against the advancing Persians. The EMPEROR, unconscious, is carried away. At the same moment JOVIAN appears on the plain with fresh troops.)*

JOVIAN: Forward, forward, brothers in the faith; give to the Emperor what is the Emperor's.

RETREATING SOLDIERS: *(Shouting to him.)* He's fallen! The Emperor's fallen!

JOVIAN: Fallen! Oh, Heaven's vengeful God! Forward, forward; the Lord wills that his people shall live. I see the heavens open; I see angels with flaming swords—

SOLDIERS: *(Storming forwards.)* Christ is among us!

AMMIAN'S TROOPS: The Galileans' god is among us! Gather round him! He is the strongest!

(Wild fighting. JOVIAN breaks through the enemy lines. Sunrise. The Persians fly in all directions.)

(The EMPEROR'S tent with a curtained entrance in the background. Bright day. JULIAN lies unconscious on his bed. The wounds in his right side, arm, and hand are bandaged. Close by him stand ORIBASES, MACRINA, and

EUTHERIUS. Further back stand BASIL OF CAESAREA and PRISCUS. At the foot of the bed stands MAXIMUS.)

MACRINA: He's bleeding again. I must make the bandages tighter.

ORIBASES: Our thanks to you, gentle lady. Your ministering hands have been of great help.

EUTHERIUS: Is he actually still living?

ORIBASES: He's definitely alive.

EUTHERIUS: But he's not breathing.

ORIBASES: He's still breathing.

(AMMIAN enters quietly carrying the Emperor's sword and shield which he lays down and remains standing by the curtain.)

PRISCUS: Ah, my dear Captain, how do matters stand out there?

AMMIAN: Better than in here. Has he already—

PRISCUS: No, no, not yet. But is it true we've driven the Persians back?

AMMIAN: Yes, completely. Jovian put them to flight. Just this moment, three high envoys from King Sapor are in the camp seeking an armistice.

PRISCUS: And you think Nevita will go along with that?

AMMIAN: Nevita's handed over the command to Jovian. Everyone's looking to him as the only one who can save us.

ORIBASES: Talk quietly, he's stirring.

AMMIAN: Stirring? Will he regain consciousness. Oh, if he should live to see this!

EUTHERIUS: What, Ammian?

AMMIAN: Both the soldiers and their leaders are voting to choose the new Emperor.

PRISCUS: What are you saying?

EUTHERIUS: What shameless impatience!

AMMIAN: The army's precarious situation is some excuse: and yet—

MACRINA: He's waking. He's opening his eyes—

JULIAN: *(Lying still a moment and gazing peacefully at those gathering round him.)*

ORIBASES: Do you know me, my lord?

JULIAN: Yes, perfectly, my dear Oribases.

ORIBASES: Lie completely still.

JULIAN: Lie still? What are you thinking of? I must get up!

ORIBASES: Impossible, my lord; I beg you—

JULIAN: I have to get up, I tell you. How can I lie still just now? I have to crush Sapor completely.

EUTHERIUS: Sapor is crushed, my lord! He's sent envoys to the camp to sue for armistice.

JULIAN: Has he really? I'm glad to know that. Then I've beaten *him* at all events.

But no armistice. I will strike him to the ground. Ah, where did I put my shield? Can I have lost my shield?

AMMIAN: No, my Emperor—here's both your shield and your sword.

JULIAN: That truly pleases me. My good shield. I'd regret them falling into barbarian hands. Put it on my arm—

MACRINA: Oh, my lord, it's too heavy for you.

JULIAN: Ah, *you?* You're right, my pious Macrina; it's a little too heavy. Lay it before me, so I can see it. What? Is that you, Ammian. Keeping watch over me? Where is Anatalus?

AMMIAN: My lord, he's among the blessed.

JULIAN: Dead: The faithful Anatalus died for me? Among the blessed, you say? Hm! One friend the less. Ah, my Maximus! I won't receive the Persian envoys today. They are fooling with me, hoping to gain time. But I'll have nothing to do with that. I'll follow up my victory with the utmost vigor. The army will turn against Ctesiphon again.

ORIBASES: Impossible just now, my lord; think of your wounds.

JULIAN: My wounds will soon heal. Isn't that right, Oribases, you promise, don't you—?

ORIBASES: Above all, you must rest, my lord!

JULIAN: A most unfortunate accident! And then just now when so many urgent claims are flooding in on me. I can't leave such things in Nevita's hands. In matters like this I can't rely on him or the others; I must do all this myself. I really am feeling a little weary. Most annoying! Tell me, Ammian, what's the name of that ill-destined place?

AMMIAN: What place, most gracious majesty.

JULIAN: That place where the Persian spear struck me.

AMMIAN: It's named after the village of Phrygia—

MAXIMUS: Ah!

JULIAN: What's it called—? What did you say the area's named?

AMMIAN: My lord, it's named Phrygia after the village there.

JULIAN: Ah, Maximus—Maximus!

MAXIMUS: Betrayed! *(He hides his face and sinks down at the foot of the bed.)*

ORIBASES: My Emperor, what is causing you such distress?

JULIAN: Nothing, nothing. Phrygia? Ah yes? Then Nevita and the others had better take matters into their own hands. Go, and tell them—

AMMIAN: My lord, they've already on your behalf—

JULIAN: They have? Well, well, that's good then. The world-will laid an ambush for me, Maximus!

MACRINA: Your wound's opening up again, my lord!

JULIAN: Oh, Oribases, why did you want to conceal it from me?

ORIBASES: Conceal what, my lord?

JULIAN: That I must leave you. Why didn't you tell me before?

ORIBASES: Oh, my Emperor!

BASIL: Julian—Julian! *(Weeping, he throws himself by the bed.)*

JULIAN: Basil, friend, brother, the two of us have shared splendid days together. You mustn't weep because I go from you so young. It isn't always a sign of the divine powers' displeasure when they snatch away a man in his early years. What is it to die? Is it anything more than paying one's debt to the eternally shifting empire of dust? Don't grieve. Don't we all love wisdom? And doesn't wisdom teach us the supreme happiness is centered in the life of the soul, not that of the body? There, at least, the Galileans are right except—but we won't go into that. If the powers of life and death had permitted me to complete a certain essay, I believe I could have satisfactorily—

ORIBASES: Oh, my Emperor, doesn't it tire you to speak for so long?

JULIAN: No, no, no. I feel remarkably light and free.

BASIL: Julian, beloved brother—have you nothing to recant?

JULIAN: I can't in all honesty imagine what it could be.

BASIL: There's nothing you regret?

JULIAN: I've nothing to regret. The power which destiny placed in my hand, and which issues from the divine, I know I've used to the best of my ability. I've never willingly done wrong to anyone. This war was launched on good and valid grounds; and although some might conclude I haven't lived up to all expectations, they should at least consider there's a mysterious power outside us which essentially decides the outcome of all human endeavor.

MACRINA: Oh, hear how heavily he's breathing.

ORIBASES: His voice will soon fail him.

JULIAN: As to the choice of a successor, I don't presume to give advice. You, Eutherius, shall divide my possessions among those who were closest to me. I won't be leaving much; for I've always held that a true philosopher— What's this? Is the sun going down already?

ORIBASES: Not at all, my lord. It's still bright day.

JULIAN: Strange. It seemed to go so dark before my eyes. Yes, wisdom— wisdom. Hold fast to wisdom, good Priscus! But be always on your guard against all that is unfathomable beyond us which—Has Maximus left?

MAXIMUS: No, my brother!

JULIAN: My throat is burning. Can't anyone soothe it?

MACRINA: A drink of water, my lord! *(She holds a cup to his lips.)*

ORIBASES: *(Whispering to Macrina.)* His wound is bleeding internally.

JULIAN: No weeping. No Greek must weep for me; I'm ascending to the stars. Beautiful temples. Images. But so far away.

MACRINA: What is he speaking about?

ORIBASES: I don't know; I don't think he can collect his thoughts.

JULIAN: *(With closed eyes.)* Alexander was granted his entry—into Babylon. I too will—beautiful leaf-crowned youths—dancing girls—but so far away. Beautiful earth, beautiful life on earth—*(He opens his eyes wide.)* Oh Sun, Sun, why did you betray me? *(He sinks back.)*

ORIBASES: *(After a silence.)* That was death.

THE OTHERS: Dead—dead!

ORIBASES: Yes, now he is dead.

> *(BASIL and MACRINA kneel in prayer. EUTHERIUS covers his head. Sound of drums and bugles in the far distance.)*

A CRY FROM THE CAMP: Long live Emperor Jovian!

ORIBASES: Ah! Did you hear that shout?

AMMIAN: Jovian is proclaimed Emperor.

MAXIMUS: *(Laughing.)* The Galilean Jovian! Well, well, well.

ORIBASES: Disgusting haste! Even before they found out if—

PRISCUS: Jovian—that victorious hero who saved us all! Emperor Jovian certainly merits a panegyric. I just hope that sneaky Chytron hasn't already— *(He goes out quickly.)*

BASIL: Forgotten before your hand is cold. And for this fleeting glory you sold your immortal soul.

MAXIMUS: *(Rising.)* The world-will shall answer for Julian's soul.

MACRINA: Don't blaspheme; even though you truly loved this dead man—

MAXIMUS: *(Closer to the body.)* Loved him and misled him. No, not I! Tempted like Cain. Tempted like Judas. Yours is a wasteful god, Galileans! He uses up many souls. Were you not the chosen one this time either, sacrificed on the altar of Necessity? What is it worth, to have lived? Everything's game and chance. To *will* is to *have to will.* Oh, my beloved, all the signs betrayed me, all the omens spoke with two tongues, so that in you I glimpsed the One who would reconcile the two kingdoms. The third empire *shall* come! The spirit of man shall reclaim its birthright—and then burnt offerings shall rise for you and for your two guests in the symposium. *(He goes.)*

MACRINA: *(Rising, pale.)* Basil, did you understand the heathen's words?

BASIL: No—but within me floods the radiant truth that here lies a glorious, shattered instrument of the lord.

MACRINA: Yes, in truth, a rare and precious instrument.

BASIL: Christ, Christ—where were your people that they did not see your manifest purpose? Emperor Julian was a rod to scourge us—not to death but to resurrection.

MACRINA: Destiny's choices are fearful. What do we know—?

BASIL: Isn't it written: "One vessel is shaped for infamy, one for glory?"

MACRINA: Oh, brother, let us not try to fathom that abyss. *(She bends over the corpse and covers its face.)* Erring human soul—if you were forced to stray, you will be received with favor on that great day when the mighty one comes in a cloud to judge the living dead and the dead who live!

END OF EMPEROR AND GALILEAN

CHRONOLOGY

1828   • **Ibsen born in Skien, Norway, on March 20.**
           • Leo Tolstoy born in Russia.

1835   • Financial problems force the Ibsen family to move out of town to a smaller house for eight years.

1843   • Ibsen leaves home, at age 14, to earn his living as an apothecary's apprentice in the seacoast town of Grimstad. Except for one brief visit, he never returns to his hometown.

1846   • A maid in the Grimstad household, considerably older than Ibsen, bears him an illegitimate son. Ibsen was to support this son financially for many years, despite his own impoverished circumstances.

1848   • Revolutions throughout Europe which are one by one suppressed. Ibsen writes sonnets in support of these revolutions.
           • Karl Marx and Friedrich Engels publish *Manifesto of the Communist Party.*

1848–50 • Ibsen writes his first play, *Catiline,* which is submitted to the Christiania Theatre and rejected.

1849   • August Strindberg born in Sweden.

1850   • Ibsen writes his second play, *The Burial Mound,* which is performed at the Christiania Theatre.

1851   • Ibsen arrives in Bergen to take up an appointment as playwright in residence and stage manager of the new Norwegian Theatre, established by Ole Bull. He was to spend six years in Bergen, learning every aspect of dramatic and theatrical craft.

1853   • *St John's Night* is performed at Bergen.

1855   • *Lady Inger of Østraat* performed at Bergen.
           • Søren Kierkegaard, Danish philosopher, dies.

1856   • *The Feast at Solhoug* performed at Bergen. This is Ibsen's first success in the theatre.

1857   • *Olaf Liliekrans* performed at Bergen.
           • Ibsen takes up new post of artistic director, Norwegian Theatre in Christiania.

1858
- June 18, Ibsen marries Suzannah Thoresen.
- *The Vikings at Helgeland* performed at Christiania Theatre.
- Gustav Flaubert's *Madame Bovary.*
- Apparition of the Virgin Mary reputed to have appeared to Bernadette Soubirous at Lourdes, France.

1859
- Ibsen's son, Sigurd, born.
- Charles Darwin publishes *The Origin of Species.*
- Karl Marx, *Critique of Political Economy.*
- John Stuart Mill, *Essay on Liberty.*

1860
- Anton Chekhov born.

1861
- Outbreak of American Civil War.

1862
- *Love's Comedy,* Ibsen's first major play, published as a supplement to a journal. The play subjected to harsh attacks as "an offense against human decency." Ibsen himself now the object of much critical abuse. The Christiania theatre dared not perform the play.
- The Norwegian Theatre in Christiania goes bankrupt and Ibsen loses his job.
- In May, awarded a grant from the University of Christiania to compile folk songs and legends. This required extensive travel throughout Norway.

1863
- *The Pretenders* published.

1864
- January, *The Pretenders* performed at the Christiania Theater. It is Ibsen's most successful production to date.
- April 5, leaves Christiania for Copenhagen and Rome. The beginning of a twenty-seven year exile from Norway, in which most of his major work will be written.

1866
- Ibsen in Rome. In March, *Brand* published and creates a sensation throughout Scandinavia. From now on, Ibsen will be Scandinavia's most prominent writer.

1867
- November 14, *Peer Gynt* published.
- Karl Marx's *Das Kapital* published.
- Emile Zola writes *Thérèse Raquin,* his first "naturalist" novel.

1868
- In October, after staying in Florence, Bologna and Venice, Ibsen moves to Dresden.

1869
- In September, *The League of Youth* published. Ibsen's first realistic prose play.
- Wyoming establishes women's suffrage.

- John Stuart Mill writes *On the Subjection of Women.*
- Ibsen begins his long intellectual friendship with the young Danish critic, Georg Brandes.

1870
- Franco-Prussian War. Napoleon III capitulates to Prussia.
- Revolt in Paris, proclamation of the Third Republic.
- Schliemann begins excavations at Troy.

1871
- Election of socialists to the Paris Commune, upon which troops, led by Thiers on behalf of the French bourgeoisie massacred over 25,000 Communards—men, women and children—in one week. Thousands more executed or deported to tropical penal colonies. Ibsen wrote to Georg Brandes about these events.

1872
- Friedrich Nietzsche's *The Birth Of Tragedy.*
- Jules Verne writes *Around the World in 80 Days.*

1873
- ***Emperor and Galilean* published.**

1874
- First Impressionist exhibition in Paris.

1875
- Leo Tolstoy's *Anna Karenina.*

1876
- First performance of *Peer Gynt,* with music by Edvard Grieg, at the Christiania Theatre.
- In April, *The Vikings at Helgeland* performed at the Court Theatre in Munich, the first of Ibsen's plays produced outside Scandinavia.
- In June, Ibsen attends a performance of *The Pretenders* by the Duke of Saxe-Meiningen's players.
- Opening of Bayreuth for first complete performance of Richard Wagner's Cycle, *Der Ring des Nibelungen.* Ibsen is living close to Bayreuth, in Munich.

1877
- *Pillars of Society,* inaugurating Ibsen's Cycle of twelve realist prose plays.

1879
- In December, *A Doll House.* The play quickly becomes notorious, first in Scandinavia, then throughout Europe. Ibsen is soon to become the most written about man of letters, internationally, until his death in 1906.

1880
- Emile Zola's *Nana.*
- Dostoevsky's *The Brothers Karamazov.*
- Rodin sculpts *The Thinker.*

1881
- Publication of *Ghosts* causes a major scandal internationally; the play is banned from public performance in many countries, giving rise to the

minority theatre movement where, in Berlin, the Freie Bühne, and in London, the Independent Theatre, will be founded to perform Ibsen's play. No established theatre in Scandinavia dared put on the play, and the bookshops returned copies of the play to the publisher. It would be over ten years before the first edition was sold out.

1882   • *An Enemy of the People* published.
         • World premiere of *Ghosts* in Chicago, performed in Norwegian by Danish and Norwegian amateurs before audiences of Scandinavian immigrants.
         • James Joyce, Irish novelist, and lifelong Ibsen admirer, born.

1883   • First European performance of *Ghosts* by August Lindberg in Hälsingborg, Sweden. Lindberg was regularly to direct and act in Ibsen's plays.
         • Friedrich Nietzsche, *Also Sprach Zarathustra*.

1884   • *The Wild Duck* published.

1886   • *Rosmersholm* published.

1887   • Andre Antoine establishes his Théâtre Libre, the first of the non-commercial theatres to take up the cause of Ibsen.
         • August Strindberg writes *The Father*.

1888   • *The Lady from the Sea* published.

1889   • Otto Brahm and Paul Schlenther open the independent theatre, Freie Bühne, in Berlin, to evade censorship and produce *Ghosts*.
         • Opening of the Eiffel Tower in Paris.

1890   • *Hedda Gabler* published.
         • Andre Antoine produces *Ghosts* at the Théâtre Libre. Lugné Poë called the production "a thunderbolt in French theatrical history."

1891   • J. T. Grein established the Independent Theatre in London which opened on Friday March 13 with *Ghosts*. The performance causes the greatest scandal and controversy in British theatrical history. Banned by the Lord Chamberlain, the play had to be performed at the Independent Theatre as a private club.
         • George Bernard Shaw's *The Quintessence of Ibsenism* published.
         • In July Ibsen returns to settle in Norway after twenty-seven years exile.

1892   • *The Master Builder* published.
         • Maurice Maeterlinck writes *Pelléas et Mélisande*.
         • George Bernard Shaw's first play, *Widowers' Houses*.

1894   • *Little Eyolf* published.
         • Shaw's *Arms and the Man.*

1896   • *John Gabriel Borkman* published.
         • Anton Chekhov's *The Seagull.*

1899   • *When We Dead Awaken,* Ibsen's "Epilogue" to the Cycle, published.
         • H.G. Wells' *When the Sleeper Wakes.*
         • Leo Tolstoy's *Resurrection.*
         • Oscar Wilde's *The Importance of Being Earnest.*

1900   • Ibsen suffers his first stroke and has to stop writing. He has his second
         stroke the following year.
         • Sigmund Freud, *The Interpretation of Dreams.*
         • Friedrich Nietzsche dies.
         • Oscar Wilde dies.

1901   • Queen Victoria dies.
         • Strindberg's *The Dance of Death.*

1903   • Shaw's *Man and Superman.*

1904   • Chekhov's *The Cherry Orchard.*
         • Chekhov dies.

1906 • **May 23, Ibsen dies.**
         • Samuel Beckett born April 13 (or May 13).